REFORMING THE MUSLIM WORLD

Reforming the Muslim World

Masudul Alam Choudhury

KEGAN PAUL INTERNATIONAL
London and New York

First published in 1998 by
Kegan Paul International Limited
UK: P.O. Box 256, London WC1B 3SW, England
Tel: (0171) 580 5511   Fax: (0171) 436 0899
USA: 562 West 113th Street, New York, NY 10025, USA
Tel: (212) 666 1000   Fax: (212) 316 3100

Distributed by

John Wiley & Sons Ltd
Southern Cross Trading Estate
1 Oldlands Way, Bognor Regis,
West Sussex, PO22 9SA, England
Tel: (01243) 779 777   Fax: (01243) 820 250

Columbia University Press
562 West 113th Street
New York, NY 10025, USA
Tel: (212) 666 1000   Fax: (212) 316 3100

© Masudul Alam Choudhury 1998

Printed in Great Britain by TJ International Ltd. Padstow

ISBN 0-7103-0575 3

British Library Cataloguing in Publication Data

Choudhury, Masudul Alam, 1948-
Reforming the Muslim World
1. Islam and the social sciences 2. Islam - Doctrines
I. Title
297.2'7

ISBN 07103305753

US Library of Congress Cataloguing in Publication Data

Choudhury, Masudul Alam, 1948-
Reforming the Muslim World / Masudul Alam Chodhury
p. cm.
ISBN 0-7103-0575-3
1. Islam--20th century   I. Title
BP163.C49 1997
297'.09'049--dc21

90-29387
CIP

DEDICATION

This book is dedicated in remembrance of my father, Professor Sultanul Alam Chowdhury, who passed away during his active academic service in Islamic Law and Jurisprudence at the Institute of Islamic Research, Government of Pakistan, in 1964.

TABLE OF CONTENTS

ACKNOWLEDGEMENT xv

FOREWORD BY
Professor John L. Esposito xvii

INTRODUCTION xix
Nature of Study xix
Particular Comparisons xxii
Summary of Chapters xxv
The Audience of This Book xxviii

CHAPTER 1: THE EPISTEMOLOGICAL PREMISE OF
REFORMATION 1
The Precept of Unity 1
A Mathematical Formulation of the Unity Precept and
Field 2
A Mathematical Formulation of Unification
Epistemology 5
Unity-Based Vs Rationalistic Perspectives of World
Systems 6
World View as a Systems Concept 8
Other Concepts of Unity in the Sciences 9
Conclusion 10

CHAPTER 2: THE SCIENTIFIC PREMISE OF
REFORMATION 11
The Questions Posed 11
A Brief Critique of Occidental Scientific Epistemology 12
    1. David Hume's Scientific Epistemology 12
    2. René Descartes' Scientific Epistemology 13

3. Leibniz's Scientific Epistemology 13
4. Albert Einstein's Scientific Epistemology 14
5. Hegel and Marx's Scientific Epistemologies 15
6. Edmund Husserl's Scientific Epistemology 16
7. Kuhn and Popper's Scientific Epistemologies 17
The Methodological Inference Gained from Occidental
Scientific Epistemologies 19
Whitehead's Process Concept in Scientific Epistemology ... 19
A Theory of Strong Interactions 21
Scientific Epistemology Premised on Unification of
Knowledge: The *Qur'anic* World View 24
The *Tawhidi* (Unity of God) Creative Order 25
Ghazzali's Epistemology and Its Scientific Construction 29
Critical Inference from Ghazzali's Methodology
Towards the Construction of Islamic Science and Values ... 32
Immanuel Kant 34
Diagrammatic Explanation of Kant's Problematique of
Heteronomy 35
Critique of Kant's and Ghazzali's Epistemologies by
Means of Evolutionary *Tawhidi* Epistemology 36
Methodological Conclusion 39
Policy Conclusion 40

CHAPTER 3: THE SOCIO-SCIENTIFIC PREMISE OF
REFORMATION: FROM MODERNITY TO
POST-MODERNITY 43
Posing the Questions for Discourse 43
The Nature of Axioms and Theories in Occidental
Science 44
Science and Post-Modernity 48
1. Critique of Post-Modernity 48

Table of Contents

2. Historicism and Post-Modernity 51
Science and Humanity 53
The Emergence of Islamic Socio-Scientific World View 56
The *Shuratic* Process 56
The Principle of Universal Complementarity Underlying
Unification Epistemology 59
What is the Concept of *Qur'anic* Historicism? 62
A Functional Presentation of *Shuratic* Process 64
1. From Polity to Market: 'Action' 64
2. From Markets to Polity: 'Response' 65
3. Interactive Circularity between Polity and
Markets: Creative Evolution 65
An Application of the Circular Causation and
Continuity Model of Unified Reality in Science,
Technology and Society 68
An Application of the Circular Causation and Continuity
Model of Unified Reality in Science, Technology and
Organization 69
The Concept of Substantive Interdisciplinarity in
Interactive-Integrative-Evolutionary Knowledge Fields 71
How Can Substantive Interdisciplinarity be
Operationalized in Society? Focus on Grass-roots 72
Conclusion 73

CHAPTER 4: THE POLITICAL ECONOMY OF
REFORMATION 75
by Masudul A. Choudhury & Abdul Fatah Che Hamat

The Inherent Inconsistency Between Economic Theory
and Economic Reality 76

1. Hegelian-Marxist Dialectics 76
2. Schumpeterian Development Dialectics 79
3. Schumpeter and Drucker on the Issue of
Knowledge 80
The Nature of Political Economy in Modernist Thought 81
From Modernity to Post-Modernity in Political Economy . . . 82
1. Wither Economic Historicism in Post-Modernity? 83
2. Gunnar Myrdal's Social Causation Model of
Development 84
Application of Deconstructionist Methodology to
Some Socio-Economic Issues: Social Justice,
Entitlement and Organization 85
1. Rawls and Nozick on the Question of Justice and
Entitlement 85
2. Hayek on the Question of Social Justice and
Organization 86
Wallerstein on the World-System and Power Dynamics 88
Economic Futures at the Advent and End of Post-
Modernity 89
Environment as a Relational System: Alternative to
Deconstructionist Approach 91
The Universe as a Relational Domain 93
The Alternative Ethico-Economic Approach in
Ecological Economics 94
The Nature of Ethics in Unification Epistemology:
Principle of Ethical Endogeneity 95
1. The Concept of Ethical Endogeneity in Political
Economy 95
2. An Ethico-Economic Reformulation of the
Ecological Problem 96
Historical Evidence on Islamic Economic

Table of Contents

Transformation: The Case of Malaysia 100
Conclusion 102

**CHAPTER 5: THE INSTITUTIONAL BASIS OF
REFORMATION: ORGANIZATIONAL THEORY OF
THE FIRM** 105
A Critical Review of Problems in the Theory of the Firm . . 105
  1. Equilibrium at the Core of the Economy 107
  2. Walrasian Equilibrium 107
From the Concept of Equilibrium to That of
Organization and Process in Economic Theory of the
Firm 109
  1. Shackle's Concepts of Equilibrium and Time in the
  Context of Organizational Theory 109
  2. Concept of Organization According to Arrow 112
  3. A Critique of Shackle's and Arrow's Approaches
  to Organization Theory 113
Herbert Simon's Organizational Theory of the Firm 114
The Concept of Process Derived from the Concept of
Organization 116
Lessons Learned on Organizational Theory in Received
Economic Theory: Toward Redefining the Concept of
Process 117
    Redefining Process 118
An Example in the Organizational Theory of the Firm 119
The Concepts of Process and Organization in Islamic
Perspectives 121
  1. Introducing the Concept of Process in Islamic
  Perspectives 121
  2. Introducing the Concept of Organization in
  Islamic Perspectives 122

3. The Nature of Islamic Firm 122
Introducing Unification Epistemology to the Islamic
Firm 123
The *Shuratic* Process Revisited 125
    1. The Concept of Equilibrium in *Shuratic* Process 126
    2. The Concept of Organization Derived from the
    Shuratic Process 129
The Islamic Firm's Menus Derived from the *Shuratic*
Process and Organization 130
Objective Criterion of the Islamic Firm as an
Organization 132
Simultaneity of Economic Efficiency and Distributive
Equity in the Islamic Firm's Production Menu 135
The Islamic Firm's Production Menu in Relation to
Organizational Behaviour 136
    The Role of Divine Attributes in Contrasting Paradigms 138
Relationship Between Wages and Profit-Sharing in the
Islamic Firm 140
Simulative Equilibrium Concept for the Islamic Firm 141
Conclusion 142

CHAPTER 6: REFORMING THE CAPITAL MARKET:
ISLAMIC CONCEPT OF MONEY 145
Various Treatments of Money in the Literature 145
Money in Islamic Political Economy 148
Simulation With Money in Islamic Political Economy 150
The Nature of Interest Rate in Monetary Valuation 150
Valuation of Money in Islamic Political Economy 152
Definition of Money in Islamic Political Economy 154
Relationship Between Money and Investment 158
The Use of Reserve Ratio in Monetary Policy in Islamic
Political Economy 160

Transactions with Currency Based Endogenous Money 161
Conclusion 163

**CHAPTER 7: REFORMATION IN THE MIDST OF
GLOBALIZATION** 165
Neo-Mercantilism 167
De-Equalizing Global Trade 168
Problems of Trade and Development Policies of the
Bretton Woods Institutions 170
Eurocentric Economic Reasoning and Globalization
Process 170
   1. Neoclassical Individualism 170
   2. Strategic Global Model 171
   3. Summary Features of Western Globalization Model . 173
Economic Problems for Muslim Countries in the
Globalization Process 173
Adverse Consequences of Interest Rate and Exchange
Rate Mechanisms by Industrialized Countries 176
The Risk to Muslim Countries in the Globalization
Process 179
The Islamic Concept of Globalization for the Muslim
World 180
   1. The Philosophical Premise of Globalization in
   Islamic Perspective 181
   2. Institutional Aspect of Globalization in Islamic
   Perspective 182
   3. Application of *Shuratic* Process to Globalization 183
State of Eurocentricity Within the Muslim World
System 185
The Way Out For Muslim Countries in Their Own
Globalization Process 187
Conclusion 188

CHAPTER 8: MALAYSIA AND THE MUSLIM WORLD: THE TWENTY-FIRST CENTURY AND BEYOND 191

Prevalent Malaysian Models of Growth and Development 191

The Issue of Labour Market and Technological Choice in Malaysia 197

Question of Productivity in a Knowledge-Based Society ... 199

Absolute Versus Relative Inequality with Skill Formation 200

The Need for a New Outlook in Malaysian Development .. 203

Alternative Paradigm of Growth With Development for Malaysia 203

Meaning of Socio-Political and Socio-Economic Interactions 204

Some Complementary Politico-Economic Policies Relating to a Future Islamic Common Market 205

Malaysia's Growth-Distribution Perspectives 207

Examples of Activities on Sectorial Interlinkages 207

Overall Interactions in Global Economy and Society 210

The Meta-Theory of Development by Application of the Principle of Universal Complementarity 211

Conclusion 212

CHAPTER 9: INSTITUTIONAL REFORMATION: THE ORGANIZATION OF ISLAMIC CONFERENCES SYSTEM 215

Critical Questions Relating to the OIC System 217

Public Choice-Theoretic Explanation of OIC Decision-Making 220

The *Shuratic* Process Oriented Transformation of the OIC System 222

1. Empowerment by Participation 222

2. Using *Zakah*, Islamic Wealth Tax as International
Finance 224
Structural Change of the OIC System in Light of the
Shuratic Process 225

CHAPTER 10: POLICY CONCLUSION: *UMMATIC*
TRANSFORMATION 227
I. How to Realize Self-Reliance? 229
II. Towards Attaining Science-Technology-Society
Interface by Means of the Methodology of Unification
Epistemology 234
III. Development of Indigenous Capital Market 236
Conclusion 237

NOTES AND REFERENCES 239

INDEX 263

FIGURES

Figure 2.1: The Knowledge-Based Evolutionary *Tawhidi*
            Epistemology 26
Figure 2.2: The Interactive-Integrative-Evolutionary
            Phenomenon of *Tawhidi* Epistemology 28
Figure 2.3: Contrasting Ghazzali's Epistemology by
            Evolutionary *Tawhidi* Epistemology:
            A Methodological Problem 33
Figure 2.4: Depiction of Kant's Knowledge Formation 37
Figure 3.1: The Interactive Process of Knowledge
            Formation 67
Figure 5.1: The *Shuratic* Process 127
Figure 5.2: Organizational Theory of the Islamic Firm 139
Figure 5.3: Case of Knowledge-Based Interactions-
            Integration-Evolution in the Organizational
            Theory of the Islamic Firm 143
Figure 6.1: Simultaneous Equilibria in the Money and Goods
            Relationship 155
Figure 6.2: Interest Rate, Price Level and Monetary
            Relationships 157
Figure 6.3: Knowledge-Induced Evolutionary Equilibria 159
Figure 9.1: The OIC System 216
Figure 9.2: The Organization of Islamic Conferences in
            Light of the *Shuratic* Process 226
Figure 10.1: The Blueprint of *Ummatic* Transformation 230

TABLES

Table 6.1:   Balance Sheets of Banks in the Case
            of Endogenous Money 160
Table 7.1:   Foreign Direct Investment in Agro-Based
            Sector in Malaysia (Percentages of
            Total Foreign Direct Investment) 171
Table 7.2:   Selected Macroeconomic External Sector
            Indicators for OIC Members 174
Table 7.3:   Interest Rates in Industrialized Economies,
            Inflation Rates and Exchange Rates
            in OIC Countries 178
Table 7.4:   OIC Country Risk Rankings and Ratings 179

ACKNOWLEDGEMENT

My thanks are to the University College of Cape Breton Research Evaluation Committee for funding the preparation of the manuscript of this book. I thank Professor Stephen Kavanagh, Dean of the School of Business at UCCB for being so very accommodative to fund many of my travels to international conferences, where some of the chapters of this book were presented as papers. My gratitudes are to the Department of Research and Development and the School of Business at UCCB to award me matching grants for preparing this book in camera ready form.

I also thank Dr Abder Rehman Zeinelabdin, Director of the Research Division at the Statistical, Economic and Social Research and Training Centre for Islamic Countries in Ankara, Turkey, for helping me out with several of the documents of the Organization of Islamic Conferences that were required in the preparation of this work. Finally, I thank the Public Relations Department of the Islamic Development Bank for providing me with their latest Annual Reports for current statistical information quoted in this book.

Masudul Alam Choudhury

FOREWORD

Masudul Alam Choudhury's **Reforming the Muslim World** stands within an evolving tradition of Muslim intellectuals and activists who have addressed the major issues facing the global Islamic community.

Throughout the twentieth century, Muslims, as all believers, have grappled with the realities of modernity and more specifically, with the relationship of religion to modernity. If some have at times rejected much of modernity, equating it simply with the Westernization of society, many others have pursued new paths in defining, or perhaps better redefining, the relationship of religion to modern life. In the late nineteenth and early twentieth centuries, Islamic modernism sought to bridge the gap between the conservatism of the religious establishment, the *Ulama* or religious scholars, and the secular liberalism of many emerging elites. Islamic modernists like Muhammad Abduh, Sayyid Ahmad Khan, and Muhammad Iqbal called for a reinterpretation or reformation of Islam. They affirmed the compatibility of religion and reason and reminded the Muslim community that reason and science were not the executive domain of Western Christendom. Islamic modernists called the community to a reawakening and renaissance to reclaim Islam's past glories: political independence and power as well as a flourishing civilization that had once been a major contributor to science and mathematics, art and architecture.

In the 1930s and 40s, a second major Islamic response occurred with the creation of the Muslim Brotherhood in Egypt and the Jamaat-i-Islami in the Indian Subcontinent. These Islamic revivalists were critical of both the conservatist *Ulama* and of Islamic modernists who they believed Westernized Islam in the process of trying to make Islam compatible with the West. Hassan al-Banna and Mawlana Mawdudi created the Brotherhood and Jamaat, respectively. They and their successors have combined ideology and political and social activism addressing a wide range of concerns, from the nature of the Islamic state and Islamic law to the relevance of Islam to economic and educational development.

In recent years a diverse group of Muslim scholars and intellectuals have continued to address issues of reforms from a variety of perspectives and schools of thought. Those who opt for a more secular approach, affirm the importance of religion but restrict it to personal life; others speak of the Islamization of knowledge and of Islamic economics. Yet, however different Islamic modernism, Islamic revivalism, and contemporary Islamic voices may be, they share in common recognition of the need to create a new epistemology to undergird and inform a process of reform that has roots and continuity with the Islamic tradition but also responds in new and creative ways to a rapidly changed and changing world.

Masudul Alam Choudhury in **Reforming the Muslim World** tackles the difficult epistemological questions that underlie any effective reconstruction of the governments and institutions of the Muslim world. Drawing on Islamic and Western sources (philosophical and socio-scientific), he critiques Western paradigms and proposes his own, a *Shuratic* process (an Islamic socio-scientific world view) rooted in the Islamic doctrine of *Tawhid*, the Unity of God. His discussion is placed not only within the context of political economic theory but also in the praxis of Malaysia and of the Organization of the Islamic Conferences.

The challenge for Muslims, as for humanity, at the dawn of the twenty-first century is to construct a post-modern age in which development is seen not only in terms of political economy but also in terms of enduring principles and values which provide a sense of meaning and purpose. Masudul Alam Choudhury's **Reforming the Muslim World** offers both a critique and a response, one which will challenge both Muslim and non-Muslim readers.

Professor John L. Esposito
Director, Center for Muslim-Christian Understanding
Georgetown University, Washington D.C.

INTRODUCTION

NATURE OF THE STUDY

Reforming the Muslim World is a study of the epistemological questions underlying authentic Islamic issues. Such questions must be understood, tackled and answered within the thought process and material reconstruction of a future Muslim world for its Islamic reformation. The range of reformation is thus shown to include economic, social, political and socio-scientific inquiries for realizing the common good of the *Ummah*, the world nation of Islam, and of the *Ummah* in relation to the global order today. The epistemological premise of the Unity of God as it is primordially understood and is practically applied for realizing structural transformation of the *Ummah*, becomes the central subject matter of this study for investigating the reformation process.

Future reconstruction of the institutions and governments of the Muslim world, most importantly the role of the Organization of Islamic Conferences and of Malaysia as a dynamic Muslim nation in the contemporary Muslim world, is critically evaluated. New institutional and developmental forms are then prescribed on the basis of the epistemological framework of Divine Unity and its application to the principle of systemic unification taken globally. This is an Idea that emanates from the Precept of Divine Unity and extends over the realm of applications and empirical reality called here as the Field of Unity. The resulting organizational structure of the globally interactive-integrative-evolutionary world view that naturally arises from the epistemological premise of Unity and unification, is termed in this book as the *Shuratic* Process. The term is coined from the generic word, *Shura*, which in the *Qur'an* is explained as a universal consultation *process* that carries the unification epistemology with it. The concept of *Shura* is thus not limited to the political arena alone as is otherwise to be found in much of recent Islamic literature.

Problems of science, political economy, firm as an organization, institutionalism in the midst of globalization, money and finance, the Organization of Islamic Conferences and the present state of political governance in Muslim countries with a special focus on Malaysia within Islamic reconstruction, are studied critically and alternatives are prescribed in light of unification epistemology. The study is comparative in nature, taken up within the broad spectrum of occidental thoughts in economics, epistemology, science and political economy.

The problems of science, society, economics and institutions are treated in this book as an evolving and pervasively interactive domain of human experience transcended only by knowledge of unification among these systems. Such a power of unification, that is derivation of knowledge, is totally founded on cause and effect in the Divine roots. With such a world view the epistemological foundations of Islamic reformation is bound to be contrary to the occidental world (Huntington 1993), what the modernists have captioned as the Hegelian world borrowed from Hellenic origins and converging to Germanic civilization (Mazrui 1993). Within the occidental order, unity is self-abiding within individuality, the particular and the universal (Kolb 1986), but coordination among these necessitates emulation of the individual self to describe and drive the principle of universal becoming (Makkreel 1990). Coordination and reformulation of the concept of universality in occidentalism is seen to be a lateral aggregation of the individual preferences in all domains of thought and experience (Crocker trans. of Rousseau [1762] 1967). That is, while pluralism is promoted, this means the lateral aggregation of agency preferences that are optimally unified within themselves. Hence, methodological unification cannot be possible among such totally differentiated agencies without giving up the intrinsic character of individualism. Conflict cannot be removed. Pluralism is thus aggregative individualism, a perspective that is truly utilitarian in its universalization across self, socio-scientific domain and human actions of the occident (Parson 1964).

Our denial of methodological individualism in the Islamic civilizational framework of unification epistemology must not be construed as denial of the individual spirit. The *Qur'an* has sanctified the individual in so many of the verses (Chapter 2, v. 30; Chapter 15, v. 29). Individuality is seen to be preserved and liberated to freedom in Islam by means of its social belonging, wherein it renders its potential through the discursive *process* of formation of rules of conduct in conformity with unification epistemology of Divine Unity (*Tawhid*). Yet the individual, and hence the test of rationalism, are not the ultimate roots of socio-scientific rationality in Islam. Humanism does not transcend the axiomatic foundation of the divinely unified world view. It is created, capacitated and re-originated within the Freedom given to humanism by the Divine fold (Boisard 1988).

The derivation of rules from the knowledge-based *process* and not *aggregation*, is referred to in this book as *Ahkam*-formation premised on the epistemological roots of *Qur'an* and *Sunnah* (sayings and actions of the Prophet Muhammad) derived by means of exercising human discursions on issues (*Ijtehad*). The domain of Islamic Laws, *Shari'ah*, is thus seen to be neither static nor narrowly restricted to social, political and economic matters alone. It equally extends substantively over the socio-scientific issues. The socio-scientific domain comprises everything where science, society, economy, institutions and the self interact, integrate and evolve by a distinctively life-giving blood of the *Qur'anic* world view in human praxis.

Likewise, the meaning of pluralism is reconstrued to mean diversity within unity. The utilitarian concept of lateral aggregation of individuated preferences is thus thoroughly rejected as being both amoral and methodologically incorrect. Furthermore, the unification epistemology applied to so many realms of human action covered in this book, presents a concept of change and freedom that is quite contrary to the positioning of individualism at the centre of the idea of modernity. The discursive *process* of unification epistemology is shown to be embedded in the pervasiveness and realization of Divine Unity in all walks of life. The functional way of creating this great 'Universal' is shown to be the medium of Islamic Laws taken up in the Freedom of the *Ijtehadi* Spirit. The cause, effect and continuity of this *process* is called in this book as the Islamic social contract, that is, the *Ummah* and the *Ummatic* Order (Choudhury 1993).

PARTICULAR COMPARISONS

Reforming the Muslim World looks at a scientific research program similar to what Husserl in recent times undertook for reviving the materialistic fallen European Spirit, to a new order of science-philosophy, which he construed as the essence of rationality (Husserl trans. Lauer 1965). Husserl saw in naturalism and overly empirical objectivism of the sciences the sign of decline of the human spirit to know and to coexist through infinities of possibilities. Husserl's transcendental spiritual order was his prescription for European reformation: This was to rise to the state of becoming the truly 'European'. Husserl equated with the concept of a universal cosmopolitanism born of the intersubjective essence of science-philosophy becoming, the bedrock of liberation for the human spirit from reductionism.

Reforming the Muslim World likewise equates the universal spirit with the Precept of Divine Unity (*Tawhid*) and its scientific explanation is carried out through the Field of Divine Unity (*Ayath Allah*=Signs of God). These two permanently co-exist. The result is the phenomenon substantively explained in this book by means of the scientific methodology of circular causation and continuity model of unified reality. The same underlying *process* of interactions-integration-evolution is also variedly referred to as the epistemic-ontic circular causation and continuity model or the *Shuratic* Process. This methodology is shown to pervade the length and breadth of all sciences and fields of human actions. **Reforming the Muslim World** calls upon Muslims as well as others to this unified world view in all human actions. This is shown to be attainable by means of the overarching knowledge-based cosmic essence of *Tawhid* and its bestowing of unification epistemology in the generic socio-scientific order.

Thus like Husserl's **The Crisis of European Sciences and Transcendental Phenomenology** (Husserl trans. Carr 1970), which saw the fall of the occidental order in its divorce of spirituality from the sciences and called for its restitution, so also **Reforming the Muslim World** sees the backwardness of the modern Muslim world in its distancing from the essential roots of the *Qur'anic* world view. It calls Muslims and the world citizens alike toward this unified knowledge-based world view for a revival of unlimited human potential. However, unlike Husserl's **Crisis**, **Reforming the Muslim World** dispels from the methodology of unification epistemology all traces of Hellenic thought. It thus aims at carrying the discourse on historicism beyond the science of culture to which both Husserl and Ibn Khaldun lend their sympathy (Mahdi 1964). A universal cultural perception is treated as an experiential phenomena existing independently of an *a priori* noumena (the soul) in Ibn Khaldun. Whereas, the soul is shown to remain in its permanent search of intellection. The connection between these levels of experience is shown to be discontinuous, since Ibn Khaldun uses Aristotelian ideas of hierarchy of perceptions, also used by the Ikhwan as-Safa (Schleifer 1985, Nasr 1978). In phenomenology too, it is difficult to see how a humanly possible methodology can be deduced to read the subjective essence of 'nature in its own right', without going through the continuity of a *process* that is fired by the Divine Spirit causing unification across systems (Hammond et al. 1991). Unification epistemology arising from the *Qur'an* treats God, nature, self and the 'environing' world as essentially objective realities composed in a purposively integral relationship (*Qur'an* Chapter 3, v. 190-91).

The methodology of circular causation and continuity presented in **Reforming the Muslim World** but developed elsewhere (Choudhury 1995), premises historicism on the *Qur'anic* principle of rise and fall of civilizations. This principle is governed totally by the degree of man's acceptance or denial of the Divine Spirit as it spreads its unshakeable roots in the moral-material and socio-scientific order. It affirms and confirms itself through the attributes of Justice, Purposes, Certainty, Well-Being and Re-Origination (creative evolution) (*Qur'an* Chapter 29, v. 19-20; Chapter 50, v. 36-37; Chapter 14, v. 24-27). In this context, the phenomenology of Islamic world view is exemplified by the Prophetic Constitution of Madinah (also known as the Madinah Charter) (al- Umari 1991). Its primordial epistemology premised on the Stock of Knowledge is shown here to reside in the Essence of the *Qur'an* (*Lauh Mahfuz*), which in the anthropic world is projected by the Prophetic intellection through the Realm of Perfect Knowledge (Tree of Perfect Know-ledge=*Sidrathul Muntaha*). The circular causation and continuity model of unified reality derives its epistemological premise from such primordial roots only to further but never to claim worldly perfection in the perpetual movement of the socio-scientific *process* towards Truth. The methodology thus rejects any link with Hellenic roots of social con-tractarianism as is true of the West. It is a pity that some Muslim scholars had so blindly followed and continue to follow traditions that do not emanate from the *Qur'anic, Sunnatic* and *Ijtehadi* core of Islamic epis-temology. This is not to deny the otherwise original contributions made by Muslim scientists in all fields. A Hellenic and rationalist state of intellection and its application in life will always prove to be a great disability in reforming the Muslim world (Berggren 1992).

Reforming the Muslim World comes at a critical time to dispel once again the gross misnomer, such as, traditionalism, anti-modernism and coercive order that the occident has held against Islam (Kolb p. 5). Yet the substantive divide between the Islamic and occidental orders is recog-nized. This book hinges around this academic recognition in order to bring forth a note of continued discourse between and within Islam and the West. Thus the same dynamics of the interactive-integrative-evolutionary methodology of unification epistemology developed in this book, suggest that knowledge sharing is a uniquely *Qur'anic* world view. It is instilled in cosmic life of the past, present and the future as permanence, wherein the human kind can hope to melt together in truth, freedom and harmony.

SUMMARY OF CHAPTERS

Chapter 1 lays down the methodology of unification epistemology as it is derived from the *Qur'anic* Precept of Divine Unity and its externalization in the living and experiential worlds through the precept of the Field of Unity. Unification epistemology and its foundational methodology now become the guiding element of the entire study undertaken in this book. Because of its intrinsically knowledge-based world view, this methodology is also referred to as the circular causation and continuity model of unified reality. This chapter was presented at the Third European Congress on Systems Science, held in the University of Rome between October 1-4, 1996.

Chapter 2 examines how unification epistemology can become the foundation of new science for all, and how such a scientific epistemology substantively differs from that of occidentalism. The dividing line between the unification and occidental epistemologies is shown to be the intrinsically unified world view of the former that admits of no individuation and the central role of rationalism causing pervasive individualism, pluralism and differentiation in the occidentalist view of the world. This foundational difference between the two epistemologies is studied critically by reference to the thoughts of Imam Ghazzali in Islamic scholasticism and Immanuel Kant in occidental scholasticism. This part of the study provides a dialectical look on the emergence of new science from the *Qur'anic* knowledge-based world view. This chapter was presented as a paper at the Annual Meeting of the Association for the Unity and Integration of Knowledge, the Learned Societies Conference, Brock University, Ontario, May 28-30, 1996.

Chapter 3 presents an analytical way of viewing the moral, ethical and social relevance of science. Hence the term, socio-scientific order, is developed. The *Shuratic* Process is developed to explain further the socio-scientific world view. Substantive explanations of science-technology-society and science-technology-organization interface are developed to show how the ethical socio-scientific domain becomes globally pervasive and meaningful. The chapter was presented as a paper at the International Conference on Science and Islamic Polity in the Twenty-First Century, OIC Standing Committee on Scientific and Technological Cooperation, Islamabad, Pakistan, March 26-30, 1995.

Chapter 4 presents the idea of Islamic political economy as a systemically interactive-integrative-evolutionary process on economic, social, institutional and socio-scientific matters. The paradigm of Islamic political economy is then applied to the concept of ecology and economics as a relational order across systems. This chapter was presented as a paper at the Eleventh World Congress of the International Economic Association, Tunis, Tunisia, December 16-28, 1995.

Chapter 5 presents a theory of the Islamic firm viewed as an organization. The concepts of equilibrium, resource allocation and optimal behaviour in received economic theory are critically investigated to bring out the basically flawed deductions in neoclassical economic theory that are derived on grounds of scientific niceties at the expense of social realism. Alternatively, dynamic concepts of moving and perturbed equilibria are introduced within a knowledge-induced order grounded on the *Shuratic* Process. The dynamics of knowledge-based process grounded in unification epistemology as it externalizes itself to the practical case of the firm, are shown to be embedded in a methodology emanating from Chapter 1. This chapter was presented as an invited lecture at the School of Management, Universiti Sains Malaysia, on September 4, 1996.

Chapter 6 brings forward the politico-economic issues to the case of money and discusses the latter's endogenous nature in Islamic political economy. The Islamic concept of endogenous money is contrasted with exogenous monetary theory and the quantity theory of money. In this way, a theory of endogenous money in Islamic framework is shown to emanate from the premise of unification epistemology, now applied to show how money as a contravention arises from interactions and integration between the financial and the markets for real goods.

Chapter 7 is a critical study of the economic, political and social states of the Muslim world in the midst of capitalist globalization. The concept of capitalist globalization is critically examined in view of the goals of social well-being, grass-roots development and socio-economic reasoning. Against the existing regime of capitalist globalization, the Islamic paradigm of globalization is presented as a process of interactions and integration followed by creative evolution of ethicized markets within a globally systemic whole. The grass-roots world view of globalization is thus developed and suggested as a socio-economic prescription for future development cooperation in the *Ummah*. This chapter is a version of the author's invited talk given to the School of Social Sciences, Universiti Sains Malaysia, sometime in July 1994.

Chapter 8 studies the case of Malaysia today with regards to her approach to socio-economic development and as a potentially important role player in socio-economic integration and development of the Muslim world. Yet the Malaysian development formula is examined critically in light of the methodology arising from unification epistemology as this presents itself in the development scene. Alternatives are then prescribed.

Chapter 9 is a critical examination of the Organization of Islamic Conferences as a prime politico-economic institution in the Muslim world and yet shown to be balked down by partisan conflicts and Euro-centric type self-interests of dominant members. An alternative framework of the OIC as a Grand *Shura* for the Muslim world guided by unification epistemology on all fronts, is proposed for the future transformation of OIC. An interactive-integrative process-oriented hierarchy of relations is shown to be possible in this new framework for *Ummatic* well-being.

Chapter 10 collects the principal implications on reformation from the various chapters of the book and presents them in the form of a series of policy recommendations. The specific areas of importance taken up are first, institutional change with the OIC as a possible venue of future grass-roots-driven example of the Grand *Shura*. Second, educational curricular and programmatic changes that can help formalize the common methodology of circular causation and continuity model of unified reality as an academic undertaking, are proposed. Third, the pressing need for Islamic capital market transformation in line with the endogenous theory of money and finance, is emphasized.

THE AUDIENCE OF THIS BOOK

Throughout this book analytical approach combined with extensive comparative coverage of literature, stem the direction of the arguments and discussions. Although the book is for mature readership, general readers will follow the thrust of the arguments presented in it. The book will be of particular interest to scholars, researchers, academicians and students at graduate and advanced undergraduate levels. It will also be useful to decision makers in national and international development organizations, who invariably need to come abreast with the changes occurring in the Muslim world. Every college, university and public library throughout the world should have this book to understand the critical questions underlying relationships between the Muslim world and the global order in the light of the Islamic world view.

CHAPTER 1

THE EPISTEMOLOGICAL PREMISE
OF REFORMATION

This chapter lays down the epistemology of Divine Unity and explains how this originary epistemology is externalized in the Islamic sciences, socio-economic and institutional matters. These two parts premised on Divine Unity are together termed as unification epistemology. This provides the methodology for the analytical framework, analysis and policy study relating to reformation of the Muslim world, the subject matter of this book. Unification epistemology is shown to be the foundation for reforming the Muslim world in terms of its thought process and its socio-scientific transformation. In this chapter we will introduce the analytical methodology underlying unification epistemology. This will be invoked in this book while treating a diverse number of issues.

THE PRECEPT OF UNITY

Religious experience of the Unity of God presents the Precept of Unity in the frame of God being the sole Creator, Cherisher and Sustainer of the worlds. Yet by Himself, God remains an uncreated Being. Thus there are two precepts of Unity to be observed as the epistemological foundation of the knowledge-based socio-scientific order. These are first, the foundational Precept of Unity, and second, the Field of Unification emanating from the Precept of Unity.

The foundational Precept of Unity signifies the a *priori*, that is, the most irreducible and immutably axiomatic existence of God as the sole Creator but one who is not created, has no equal. We will call this state of completeness of knowledge of the Supreme Creator as the Stock of Knowledge (Choudhury 1995a). We will also equate this primal premise with the Complete Knowledge embalmed in a Final Event, which we call hereafter (*Akhira* in *Qur'anic* terminology).

Hence in this primal state of the Precept of Unity we show that Creation incessantly springs from the Stock, wherein the following equivalence holds:

God=Stock of Knowledge=Truth=Cumulative Stock of Knowledge in Hereafter.

A MATHEMATICAL FORMULATION OF THE UNITY PRECEPT AND FIELD

In the above-mentioned way, the Precept of Unity as the immutable and pervasive springboard of creation bestowing meaning and form, becomes a mathematically closed mapping of the Stock of Knowledge into itself through the process of creation cumulating to the same complete Stock of knowledge in hereafter. In other words, the Precept of Unity is the axiomatic foundation of belief, which subsequently, assumes the meaning of knowing and certainty followed by advance in every facet of life and thought.

By way of establishing the axiomatic premise of Divine Unity we will now inquire, as to what consequences the universe would face if the Divine origin of Unity as the primal epistemology of existence was not there? The answer to this query is of mathematical ushering. God is self-referenced in the revealed texts to mean the true Reality. Thus there are now at least two premises of coherent correspondences that are found to emanate from the Divine root of primal Unity. These are first, the question that we must now tackle, although briefly, on the logical self-referencing of God as the origin of all creation. Secondly, the conjoint meaning of Reality that emanates from the same self-referencing root

2

must be explained. We proceed as follows:

Let T denote Unity as a topological space (Maddox 1970). The mathematical properties of a topology must characterize T as being a collection of all subspaces, say X, and endowed by a field or encompassing space, say t. Hence T=(X,t). Furthermore, t has the property that it includes both X and the nullity of X. All possible mathematical unions (denoted here by the symbol ∪) and mathematical intersections of all subspaces of T (denoted here by the symbol ∩), belong to T. However, there is an additional characterization that must be included with T. That is to allow for the possibility of infinite intersections, and hence for the possibility of infinite union of infinite intersections of subspaces of T. This additional property is not found in a standard definition of topological space, with t say, as the topology over the subspaces of T.

We define here the space X belonging to t as the space of all worlds that religious experience spans. God is taken as the Lord of all the worlds. There are uncountable number of these worlds. Therefore, ∪X must also belong to t for infinite unions of X's.

Next we will define t as the set of Divine Laws, which are understood as relations between knowledge and creation (the worlds). Since t itself is also infinite in its capacity for generating relations (Hawking 1988), therefore, ∪t belongs to t. As well as, ∩t for all possible t's, belongs to t. That is, ∪∩t belongs to t. But since X and ∪X belong to t, therefore, (∪∩X) belongs to t. t now becomes the carrier of the Stock of Knowledge into the creation of material forms that are signified by X's.

In the limit of infinite possibilities for X's and t's through combinations and evolutions in them, the following relations must hold:
$\lim\{[d[\cup\cap X(t)]/dt\} > 0$, in the limit as t increasingly gets contained in T. X(t) here denotes the functional dependence of X on t because of the topological inclusions. Hence two dynamics are involved here. First $\lim[\cup\cap t]$ comprehends the whole of T and along with this the positive

3

mapping of t on X must also make $\lim[\cup \cap X]$ comprehend the whole of all X's. In the infinite limit therefore, intersections of infinitely limiting subspaces coincide with the union of such subspaces. This is the meaning of the irreducible character of T. T comprehends both the subspaces as well as the total space of X's and t's and interrelationships in these.

The concept of irreducibility is also equivalent to that of self-referencing. This is a methodology of revealed texts through which God establishes Himself as the Supreme Being. Self-referencing is possible only in the infinite limiting domain. It cannot exist for the localized subspaces due to the limited power endowed in the subspaces. Self-referencing therefore means the equivalence of truth with the Stock of Complete Knowledge. This is the limiting topology of t as the topologically 'complete' subspace of T. On the other hand, in the local subspaces that allow for the invoking of temporal flux and changes of knowledge, it is the recursive phenomenon of combinations of t's and X's through their incessant movement toward greater certainty, that translates into cognitive phenomena and flows of knowledge.

However, every new creation in this sense must derive its existence from T. Hence, we deduce the two dynamics: One is of T being complete, impacting and creating (mathematical inclusion) the t's and X's and their varied combinations. The other is the movement of t's and X's incessantly in subspaces. But even in this case there is no independence between the t's and X's, among their combinations, and hence, among re-originations from the primal impact of T as the first cause of the dynamics. However, T remains primal, complete, irreducible, self-referencing, re-creating, but never created, never changing. Whereas, (X,t) and their combinations are forever changing and are never self-referencing except by way of primal reference to T.

Finally, self-referencing must also mean that the end-all or the cumulative process of temporal order is attainment of T. This phenomenon as we have mentioned, is established in hereafter. That is, while

4

the openness of the human mind as the primordial praxis. While God and His Divine Laws as manifested in the worlds, become the Supreme Ontology of the Unity order, in the domain of rationalism and perception, humanistic philosophy and outlook assume the primal praxis.

Evolution in non-Unity systems is not from the episteme of knowledge that can then carry with it the topological mappings into materiality, seen here as knowledge-induced events enabling entities to recreate fresh flows of knowledge. Rather, they emerge from materiality either in the Humean or Cartesian sense of *a posteriori* category or in the Kantian sense of *a priori* isolation of the Divine as the abstract domain removed from the field of material realism. The two methodologies of the *a priori* and the *a posteriori* do not interrelate with each other. This creates systemic dualism in the methodological approach and perceptions of the sciences. It is in this sense that unification between the *a priori* and *a posteriori* cannot be attained. Perception in rationalistic framework remains a phenomenon distinctly opposed to the concept of world view.

OTHER CONCEPTS OF UNITY IN THE SCIENCES

Other forms of unification methodology in the sciences have meant systemic perpetuation of Darwinian type competitive evolution (Hawking 1988). This causes interactions to lead into non-integration, competition, differentiation and resultant diminishing interactions. Darwinian evolutions repeat this dynamics. Endogeneity in this system means the recreation of the inter-systemically exogenous nature of Darwinian, falsificationist and dualistic order across systems (Neurath 1970). This is the ethics that is manifest in the theory of utilitarianism. On the other hand, endogeneity in the knowledge-induced world view means the inter- and intra-systemic interactions leading to integration and evolution premised on the Principle of Universal Complementarity (Daly 1991, Choudhury 1995b).

9

CONCLUSION

In this chapter we have introduced the meaning and methodology of unification epistemology as the central idea of knowledge in Islamic world view. We identified the Stock of Knowledge with the Precept of Unity. Likewise, we refer to unification of knowledge premised on Unity as the Field of Unity emanating from the Stock. In the *Qur'an*, the Field of Unity is referred to as the Signs of God (*Ayath Allah*). World systems are established by a topological relationship between the Stock and flows of knowledge in the interactive, integrative and evolutionary sense.

CHAPTER 2

THE SCIENTIFIC PREMISE OF REFORMATION

The beginning of any scientific revolution owes itself to the construction of or revisitation in epistemology, the theory of knowledge pertaining to the discipline under investigation. This has been the trend with scholarship both among the occidental schools and the Islamic thinkers, who themselves had contributed to the scientific epistemology of the occident in certain ways. Therefore, while it is important to discern the origins and foundations of scientific reconstruction on epistemological questions, it is equally important to note what the principal undercurrents of scientific revolution have been historically to modern times. This is to assess whether the epistemological directions of scientific inquiries are being well directed or not.

THE QUESTIONS POSED

What are the roots of the scientific problematique in their modern content? What scientific alternatives exist in the face of such problematique? By an answer to these questions the comparative world view of Islamic scholarship against occidentalism in the area of scientific epistemology can be understood. The search for such answers is the objective of this chapter. Within this objective we will undertake a comparative study of various scientific doctrines. Our particular focus will be on the epistemology of Kant for the occidental order and of Ghazzali's for Islamic scholasticism. We will also cover other scientific thoughts. Our examination of all these doctrines will be carried out critically in light of the scientific world view presented by the *Qur'an* on unification of knowledge, which we have formalized in Chapter 1.

A BRIEF CRITIQUE OF OCCIDENTAL SCIENTIFIC EPISTEMOLOGY

The great relevance of epistemology in scientific paradigm shifts has been recognized in the Western world by Kant, Hume, Descartes, Husserl, Hegel, Marx, Leibniz, Einstein, Kuhn and Popper, among so many others. In this chapter we will take up the legacy of Kant in some depth, for we claim that there exists a systematic pattern of scientific dualism premised in Kantian thought, that has pervaded modern science. Thus our claim is that there exists a post-Kantianism and pre-Kantianism in occidental scientific epistemology that mark the continuity of Hellenic influence in such inquiry. Hellenic thought, Kant and Islamic rationalism thus link up in the rationalistic approach to scientific inquiry. We will return to Kant's epistemology in depth later in this chapter. We now turn to some other leading doctrines that have shaped the development of scientific thought in the West.

1. David Hume's Scientific Epistemology

Hume was an epistemologist with an inductive reasoning. His concept of the nature of human understanding was based on sensate premises that perceive of touch, feeling, seeing and inference (Hume 1992). Material-ism for Hume as to Bacon, became the premise of induction and abstraction for a quantitative approach in science. Rationalism took its roots from the bedrock of the sensate order in Hume, and inductive philosophy became the basis of science either as a positive field of inquiry or as normative metaphysics based simply on the infinite recesses of inductive reasoning. In Hume the ontology or existence of a scientific reality was seen to emanate from a cognitive premise that was sensate.

12

Thereafter, the world was rationally explained by the continuity of inductions infinitely regenerated on the premise of the ever-emerging cognitive identities.

2. René Descartes' Scientific Epistemology

Hume was the legacy of Descartes in the field of scientific dualism. Cartesian dualism has to do with the infinitesimal dissection of the space of reality. Each part so dissected is mapped upon by an infinitesimal part of reason. In this way, the domain of scientific reality is made to comprise non-intersecting poles of the body-mind dichotomies with differentiated and localized action spaces. Such body-mind dualism spans the Cartesian space and forms the concept of scientific duality (Descartes 1952). Descartes was like Hume in his sole reliance on reason as the conveyor of scientific truth. Through this primacy of reason the scientific epistemology in Descartes was made to depend on localized phenomena caused by the mapping of cognitive faculty 'onto' the space of observed things. The difference between Descartes and Hume in the delineation of the originary roots of rationalism, was the former's reliance on deductive reasoning, while Hume premised reason on induction.

3. Leibniz's Scientific Epistemology

Leibniz carried on the infinitesimal concept of space in his monadic philosophy. According to this concept, all actions in space-time are seen to commence by activating an isolated space into social action. To configure his space of monads, Leibniz like Descartes had to isolate the scientific domain into infinitesimally non-interactive parts (Leibniz 1989). This enabled monadic philosophy to observe actions fully in the absence of externally induced interactions. Leibniz thus viewed science as a minimal-axiomatic body of inquiry. He argued that if a point was

13

capable of explaining the universe, then this monadic point was seen to be more real than the universe itself. Leibniz's epistemology was ontological in terms of the existence of the primordial essence in creation. But in his monadic universe, this essence was not readable as a totality. It could be read only in an infinitesimal part of the universe with a tiny embodiment of the essence of creation (monad). This infinitesimal monad configured a geometrical existence for itself in isolation of others. Leibniz's space like Descartes' was thus a mathematical 'union' of non-interacting sub-universes, while their mutual intersection remained void.

4. Albert Einstein's Scientific Epistemology

Einstein's view of space-time reality was of a deeply epistemological type. He remarked that there can be no science without an epistemology (Einstein 1949). Yet Einstein's large scale geometrical configuration of the universe stood on an epistemology that saw time and the speed of light as the basis and the limits for determining change. The principle of simultaneity of time and event in general relativity theory uses the instantaneity of the impact of light on moving frames to establish the relative truth of physical laws with respect to the relative velocity of these geometric frames. Natural laws could then be explained relatively with reference to any of these geometrical frames. This principle of the equivalence of time and event by the medium of the relative velocity concept, is stated in Einstein's words: "According to the theory of relativity, actions at a distance with the velocity of light always takes the place of instantaneous action at a distance or of action at a distance with an infinite velocity of transmission. This is connected with the fact that the velocity c (velocity of light) plays a fundamental role in this theory" (Einstein 1954a, p. 48).

What is important for us to note in the epistemological basis of general theory of relativity is the endogenous nature of time in the four-dimensional geometric configuration, which is unlike the geometrically independent nature of time in classical physics and in Euclidean geometry. The idea of endogeneity of time leads to continuity in space-time structure by means of the principle of equivalence of event and time in moving geometric frames. In other words, what relate one frame to another are their velocities relative to the velocity of light, and such velocities are determined by the 'time-like' movements of the frames.

Relativity theory that has engaged the originary episteme of much of modern theoretical physics leading to the quest for grand unified theories, fails to realize a distinctive claim of universality of the equivalence principle in the local field of Euclidean space and micro-universes of quantum physics. This is due to the way a material field is conceptualized in relativity and in quantum physics. A physical field appears as a domain of gravitational matter in relativity physics and as a field of electrical attractions in quantum physics. The endogenous nature of time depending upon the relative velocity concept, is then marginalized, as particles reach the velocity of light in quantum fields. The equations of Lorentz transformation on space-time structure, so fundamental to general relativity, now turn out to be indeterminate. Singularities occur as is known with regards to the event horizon (Hawking 1988, pp. 81-97). It then becomes futile either to hold on to the limitation of the velocity of light or to the description of material field with Cartesian type extensions (*res extensa*) given in general relativity for understanding physical actions at a distance.

5. Hegel and Marx's Scientific Epistemologies

In Hegel and Marx we observe the relativistic argument being extended to the field of social theory and political economy. To them history was a dialectical movement of either deductive rational arguments or of inductive forms of rationalism gained from economistic experience. In either of these approaches, modernity is seen as a state of presencing, annihilating and recreating thought by continuous movement in human environments. What the velocity of light was to Einstein as the limiting premise of physical explanation, so was economism the limiting premise of historical explanation to Marx. To Hegel the convergence of history on these similar kinds of dialectics was toward his ultimate order of Germanic civilization, where rationalism is seen by Hegel to abide (Hegel 1956, pp. 341-457).

The epistemological meanings of these theories of social sciences, historicism and evolution are dimmed by the limited scope of the premise and hence of the nature of scientific inquiry. On the one hand, the rationalism of the dialectical process causes Darwinian type individualism arising from differentiation by power. On the other hand, any reference to interactions in this mode of understanding scientific socialism is reduced to conflicting hegemony of power groups that span the total social space. The result is thus similar to the scientific dualism of Cartesian philosophy. It marks the end of scientific endogeneity. Einstein experienced this by his inability to incorporate timal endogeneity in his scientific understanding of space-time structure in spite of his desire for treating this primitive concept in a grand unified field (Einstein 1954b). Marx experienced his failure by reducing social ethics to the one-dimensionality of economism (Marcuse 1964). Hegel failed to explain universality of historical process due to his idea of hegemonic convergence of all social processes to the Germanic penultimate state.

6. Edmund Husserl's Scientific Epistemology

The extrapolation of Hegel and Marx into yet another problem that Einstein attempted to accomplish, namely the structure of scientific theorizing, came to a head with Husserl's phenomenology. This was an attempt toward combining the epistemological with the ontological

16

premises of theory construction over states of nature taken in perpetuity. Einstein explained this idea by envisaging the structure of theory as the Cartesian type extension of a reduced number of axioms, to a mix of inductive and deductive planes of knowledge (Holton 1979). To Husserl likewise, phenomenology meant the process of explanation in science by invoking logical types that are premised in both deductive domain (transcendental ego) and inductive domain (phenomenal world of experience). By combining these two in continuity over space-time, phenomenology becomes the study of unification between appearance and reality using extensions over states of nature and society (Hammond et al. 1991, pp. 1-13). Yet Husserl and the phenomenologists like Descartes, separate the domain of transcendental ego from the perceptual world of cognitive realism. Such a dichotomy consequently dissolves any interactions between these two domains. It subjects philosophical explanations of scientific theories to the vagaries of individualistic human praxis and to pluralism in the sense of systemic differentiations. Science is thus demarcated between private science and public science, on which Holton comments. Scientific inquiry becomes an institution of power (Holton 1975).

Hegelian concept of the supremacy of Germanic civilization, the present days idea of Western scientific Eurocentricity, Marx's economism for explaining historicism and Einstein's closedness of space-time structure by the ultimate reduction to the velocity of light, are all examples of such powerful manifestations of peer groups within scientific culture. In such manifestations of scientific plurality as power driven differentiations and not forms of diversity, scientific truth becomes seriously contested by its relativism and pluralistic design.

7. Kuhn and Popper's Scientific Epistemologies

Kuhn recognized the powerful role that peer groups play in reinforcing their ideas to generate paradigm shifts. Popper formalized his theory of scientific falsificationism to instill the dynamics of rationalistic methodological individualism in the truth-statements of science. The openness of the conjectural universe bears testimony to these facts (Kuhn 1970; Popper 1963).

It is interesting to note the contradiction between Kuhn's idea of paradigm shifts that are attained by rejecting old beliefs by revolutionary new crisis-aiming ideas, and Popper's falsificationism that sees scientific evolution to be premised on a continuously falsifying trend of old theories. One can formalize to show that the continuity property of falsifying change in Popper must negate the character of scientific gestation to establish a paradigm in Kuhn. Besides, Popper's falsificationism leads to a dilution of the action space of scientific theories into infinitesimal segments, each falsifying the other. In this state of scientific evolution too, a gestation period of power and reinforcement of Kuhnian revolution cannot be permitted.

Kuhn's scientific revolution leads to the formation of powerful but conflicting groups. This is an idea of scientific convergence. Popper's falsification leads to plurality by scientific differentiation that conflict and marginalize each other and finally form Darwinian clusters. This gives the idea of methodological individualism negating interactions. Thus methodological individualism may be seen as a convergence in the small domain; whereas Eurocentric convergence is methodological individualism in the large domain (Choudhury forthcoming). The two taken together once again bring us to the idea of conflict between private and public science mentioned by Holton. In recent times too, we find that much of the government sponsored research grants is the United States must be approved finally by the Research Department at the Pentagon. Highest ranking is given to those research proposals that promote the American world views.

THE METHODOLOGICAL INFERENCE GAINED FROM OCCIDENTAL SCIENTIFIC EPISTEMOLOGIES

The methodology of scientific inquiry in occidental order can be endlessly critiqued by including so many other doctrines. But wherever we turn in this spectrum there is a unique message to be found. This is also the singular conclusion that we derive at this point by summarizing the common methodology in all of the doctrines we have examined above. We find that in every one of these, the primacy of rationalism and individualism taken in the very small or the very large systems, makes scientific truth a relative form of comprehension of reality. Human societies are led to search for such relative truths by the advance of science. Knowledge is thus not necessarily advanced in the direction of certainty. The world of science is thereby seen to be an uncertain domain of knowledge acquisition, when ethics, values and morals are considered to remain exogenous to the scientific domain. Consequently, the socio-scientific impact that is left behind by such a random idea of truth, assumes an equally uncertain nature.

We also deduce that in either the Darwinian concept of interaction and evolution or in the endogenous nature of continuity of certain intrinsic elements of the systems under study, the limiting and reduc-tionist premise of cognitive elements, such as, the velocity of light, economism, transcendental ego and experiential realism, finally annuls interactions and endogeneity. Such systems then fail to acquire ethical and moral relevance. Our search for these essential elements within a new scientific epistemology must therefore continue.

WHITEHEAD'S PROCESS CONCEPT IN SCIENTIFIC EPISTEMOLOGY

Our search still proceeds on in the comparative framework of occi-dentalism for a concept of *process* in scientific methodology. We will

19

commence by defining the precept of *process*, and hence of processual systems, by invoking the works of Whitehead and others.

Using the ontological categories of existentialism, Whitehead defines a process as a field of ever-widening extensions arising from interactions between ontological categories and the temporal state of physical realities. This processual idea is further explained by taking three fields of actions that combine with each other by sets of causal relations.

First, an entitiy, E, is endowed by its concrescent presense, E_0. This defines the given geometric position. Then there is the past data base - the prehensions of E_0, denoted by E-. There are also the future consequences of E_0, denoted by E+. Above these are the overarching interactions induced by contemporaneous entities C. A process is now seen as an extension of information through cause-effect relationships among these entities (Whitehead 1979, pp. 123-26).

Let us define E_0 as the entity caused by interactions among all the entities, by $E_0=[E \cap (E-) \cap (E+) \cap C](t)$, t denoting extensions that may be over time, space or space-time. Besides, all possible variations of the above interactions denoted by the functional, f(.) defined over E_0, are possible. That is, $f(E_0)$ is an equivalent processual system. The directions of the relations are also to be noted in Whitehead's conception of processual systems: E- $\rightarrow E_0$, E $\rightarrow E_0$, E $\rightarrow$ E+, C $\rightarrow$ E, and since E is a contemporary with regards to the other entities, therefore, E $\rightarrow$ C as well. t is then the realization of each and every such interaction. That is, $t_0=E(E_{-0})$ is the initial point of the nexus of relationships, prior to which no prehension exists. Besides, $t_0 \rightarrow E_0 \rightarrow t_1$ etc. $t=(t_0,t_1, ...)$.

It is now important to note that the critical originary functionals, t_0 and E_0-, that subsequently influence all processual elements, are sensate according to Whitehead. Consequently, either like Hume or Kant or in terms of the limitation of the physical properties of epistemological entities that we have seen, the sensa acquire the same kinds of epistemological limitations. The result is that the emanation and the end of extensions are within simply the physical domain. This is equivalent to the concept of material field in physics of which Einstein like Descartes and Hume, wrote,

"It requires the idea of the field as the representative of reality, in combination with the general principle of relativity, to show the true kernel of Descartes' idea, there exists no space 'empty of field' " (Einstein 1954a, p. 156).

It was also the material idea of such concrescent fields that led Whitehead to conceptualize God as a created though permanent thing. Such ideas of sheer metaphysical groping led Whitehead to belittle the theistic originality of Islam and orthodox Catholicism. He wrote, "...the doctrine of an aboriginal, eminently real, transcendent creator, at whose fiat the world came into being, and whose imposed will it obeys, is the fallacy which has infused tragedy into the histories of Christianity and Mahometanism" (Whitehead 1979, p. 342). Thus at the end, out of the grandiose metaphysical groping of Whitehead for a substantive explanation of processual system, his characterization of God as a created divine order, hurls divinity into the domain of the created (but permanent things). Whitehead's treatment of God is pantheistic in terms of time, space and energy. The *sui generis* of causation, universality and processual meaning thus ends up in the same quagmire of emptiness earlier argued out regarding the demise of ethical endogeneity and systemic interactions.

A THEORY OF STRONG INTERACTIONS

A theory of strong interactions as reciprocal interactive relations between agents, has been provided in the literature (Smith 1992, pp. 67-104). The formalism of strong interactions proceeds as follows: Let the interacting variables be X_i, Y_i, $i=1,2,..n$. The concept of strong interactions means that $(X_1,Y_1) \cap (X_2,Y_2) \neq \Phi$. This comes about through a maze of interrelationships among the component variables. Yet if we are to express these vectors by means of feedback equations in time-dependent variables, the problem of initial and terminal conditions would epistemologically result in a non-interacting system. It then becomes epistemologically unexplainable as to how interactions start and persist on globally, once non-interactions exist in the initial and terminal states.

This is the problem seen with optimal control theory problems, where the need for optimization necessitates initial and terminal conditions on the state variables to be preassigned. The result is that the scientific urge for optimization in turn annuls the possibility for interactions in the system.

The problems of optimality was faced in relativity theory by the assumption of the limiting velocity of light (world-line). This in turn caused ethical endogeneity and interactions to become finally ineffective in the physical order. So also now in any social system, the presence of an assumed hegemony or steady state behaviour of state variables and policy variables, makes interactions in such a system ineffective in the global sense. The idea of strong interactions is lost.

This result can be briefly formalized as follows (Intrilligator 1971, pp. 306-25) Let $X(0)=X_0$, $X(T)=X_T$, $Y(0)=Y_0$, $Y(T)=Y_T$ be the initial and terminal conditions on these state variables. Then the criterion objective function is,

$$\text{Max. } J = \int_0^T f(X(t), Y(t))dt,$$

subject to the initial and terminal conditions on state variables. The optimal values of the state and policy variables obtained by solving the Euler-equations, when substituted in the J-function, will yield the value of Max J in terms of X_0, Y_0, X_T, Y_T. Thereafter, $(d/dY)(\partial J/\partial X)=0$ and $(d/dX)(\partial J/\partial Y)=0$. This implies that no further interactions between X and Y variables can be possible. Now since arbitrary values of the terminal time-points can be chosen for micro-systems, therefore by generalization, the entire system reverts to individualized singletons in the limiting sense. All interactions now cease.

The basic problem in substantively establishing globally interactive systems and in viewing systems as organisms of strong interactions taken globally by extensions, is the absence of evolutionary type embodied knowledge in learning systems. This problem is compounded by the assumption of optimal systems, the assumption of globally equilibrium systems and of the independence of the time variable. Scientific epistemology requires axiomatizing of an originary element that remains permanently endogenous in the system, thus causing interactions to occur in perpetuity and extension. The resulting exchange of knowledge across agents, variables and boundaries of systems in perpetuity, further unifies them according to certain patterns of universalized knowledge variables. Strong interactions cannot allow for discontinuities in the inter- and intra-systemic relationships. Neither can there exist hegemony nor methodological individualism (pluralism) to enforce consensus, as are implied by the preconditions of the terminal variables in optimal control problems.

The discovery, explanation and pervasiveness of certain knowledge parameters in realizing systemic unification, are the essence of the concept of process and of the processual universe. This is a perspective that occidental order cannot address because of its peculiar methodological conception of causation and inference. The problem of methodological individualism or pluralism, both of which are forms of systemic dualism, in opposition to the Precept of Unity as the epistemological premise and character of systems, poses as the principal debility of scientific epistemology in occidental order. On the other hand, the answer to this epistemological problematique is the dividing line between occidental and Islamic scientific epistemologies. This problematique is so deep and so pervasive between Islam and the occident, that it shakes the basis of scientific inquiry in both the natural and social domains. It is a total change in our conception of reality. To this topic we now turn. The epiphenomena of reality here means the epistemological basis of understanding interactions between science, society, economics and polity. Hence such a concept of reality embraces the world view.

SCIENTIFIC EPISTEMOLOGY PREMISED ON UNIFICATION OF KNOWLEDGE: THE *QUR'ANIC* WORLD VIEW

Unification of knowledge has been the pursuit of serious scholars of the sciences since a long time now. The classicals and scholastics in the Islamic and occidental schools pursued it in varying folds of Hellenic and other traditions. The modernists are found to have added nothing new but simply an extension to the metaphysical roots of specific disciplinary areas. What has then emerged out of these old metaphysical orientations is increasing independence between the disciplines. This has created an increasing problem for the project on unification of knowledge in the sciences. In post-modernity a rebirth of interests for discovering common and different roots to the unification question has arisen. This is particularly to be found in the Grand Unification Theories of theoretical physics, in the emergence of interdisciplinary texture of pedagogy and in turn to ethical questions of the social and scientific disciplines. Similar trends are also being observed in the present movements of pressure groups and in a reorientation of public policy under the sustainability agenda.

To investigate the project of unification of scientific knowledge in a comprehensive socio-scientific world view, we now first formalize the basis of that unification model as derived from the *Qur'an*. This measure is then used to evaluate both the scholastic Islamic and the occidental approach to scientific epistemology. We have selected Ghazzali to represent the scholastic Islamic approach, because Ghazzali's conception of Divine Unity in the sciences is singularly different from that of the Islamic rationalists. We have selected Kant as the high watermark of occidental rationalism. Kant developed his ideas of rationalism around Hellenic traditions and these ideas remarkably influenced the development of scientific traditions in the West. Of those today who are strongly influenced by Kantian epistemology are Rawls and Nozick.

The *Tawhidi* (Unity of God) Creative Order

In Figure 2.1 we depict the *Tawhidi* world view (Divine Unity) of the creative order by means of the interactive core of unification. In this figure we show the Stock of Knowledge (invariant by being a Stock) to emanate from the uniquely Divine roots of creation, G_0. G_0 maps 'onto' the world, W, by the arrow G_1. This impact creates a knowledge-induced reality in W, called in the *Qur'an* as the Signs of God (*Ayath Allah*). Knowledge derived as a flow (change in knowledge in the animate world) from Θ in the Stock form at G_0, is now realized in the transformation of G_1 into a created bit of the universe. This is shown by the evolution from G_1 to G_1'. Since G_1' is now a knowledge-induced universe with a part of the Stock in it acquired by means of the flow that has taken place, therefore, G_1' can correpond with G_0. This process means the affirmation of the universal law of Divine revelation in realizing creation as signified by the transition from G_0 to G_1. Subsequently, G_0 maps 'onto' a higher universe induced by earlier flows of knowledge. In this way, we obtain the circular relationship from G_0 to G_2, which subsequently evolves to G_2'. This evolves on to G_0. The process of circularity continues on to G_3 evolving subsequently to G_3', etc. These circularly continuous processes describe evolutionary epistemologies derived by means of interactions among universes, caused by the Stock converting into flows and cumulatively moving toward the Stock again. Unification through interactions in this order is brought about by each process referring back to the Stock while new flows are generated for learning from the Stock.

The lower unbounded region of G_0 means the temporal inability to approximate to the Stock. Only cumulative flows will exist and in the final reality of hereafter (*Akhira*), G_0 is attained fully. Knowledge is completed.

In the above circular process, it is to be noted that since all interactions first return to Stock and recreate the flows, therefore, universal interactions are established inter- and intra-systems. The common root is the Stock. The universe emanates from and then converges to the Stock through the function of flows. Thus unification remains the be-all and end-all of creation in this knowledge-centred epistemic-ontic circular causation and continuity model of unified reality (Choudhury 1994.)

Figure 2.1: The Knowledge-Based Evolutionary
***Tawhidi* Epistemology.**

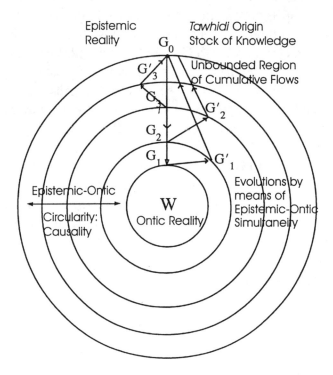

The inter- and intra-systemic interactions and integrations in the evolutionary *Tawhidi* order are described in Figure 2.2. We note the following functional relations inherent in these interactions:

Consider the compound mappings (denoted by o), $g_{01}og_1=g_{02}$; $g_{02}og_2-g_{01}$. Between these, by substituting for g_{01} from the second equation into the first one, we obtain, $g_2og_1=1$. This shows, that there must exist a well-defined inverse relationships between the evolving systems S_1 and S_2. These finally intersect each other with the advance of knowledge, as shown by dotted extensions in the direction of the arrows. This denotes inter-systemic interactions.

The same method can be invoked to establish intra-systemic interactions. Finally, since both of these systems are G_0-based, therefore, inter- and intra-systemic interactions must both be based on and converge to G_0. We call this last characteristic of the evolutionary *Tawhidi* knowledge-centred universe as the interactive-integrative-evolutionary phenomenon of reality.

In the intra-systemic case, the mappings $g_{02} \rightarrow g_2' \rightarrow g_{02}' \rightarrow g_{02} \rightarrow$ etc. are shown to be circular in the knowledge-based evolutionary epistemological order of *Tawhid* (Unity of God). Since these are functionals of both socio-scientific variables and policy/ institutional variables, all being centred in the knowledge domain of Stock and flows, therefore accordingly, the specific pattern of movement of the knowledge parameters, $\{\Theta\}$, over sequences of interactions, will determine the similar pattern of evolution of the variables and their functionals. This is a one-to-one relationship. The dotted regions intra-systems show the evolutionary effect of the total evolution.

Finally, the lower unbounded region of G_0 carries an explanation as before. That is, the human world in the temporal domain is perpetually experiencing simply the flows cumulating to the Stock of knowledge. The latter case is possible only in hereafter (*Akhira*). Hence a closed mapping is established from the originary Stock to the terminal Stock through the medium of flows.

27

The implication of this closed mapping is a deep one. It proves the knowledge-centred ontology of God's (i.e. *Tawhidi*) existence. The same point also proves the uniqueness of the unification epistemology in the universal order and its capacity to attain moving equilibria over knowledge flows. These results answer the ontological questions of socio-scientific systems.

Figure 2.2:   The Interactive-Integrative-Evolutionary Phenomenon of *Tawhidi* Epistemology.

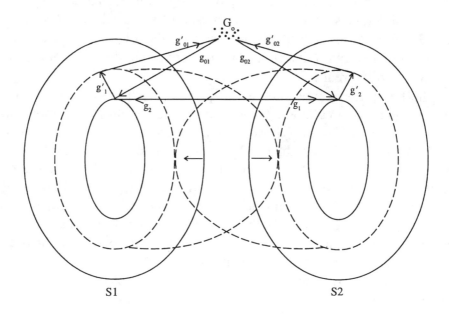

GHAZZALI'S EPISTEMOLOGY AND ITS SCIENTIFIC CONSTRUCTION

Our case studies in this chapter is of Imam Ghazzali's concept of acquisition of knowledge in relation to the project of knowledge-based unification on the plane of *Tawhid*. This grounds the basis of the epistemology in Ghazzali's immortal work **Ihya Ulum-Id-Deen** (Karim undated). Of importance here to note is the primacy that Ghazzali attaches to religious knowledge, and thus treats revelation as premised in the *Qur'an* and *Sunnah* (Prophetic traditions), as the foundation of Islamic epistemology (Karim undated, p. 7). Such a category of knowledge is termed as *Fard Ayn* (obligatory). It comprises the praiseworthy sciences along with the *Shari'ah* (Islamic Law) sciences.

On the other hand, there are the highly recommended but non-obligatory sciences that are necessary for the welfare of society. This branch is called *Fard Kifaya* (recommended). Disciplinary subjects, such as mathematics, natural sciences, social sciences, medicine etc. are taken up by this area.

Islamic epistemology is further extended to comprise also the sources of social consensus, called *Ijma*, arising from discursions on specific matters dealing with the knowledge of *Qur'an* and *Sunnah*. Yet a fourth source of Islamic epistemology is taken up by Ghazzali. This comprises the sayings of the companions of the Prophet Muhammad, as the companions witnessed the actual enactment of Divine revelation to the Prophet.

In Ghazzali's opinion, deriving from his devotional practice of *Sufism*, real knowledge of the sciences lies as a secret to the heart and mind (Karim op cit, pp. 14-118). The heart and mind can fathom these secret recesses a little at a time, only by associating with Divine knowledge the attributes of God, the understanding of His creative purpose, the meaning of prophethood in these functions and in the eternal link between temporal life and hereafter. The creative order with the purpose of knowledge, the gradual unveiling of the mind and heart to the

29

knowledge of Divine attributes and moral self-reformation, are seen to establish the link between such revealed premises and the real world of human conduct and cognition. This functional relationship between revelation and reality is called in **Ihya** as practical religion. The Prophet Muhammad said in this regard, "Take to learning as far as possible, but God will not give its rewards till you translate it into action."

In the area of practical religion, **Ihya** goes on to define the rules of moral conduct in commerce, earnings, work and transactions (Karim op cit, pp. 53-96). A model of the social economy is laid down on the premise of moral self-actualization. This is shown to be the linkage between the commerce of the temporal world and the rewards of hereafter. Three classes of transacters are categorized. First are those who earn livelihood only for this world and reject the returns of hereafter in relation to temporal actions. Second, there are those who focus life's purpose solely for the hereafter, and their link to worldly activities is by way of marginal earning of livelihood. Thirdly, there are those who are midway between the above two. The first case negates the model of Ghazzali's social economy. The second two comprise the model of the social economy. Hence, the world is seen as the groundwork for attaining felicity in hereafter through the benefits that practical religion in this case, bestows on the Islamic social economy (Hassan 1992, pp. 59-82).

The psychological uplift of the heart and mind toward acquisition of knowledge, is brought out in **Ihya** by way of stages of growth of moral self-consciousness. The ultimate spring of this moral consciousness is shown to be premised in the Precept of Oneness of God (*Tawhid*). Yet here too, there are stages for comprehending the essence of *Tawhid* (Faruqi 1977, pp. 45-84).

The Precept of *Tawhid* is taken up in four stages in **Ihya** (Karim op cit, pp. 234-96). First there is the outer husk of *Tawhid*, which is manifested in terms of the human utterance of God's Oneness. The second stage is to confirm that proclamation of Oneness by the heart. The third stage is to feel the essence of *Tawhid* as an inner light, and this power is said to come to truly God-conscious people. The fourth stage is to have the feeling of being in the presence of God, which is the highest stage of moral consciousness.

In all, the epistemology of **Ihya** is shown to be premised totally on the roots of *Tawhid*, and then to externalize this primordial root into action. In this way comes about the meaning of practical religion as a sum-total of belief forming moral consciousness, defining human conduct in practical life and experience.

Finally, it is important to note how Imam Ghazzali treats the relationship of temporal life with hereafter in his epistemology (Karim op cit, pp. 532-36). The following saying of the Prophet is invoked to convey the moment of the supreme most proof of self-actualization and its rewards when God will reveal His vision to the believers in hereafter. This will indeed prove to be the moment of fullest manifestation of perfect knowledge as embalmed in God Himself and presented to creation in small flows at a time. Flows would ensue in this way until the moment of the Divine Vision in hereafter. The Prophet's saying in this regard is as follows: God will fulfil His promise to the believers when He will lift the heavenly screen and the believers will see the Glorious God in the fullness of gaze. At that time, all bestowed heavenly enjoyment and happiness will be forgotten for this supreme most experience. There will be no limit to happiness acquired from such Divine presence. Thus, perfection of knowledge is equated with this supreme most event and is shown to be derived from the foundation of *Tawhid* to its transformation into practical religion through the attainment of moral consciousness.

We can now derive the key points of the above summary of **Ihya** in respect to the foundation of knowledge. The key points here are relationally expressed as follows:

(Tawhid, Risalah, Ijma, Lives of Companions) → Practical
Religion → Hereafter

31

Risalah means the life of the Prophet Muhammad taken up in its entirety of *Sunnah* (actions) and *Ahadith* (sayings).

In this relationship, the intensity of Islamic socio-scientific movement across stages depends upon the depth of belief and moral consciousness toward discovering the inner secret of the sciences. This in turn is shown to relate belief to external conduct, without which a comprehension of reality remains impossible.

CRITICAL INFERENCE FROM GHAZZALI'S METHODOLOGY TOWARDS THE CONSTRUCTION OF ISLAMIC SCIENCE AND VALUES

The requirement by the individual to attain ethical perfection to be capable of the comprehension of *Tawhid* in action in the personal and social order, is an obvious limitation of Ghazzali's methodology when applied to the reconstruction of an Islamic scientific epistemology. Problems arise from the reality of the inherently imperfect knowledge order of the universe and hence from the imperfections of systems that are regulated by such knowledge flows. In the *Tawhidi* circular causation and continuity world view of creation, only the Stock of Knowledge is complete and absolute. It creates the flows as our humanly possible comprehensions of the Divine Laws through the formation of *Ahkam* (rules). In this way, randomness of rationalism is replaced in the derivation of such rules by the *Qur'anic* essence of diversity and complementarity as a globally interacting, integrating and evolutionary (creative) phenomena.

On the other hand, the aggregation of ethically perfect entities of the kind conceptualized by Ghazzali would lead to the utilitarian kind of aggregation of agents and their preferences. The result is the optimization of some notion of happiness. Optimality of this type must reduce the whole system under consideration to a field devoid of interactions and endogeneity of ethics, as we have earlier explained in regards to the scientific epistemology in occidental order.

The above methodological critique of Ghazzali's thoughts creates the reformulation of the relationship (1). This is shown in Figure 2.3:

Figure 2.3: Contrasting Ghazzali's Epistemology by Evolutionary *Tawhidi* Epistemology: A Methodological Problem.

[Lauh Mahfuz]
[as primordial]
[Essence of *Tawhid*] →
[: Complete Stock]
[of Knowledge] ←

[Functional]
[Comprehension]
[of *Tawhid*] →
[in Islamic]
[Life: Flows] ←
[of Divine]
[Knowledge]
[Premised in]
[of happiness]
[the Stock of]
[Primordial]
[Knowledge.]

[Derivation of]
[Flows for]
[practice of] →
[practica]
[religion in] ←
[socio-scientific]
[order]

[Cumulative]
[completion of]
[Stock of]
[Knowledge in]
[Hereafter:]
[Vision of God]
[and perfection]

| ↓ | ↓ | ↓ | ↓ |

This worldly and other worldly interactions.

Interactions and integration in the formation of flows knowledge.

Evolutionary epistemology of *Tawhid* by cause effect between temporal order and hereafter (*Akhira*)↓.

| ↓ | ↓ | ↓ |

Al-Qur'an and *Sunnah* considered to be interpretation

Belief formation, *Qur'anic* interpretation, *Sunnah* not of the category of Divine inspiration.

Formation of rules - *Ahkam* on specific issues as they arise; exercise of *Ijma.*

Proof of unification of knowledge and its completion.

↓----------------------↓   ↓----------------↓   ↓------------↓

33

| The Prophet's Experience of *Sidrathul Muntaha* (celestial flight to the domain of perfect knowledge) | Worldly example of Divine perfection in the Madinah Charter | Increasing proofs of Divine from temporal order to ( ) |

NORMATIVE AXIOMATIC ROOTS
OF KNOWLEDGE

Akhira and
derivation of
tenets of
practical
religion.

↓ ------------------------------- ↓

UNIFICATION OF KNOWLEDGE   NORMATIVE-POSITIVE ROOTS OF
KNOWLEDGE

IMMANUEL KANT

Next we turn to Kant. In Kant we focus on his theory of heteronomy, that is the problem of dualizing the space of rationalism between the *a priori* domain, the *a posteriori* domain and the synthetic domain between these two. We find in Kant's problem of heteronomy his understanding of the subject matters of revelation, religion, belief and pure and practical reason. Here there exists a dichotomy that separates the domain of knowledge into non-analytical forms (Friedrich 1949). Then too, the synthetic nature of pure reason in the realm of the moral law, makes this law at best a creation of reason alone, and reason as the prime determiner of the nature of divinity and the moral law. God as the Lawgiver, remains an existential but a numinous reality in this total framework. On the other hand, the natural world is seen as the creation of the moral and universal laws, a notion that is acceptable under Kant's categorical imperative (Infeld 1963). But in itself, the natural world cannot reflect any element of the moral law in this analytic domain. On the other hand, if the *a priori* and the *a posteriori* domains are segmented from each other, then they must be synthetic within themselves only.

34

Such a characteristic of segmentation of knowledge is the sign of moral-material dualism in Kant. It raises serious questions relating to the moral relevance of scientific epistemology. It creates methodological problem of gigantic proportions. Thus the emergence of these problems from Kant's methodology raises serious questions on the applicability of Kant's metaphysics in socio-scientific reconstruction and in the construction of a universal moral law (Paton 1964).

DIAGRAMMATIC EXPLANATION OF KANT'S PROBLEMATIQUE OF HETERONOMY

In Figure 2.4 we point out the problem that appears in Kant's heteronomy seen from the synthetic and analytic points in the domains of pure reason and the *a posteriori* domain. K_0 denotes Kant's *a priori* or categorical imperative. K_0 maps onto the *a posteriori* domain, K_1, as shown by the arrow to create the sensible or empirical world, W. The regions of pure reason and practical reason are shown by their separation by means of dotted line. Within the region of pure reason, the arrow K' denotes the function of reason to determine the categorical imperative. The problem of heteronomy is shown by means of the separation of the regions of pure and practical reason.

We have earlier explained that it is this epistemological basis of all of occidental scientific epistemology that leads into systemic dualism, pluralism and methodological individualism. Kant entrenched that dualistic epistemology through his heteronomy and rationalism into the future evolution of science. Likewise, as we have seen in the case of Hellenic philosophy emanating from Aristotle's **Nichomachean Ethics**, ethics belonged to the perceptual world of happiness, which Aristotle took as the supreme most good and God as a relative good in the midst of happiness. There was therefore, no functional relationship of universal goodness with the principal Cause of all causation, namely the Divine

35

order. Ethics to Aristotle was thereby a relative form of goodness (Welldon 1987).

The Divine order was not rejected by any of them, but its functional capacity in the creative order was marginalized. This is an inference that is equivalent to Whitehead's notion of created Being as God. It is also found in the inertness of Divine laws to influence the natural laws, on which Hawking writes, "These laws may have originally been decreed by God, but it appears that he has since left the universe to evolve according to them and does not intervene in it" (Hawking 1988, p. 122).

CRITIQUE OF KANT'S AND GHAZZALI'S EPISTEMOLOGIES BY MEANS OF EVOLUTIONARY *TAWHIDI* EPISTEMOLOGY

We have stated above the circular and evolutionary nature of *Tawhidi* epistemology in the creative, purposive, balanced, felicitous and certainty order of life. The problems we note in both Ghazzali and Kant is that of heteronomy. In Ghazzali the heteronomy problem persists by the evolution of self toward *Fana'* (state of self-renunciation). That perfection of self may carry with its dynamics an increasing knowledge of the world, but the world in its evolutionary imperfection cannot respond to this demand, at least not fully. Such a delink causes non-interactive relation between *Fana'* and the world. In Kant, a similar heteronomy problem was explained before.

Heteronomy in Kant's and Ghazzali's epistemologies thus leads into a non-interactive world. This is a methodological problematique with deep social, political, economic, institutional, contractarian and scientific consequences (Choudhury 1993a, pp. 49-88). Non-interaction also has the result of simply assuming but not explaining, the central attributes of the 'universal'. This 'universal' that is the essence of knowing by means of universal laws and human senses interacting with each other, is defined by its attributes interacting and unifying among themselves inter-

36

Figure 2.4: Depiction of Kant's Knowledge Formation.

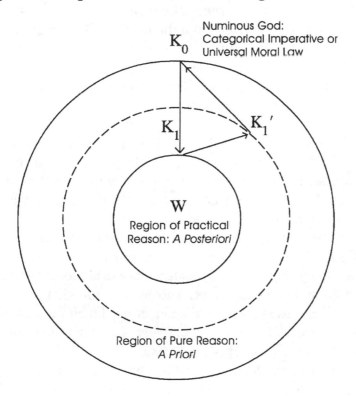

and intra-systems. The attributes in turn, by establishing causality with unification, define the dynamic essence of the universal. These attributes are given by the vector as derived from the *Qur'an* (Balance, Purpose, Felicity, Certainty, Creation). Furthermore, each of these attributes are interactively unified together by means of the primal source, the most irreducible knowledge domain, i.e. the Stock. This domain is nothing but *Tawhid* itself. We denote it by the Θ-symbol.

Furthermore, the nature of $\{\Theta\}$ is twofold. First, in the creative order it is primordially equated with the Stock, which in the *Qur'an* is identified with *Lauh Mahfuz*, the Divine Tablet in primordial universe of knowledge in which the Most Perfect Knowledge of the *Qur'an* is embalmed. Secondly, this parent Stock generates the flows of knowledge, $\{\Theta_i\}$, as interactions, i, emerge from the Stock into the flows with respect to the vector of attributes of the universal, as mentioned above.

Neither Ghazzali nor Kant considers this function of their epistemologies methodologically. Both implicate a dialectical process going on between God (=numinous for Kant; substantive for Ghazzali) and creation. Ghazzali and Kant also converge in terms of their ideas of practical religion and practical reason, respectively. These are the results of either revealed law or *a priori* epistemic, respectively.

It must however be pointed out here that Ghazzali treated the subject matter of intellect in light of the Prophet Muhammad's saying, "The first thing which God created was the intellect." What was intellect to Ghazzali is flow of knowledge in the sense of evolutionary epistemology of *Tawhid*. Faris explaining Ghazzali's theory of knowledge writes on the latter's third category of intellect as follows (Faris 1991, pp. 221-36, edited) "In the third place the word *'aql* (faculty of reason=intellect) has been applied to that knowledge which is acquired through experience [empirical knowledge], in the course of events. Thus he who has been taught by experience and schooled by time is generally called intelligent (*'aqil*), while he who lacks these qualifications is called unintelligent, stupid and ignorant. Here, therefore, is another type of knowledge which is called *'aql* (intellect)."

Both Ghazzali's concept of 'intellect' and our concept of flows of knowledge are created entities ensuing from the Stock. In this sense, Truth, Reality, God, *Qur'an* and Stock of Knowledge as embodied in the *Lauh Mahfuz*, are equivalent things. All of these have simply relational consequences through Divine Laws, the Signs of Allah and the creative order. Otherwise, they remain behind the veil of human comprehension, except in the hereafter. In spite of this recognition by Ghazzali, intellect is shown to be an epistemic reality causing sensation in the ontic sense. But there is no mention in Ghazzali of the phenomenology of the reverse mapping from the Signs of God (*Ayat Allah*) to new springs of intellect. That is, there is no methodological explanation of flows cumulating to the Stock as the universe continues to learn.

METHODOLOGICAL CONCLUSION

Finally now, in this methodological conclusion we will take up Kant's and Ghazzali's perfect states in the momentary transformation that must take place in the mapping, $g_{02} \rightarrow g_2' \rightarrow g_{02}' \rightarrow g_{02}$ etc. shown in Figure 2.2. We note here that g_{02} is a function of the Stock; whereas, g_2' is a function of flows generated by the Stock. g_{02}' is a function of the flows cumulating to the Stock. But since this cumulative process is not completed in any sequence of interactions, therefore, g_{02}' is simply a creative flux of flows. To denote this process incompleteness in the temporal order, we have included G_0 in a lower open space shown by the dispersion of dots. Thus although we go back to God, this knowledge process exists in a state of continual incompleteness, humility, human limitations. In the *Qur'an* is the continual pronouncement made to assert this submission of human imperfection before the Divine order: "In the Name of God, the Beneficial, the Merciful". The *Tawhidi* universe is then described by the *process*:

Stock → Flows → Temporal Cumulating Flows → Stock in Hereafter.

In this perspective of mappings in the evolutionary *Tawhidi* universe, Kant's region of pure reason in Figure 2.4 is opened up to interact and integrate with the process, $g_2' \to g_{02}'$. Ghazzali's region of *Fana'* is opened up to interact, integrate and dynamically evolve into higher levels of beliefs and actions by the self-same mapping. The problem of *Fana'* is also explained by the lower open-ended space of G_0; but the same does not apply for the concept of the numinous and external God in Kant's categorical imperative.

The commencing of flows of knowledge from the ontic reality in an imperfect state of an Islamic society, does not mean that a Humean type ontic connection is being implied. On the contrary, any commencing state of *Ahkam*-formation (rule formation) means invoking the Stock to give rise to the flows. In this way a problem of ethical transformation under sustainability must mean the invoking of *Shari'ah* for guidance in the underlying *Ahkam*-formation that ensues. But in such a case, the connection from the ontic to the epistemic premise is generated by realization of the worldly impact of the universal laws. The end result is certainty, which in turn causes felicity and creative order to emanate out of the attributes of purpose and balance. The concept of certainty here implies reduction of risk as also the realization of security and sustainability.

POLICY CONCLUSION

It is now time to show the relevance of the Islamic scientific epistemology in the construction of new scientific futures in a world that is fast changing every moment. This new epistemological future would be equally applicable to all in the scientific profession. The new vision as projected by unification epistemology of the *Qur'an* points to the formalization, teaching, research and application of the circular causation and continuity model of unified reality in all domains of socio-scientific inquiry. The goals here are the interactions, integration and creative evolution of all sectors of society, sciences and their agents in a meaningful community devoted to the establishing of complementarity among opportunities. This is the essence of ethical endogeneity in a unified order under systemic interactions, integration and its creative evolution to greater heights as pronounced by the *Qur'anic* knowledge-based world view. It is also this unique methodology that is distinctly different from the one based on dualism and pluralism by differentiations in the occidental mould, which thus becomes ethically void. So far, the *Qur'anic* circular causation and continuity model has been extensively applied to issues of pure science (Choudhury 1995a), economic development (Choudhury 1993b), political economy (Choudhury et al., 1996), econometric systems (Choudhury 1995c) etc. This proves the versatility of this distinct methodology to scientific generalization with empirical (policy) content. Indeed, as Stigler points out (1967, p. 12) "A science progresses, then, when a new generalization is discovered, or is made more discoverable, when an existing generalization is refined analytically, or when an existing hypothesis is 'confirmed' or shown to be false." The refutation accomplished by the circular causation and continuity methodology of unified reality is of dualism, pluralism and neo-classical marginalist substitution concept.

The values and attitude to science and technology in the Muslim world are to be premised on the opening up of opportunities and by taking up international leadership towards establishing the *Qur'anic* scientific epistemological approach as presented by the circular causation and continuity model of Divine Unity in the order of things. This transformation would take up the form of pedagogy, research and application in virtual reality laboratories at all levels in the natural and social sciences. Its development is also to be collaborated with the private sector and must take up global involvement with the whole scientific community in an open spirit of dialogue at the highest level.

Islamization of curriculum in the natural and social sciences using the circular causation and continuity model may be found in Choudhury (1995b, pp. 89-102). On a general note of Islamization of academic curriculum see Bakar (1991, pp. 243-51).

CHAPTER 3

THE SOCIO-SCIENTIFIC PREMISE OF REFORMATION: FROM MODERNITY TO POST-MODERNITY

POSING THE QUESTIONS FOR DISCOURSE

The problem we have at hand is expressed as a search for answers to the following questions: Is the post-modern trend towards deconstructive historicism a move to legitimate once and for all the occidental foundations of science, thought, socio-economic power and institutionalism? Is post-modernity anything different from the Eurocentric model of occidental world-system? Hence, has there been anything different in the convergence process or is it simply a re-theorizing of the structuralist, empiricist and epistemological-ontological biases of Western foundation of science, thought, humanity and institutions? What is the premise of conflict and the ultimate contradiction in the scientific and socio-economic, socio-political ideas of occidentalism?

If the answers to the above question lead to strong nihilism on the possibility for continuity and survival of occidentalism in the future, then we have opened up an authentic ground for discourse in human possibilities. Such possibilities make up a future that is liberated from Eurocentricity and dominating epistemological convergence of Western materialist culture; and from the latter's impossibility in 'completing' knowledge. The question of epistemology must then be taken up with the concept of historicism, and the questions of science and humanity must be addressed in this relationship.

This same juncture of substantive difference between civilizations must mark the emergence of the new age of epistemological themes. In its midst we must raise and answer similar questions: Is the final convergence of humanity and science made possible by the new epistemology and its scientific, institutional and socio-economic implications? What is the structure of the new world view and how does it negate the occidental nature of historicism? How does it implant a new world view of historicism?

In the answers to this last set of questions is found the mainstay of *Qur'anic* world view. Its epistemological and constructive foundations present that world view in the framework of a world-system emanating from primordially given moral premises and then structures the sciences and society on these moral premises. Its mainstay is also to be proven by the universality of these new forms of historistic constructions. The concept of universality here is taken up in the sense of its global episteme and application. The concept of historicism in this sense must then be understood as a continuity of dynamic relations among axioms, theory, structure, form and application. Real time is brought into such a relationship as a positional variable simply for recording data. Time by itself has no creative power. It is by itself the result of the same types of interactions. Islamic historicism, in which is premised Islamic scientific and societal world view, is thus primordially timeless. It is temporal only in the sense of an empirical possibility for recording observations.

THE NATURE OF AXIOMS AND THEORIES IN OCCIDENTAL SCIENCE

The axioms and theories of all occidental scientific systems arise from the nature of individuation and conflict based on rationalism as essence. They bestow institutional power to prevalent groups. The axiomatic foundation of occidental scientific theories is derived from the *a priori* status given to Reason. In metaphysics as in science, occidentalism treats this *a priori* category dualistically in its relationship with the moral and ethical order. This is because sustaining the dialectics of reason and the power of interest groups, individuated trajectories of scientific research programs must make their reason-based categories as premises determining power and further individuations as well. Without this power structure, the conflicting differentiations and individuation enabling the emergent process of historical evolution of rationalism, cannot be materialized.

Metaphysics during the Age of Moral Philosophy thus borrowed from Greek philosophy and gave rise to an artificial differentiation between Reason and Divinity. This was a systemic consequence of Greek belief. In the Age of Moral Philosophy it was transmitted through the establishment of Church. Science and state used the same Greek model of rationalism to premise their perspectives of this dichotomy between reason and the moral order.

With the coming of the Age of Enlightenment, the Age of Moral Philosophy disappeared. Along with this the concept of universal law was dichotomized between Natural or Positive Law and Normative Law (Schumpeter 1968). This was a continuing manifestation of that Greek confusion between absolute and relative goodness.

In Aristotle's **Nicomachean Ethics** we find the utter impossibility for describing the Absolute, and hence the nature of Divine Law (Welldon 1987). Only the relative idea of goodness takes meaning in **Ethics**, creating thus a relative idea of Divinity itself. These are the origins of dualism between reason and the capacity for moral perfection, in spite of the fact that **Ethics** dwells so profusely on the topic of morality and ethics. In the same light of the dichotomy, freedom premised in relativity of reason gives a relative meaning to the idea of happiness.

The question remains: Is the object of scientific pursuit an emanation from the theoretic constructs with logical consistency to its moral conse-

45

quence in bestowing the good? Contrarily, is the relative understanding of morality instrumental in defining what individuated systems are to deliver, be these hedonic consumption (as in utilitarian economics), benign morality (in monadism), or moral conformity with the material order (Islam)?

The ontic implication of *a priori* reason domain is the one-directional mapping of *a priori* comprehension to the realm of being and form. Thus, a mathematical reason is assumed to form reality. The *a priori* domain is then referred to as the epistemology of the emergent thought process. The *a priori* yields the *a posteriori*, which is the empirical comprehension and hence the ontic reality (Sherover 1972). But in this epistemological orientation of the *a priori* there exists no capacity to determine substantive reality from the domain of the empirical - that is the mapping from the *a posteriori* to the *a priori*. In other words, materiality in some sense has no capacity to form substantive knowledge in this Kantian type *a priori* epistemological orientation (Kant 1977).

The origins of Newtonian and Relativity Physics are of the type of *a priori* epistemological approach. The *a priori* or axiomatic foundation of the former comprises the Newtonian Laws of Motion. The *a priori* axiom of Relativity is the limiting cosmological constancy of the velocity of light. The general assumption of science is premised on the invariance of the physical constants (Breuer 1991). All subsequent developments from these schools of physics therefore owe to the same epistemological orientation.

The origins of Bohr's Complementarity Principle of Atomic Physics and of Hiesenberg's Uncertainty Principle in Quantum Mechanics owe to the *a posteriori* roots of science in clear differentiation to *a priori* epistemology. Cartesian foundation of logical positivism was premised on the same roots. Hume and later on Hiedegger premised their explanation of human nature and scientific reality on similar ontic relations (Hume 1992).

46

The *a priori* and *a posteriori* perceptions of occidental science, both being premised in the Greek roots of rationalism intensifying dualism and plurality, are embedded in scientific foundationalism. This deep-rooted nature of scientific foundation at once determines the dichotomous development of science in its micro- and macro- disciplines, such as microeconomics, macroeconomics, microphysics (Quantum Physics) and macrophysics (Relativity Physics) (Bohr 1985). There exists no particular methodology for unifying these two distinct approaches, except for introducing mathematical methods of one into the other areas.

Thus the inherent individuation, a denial of universality by the process of systemic dualism caused by distinct rationalistic developments competing with each other as certain perception of universal reality, continue in all facets of scientific relations. Science in the midst of such a perceptual view becomes a development of local forms in disjoint domains. This perception is true of science as of the social and economic order in occidental conceptualization of scientific categories (Nagel 1961, Dampier 1961).

At the end, what emerges regarding the nature of scientific inquiry is a generic foundationalism premised on rationalism gaining its legitimacy in a conjectural world of differentiated and localized epistemes. In this, empiricism is made to impact upon the *a priori* conditions of logical description of nature. Science in this context is therefore not value free inquiry, as it must hegemonically forbid any theory transcending rationalism to be unscientific. The institutional order will then incline on behalf of such differentiated characterizations in various ways. Science becomes a privileged pursuit defended by power and differentiated specializations forming scientific research programs (Holton 1975). An example in case is of alternative medicine that is not promoted within mainstream medicine, so as to perpetuate hegemony of the latter in this area. The medical profession gains a monopoly by this. The education system and the institutions of public policy promote such a disciplinary hegemony.

SCIENCE AND POST-MODERNITY

The call for a science freed from the clutches of its own hegemony, does not mean ignorance of the analytical method. Moral and ethical universality in science is necessary to formalize a methodology that axiomatically appeals and applies equally to the organization of natural and social realities. Between these, interactions are not exogenous in type. They become endogenous, being of the nature that a unique and unifying law grounds all knowledge and thus enables systems to interact on the premise of that unique knowledge. This nature of science enables systemic unification to occur by cause and effect.

1. Critique of Post-Modernity

We will now investigate how the perceptual and localized nature of science in the *a priori* and *a posteriori* distinctions, also embodies the understanding of post-modernity. First what is post-modernity?

Occidental theory of development identifies three phases in the transformation from a modern state to a post-modern one. We take them up below.

First, there is the structural phase. Within this phase a body of thought is seen to predominate, that focuses on explaining the structure of change. Structuralism assumes a static view in the literature with regards to societies sharing at any given period of time a convergence to an unique organizational structure (Bennington & Young 1990). For example, the transformation of agrarian societies to industrial ones was a convergent structure of all economies, marking the emergence of modern state. Marxism is the product of structuralism, as it attempts to prescribe an explanation of the nature of capitalist transformation. Fukuyama's thesis of global convergence to capitalism as the end of the historical process is a structuralist hypothesis (Fukuyama 1992).

48

The second phase of post-modernist transformation is marked by post-structuralism. This is the phase of denial of foundationalism and uniqueness of structure by the emergence of divergent forms of organizations (Wordsworth 1990). An example is the negation of Marxist political economy by recent developments during post-Cold War period.

Post-structuralism in this sense of intellectual discontent is strongly manifest in the rise of Islamic movements during the post-Cold War period. Huntington points to this as a serious challenge to Western legitimacy. Esposito qualifies the rise of Islam in post-Cold War period as a legitimately strong natural expression that is different from and often opposed to Western values, civilization. The media sees this as a dangerous development against Western values and democracy (Huntington 1993, Esposito 1992, Economist 1992). The historical process thus ceases to be a well-ordered, systematic and convergent process as contrived by the structuralists. Individuation as opposed to convergence marks the growing order of post-structuralism. This is contrary to structuralism not in substance, but simply in the shift of methodological individualism as the occidental way in all behavioural, intellectual and institutional explanations, developments from the megalothymic (monolithic) core to the isothymic many (individuated).

The third phase is post-modernity. This is the process of transformation from megalothymic dominance, as of capitalist transformation in Western mould, to intensifying individualism, arising either as individuated dissent or diversities. The dissent acquires the perspective of cultural pluralism as the deconstructive force behind new methodological individualism construed by post-modernist theory. The presence of foundationalism to be found in a structuralist orientation of science, is now increasingly replaced by its questioning and abandonment. Eurocentric institutionalism as a megalothymic order is increasingly challenged and replaced by isothymic dominance. Thus, the process of globalization as megalothymic arrangement is seen to be increasingly challenged by the emergence of regional pacts (isothymic). An example here is the opening up of South East Asia Trading Region as a strategic economic response to North American Free Trade Agreement and the European Community. In the sciences, post-modernity is a move away from accepted paradigms to newer ones. This marks the emergence of a new epistemology.

The critical question to contend with is whether the transformation to post-modernity can render anything new within the occidental mould even as the scientific focus drifts from foundationalism to non-foundationalism? This is equivalent to questioning whether the intrinsic nature of systemic independence, individuation, conflict and power that characterizes the unrelenting subservience to rationalism in occidental mould, can be replaced by a substantively interactive behaviour?

For this great transformation to happen, the epistemological orientation must unequivocally move away from its rationalistic premise to a unified premise, taken both in the small and large scale systems. The *a priori* episteme and the *a posteriori* ontic form are then replaced by a unified way of comprehending reality. The emergence of the mind, systems and continuity in this interactive-integrative order of unification as the unique premise of comprehension, is the concept of World View. It is a world view also by virtue of its essence of universal axiomatic-theoretic applicability for foundationalism. The phenomenon of perception, which organizes itself in the random world of Popper and the pluralistic order of post-modernity, is replaced by certitude. Science is then seen as a reformulated system of relations conceptualized in this realm of systemic interactions. It abandons the *a priori* axiom of rationalism and replaces it thoroughly by the unifying epistemology of globally interactive forms. Structure is replaced not by dominance but by interrelations. The isothymia of individualism in post-structuralism and post-modernity of occidental conceptualization is replaced not by mega-lothymia, but by the immanence of interactive preferences transcending organizational scale.

50

It is impossible for occidentalism to acquiesce to this polar state of interactive-integrative order after finalizing its establishment in Greek philosophical culture for so long. Indeed there are those who claim that occidental epistemology has established its finality in post-structuralist and post-modernist transformation (Wisman 1990).

2. Historicism and Post-Modernity

How does historicism relate to post-modernist transformation? In the precept of a science of rationalism, historicism is premised on the relationship between structuralism and post-structuralism (Smith 1989, White 1989). Historicism is then a study of the cumulative processes that intensify the interrelationship. Yet for any ascertaining convergence to occur, there must abide a sense of convergence to a definitive state. Hence, if the isothymic process is to be the order of day, then this must define the convergent process. Yet this will conflict with megalothymia, and vice versa. Thus a contradiction arises in the formation of an obvious historical relational convergence in post-modernity.

Argued differently, if the preferences and behaviour of both isothymia and megalothymia are governed by the same nature of individualism, differentiation, power and conflict, then the forms of change become unimportant. They are superseded by the significance of a convergent psychology of the system.

Historicism in this sense of post-modernist transformation must then mean perpetuation of an order that remains intact in occidentalism during post-modernist period. This is the message of Eurocentricity entrenched in the Hegelian idea of Germanic supremacy and in the old Marxist clamour of global socialism. It is now the topic of Fukuyama's thesis of the end of history and the last man according to global capitalism; and of the idea of embedded liberalism (Callaghy 1993).

51

Occidentalism is thus incapable of change from its embedded character of methodological individualism. Hence, the intellectual pursuit of historicism has reached a maximal point. It is incapable of acquiring newer forms and dynamics apart from repetitions within its own confined order. Popper's idea of historicism is now delimited to such an occidental constriction. A self-contradiction is perpetrated to Popperian dialectics by the consequence of self-referencing that is taking place within post-modernist historicism in occidental culture.

The limits of individuation in the midst of deconstruction acquiring pluralistic forms, leave historicism in the grips of atomistic reductionism. The passage of historistic system as a scientific relationship between structuralism, post-structuralism and cultural dynamics in post-modernity, is seen now to configure the historical process as a sequence of localized preferences. These preferences when reduced to the limit of atomism or made to converge by the power of dominance, mark the additive form of social preferences signified by liberalism. Methodologically, such a pattern of systemic and academic interrelationships represents the passage of evolution toward atomism. Historicism as a scientific study of the process of systemic interrelationships between universal principles and human situations, becomes impossible. With this evanescent consequence on historicism, the epistemes of Marx, Hegel, Foucault, Derida and Nietzsche, so much talked about in new historicism, become dead-ends on the question of alternative to atomism on the one hand, and to institutional or scientific dominance on the other (Giddens 1983).

A critique of such a historicity in the scientific process is provided by Hubner (Hubner 1983). His theory of system-ensembles necessitates inter- and intra-systemic interactions. Hubner writes, "The movement of the sciences is essentially a self-movement of system-ensembles." The continuity of such systems by evolution and complementarity requires substantive interactions to occur. Any state of independence cannot be logically accepted either in the small or in the large. Hence, a systemic evolutionary possibility must be the result of circular interactions between mind and form in order to realize evolutionary knowledge. In this substantively interactive form, historicism can be explained by evolutionary dynamics. Yet the question remains, where does this evolution stop?

If the trajectory of such evolutionary epistemologies crosses the bounds of occidental historicism, then the system-ensembles theory of scientific historicity must negate the axioms of rationalism. A meta-theory of universal reality is then required. Rationalism must be seen as a cognitive determination by a higher transcendental form, by means of which, unification of knowledge can be made possible. Now a circular causation and continuity model of world view becomes the ultimate epistemology of unified reality. It is the ultimate process of all historicism because of its capacity to integrate rationalism with the unified moral order, which the localized nature of human perception cannot bestow. Form is transcended by knowledge; explanation and empiricism become chains of cause-effect in the circular causation and continuity model of unified reality (Choudhury 1994a).

In our quest for the new science premised on unification, scientific historicism in its post-modernist interpretation means the study of historical processes as globally interacting and integrating nexuses of relations. Such a unification is premised principally on epistemological grounds. Hence the *a priori* and *a posteriori* dichotomy of occidental science is unified in the new epistemology by a universally interactive-integrative-evolutionary model of world view (Choudhury 1993a).

SCIENCE AND HUMANITY

The question naturally arises how and why occidental science appears to be so successful even in its Judeo-Christian roots of modernity? The answer to this question is premised on the nature of occidental science. Science as an academic discipline is the method of deriving ultimate laws of the universe with rational and consistent explanatory power and to bring out the application of such laws for the benefit of the physical and human environment. The methodological nature of science also requires explanatory power to be premised on the minimum of axioms and assumptions. Thus, in recent times with the rise of many unified field theories, the pursuit of science has become that of discovering the laws of unification (Hawking 1988, Barrow 1991).

In the differentiated nature of occidental scientific methodology, we find unification as the central law of nature and humanity to be impossible both inter- and intra-systems. The basis of scientific methodology is premised on competition and substitution between entities.

In genetics, the scientific method is shown by mutation, inheritance and evolution. Mutation reflects the power to survive; inheritance signifies the structural moment of continuity acquired by power; evolution shows dynamic movement of life on the basis of acquired power and structure.

In neoclassical economics, this scientific method is called marginalist substitution in resource allocation among competing ends. This is a structural property having no dynamic essence. The same nature of methodological individualism is used to legitimate political power and organization in occidental perspectives (Minford & Peel 1983, Buchanan & Tullock 1962, Childers & Urquhart 1994).

Moral and ethical neutrality of scientific methodology is thus established by the marginalist substitution principle arising from the inherently individualistic outlook of science. This moral neutrality starts from the methodological core. It then externalizes itself to the applications.

For instance, the organic composition of modern medicine inherits a costly way of producing output by the method of substituting medicinal resources. Such costs turn out to be ecological social costs and private costs to producers and consumers. The medical system we have inherited is seen to be a privileged and costly economic endeavour. Its outer manifestation is carried out in the form of power and control over a certain monopolized technology. Industrialized nations are thereby found to oppose biodiversity agreements with the developing countries for fear of losing their patent rights on medicinal products (Choudhury 1994b, Choudhury 1995).

On the other hand, the methods of medical science based on complementarity of its resource use, should encourage biodiversity in medicinal provisions. The complementary nature of resource use would reduce the total cost of developing in delivering medicine. This is the reason today for the popularity of alternative medicines, particularly in the developing world.

The applicative feature of modern science derives from controlled experimental situations. These conditions can be made available to any alternative system to produce a certain output. Thus with complementary methodology in medicine entering the development of alternative systems, controlled experiment on genetic subjects will yield desired results by methods that replace the substitution principle to a principle of interactive and unifying world view. Costs are minimized by cause and effect in such a system. It is logical then that the output of such a system will be larger; the prices and delivery will be cheaper.

Alternative medicines are also appropriate by their method of experimentation and accessibility. Effectiveness of an alternative medical system would be derived from this jointness among cost control, output development and effective experimentation.

Therefore, there exists no magical uniqueness in the efficacy and delivery of modern medical science. There can be no human, social and economic considerations where the methodology of science rests upon Darwinian type substitution principles, because of its consequential costly nature of the substitution. The moral and ethical orientation of new science is premised in the unified way of developing scientific axioms, analytics and applications. This becomes all the more feasible when developing countries today can benefit from their development coop- eration pacts to move into alternative medicines. They can also invite the world scientific body to work in this direction.

What is true of medicine as an example here is equally true of all areas of occidental science, because of the uniquely substitutional methodology they invoke. In the sciences this methodology aquires the essence of methodological individualism inter- and intra-systems. Thus, contrary to the remark made by Davies on Islamic science (Davies & Gribbin 1992); by Fukuyama's worship of Hegel on the topic of global convergence to Western capitalism; and Huntington's assertion on the end of epistemology in occidentalism, there remain substantive reasons for categorizing science alternatively, just as it is necessary in the post- modern age to develop alternative social, economic and political systems.

THE EMERGENCE OF ISLAMIC SOCIO-SCIENTIFIC WORLD VIEW

At this departing point between the occidental perception of historicism premised on its construction of rationalistic doctrines and the rise of new epistemology in the circular causation and continuity model of unified reality, comes the historistic immanence of Islamic world view. We identify the concept of world view with Divine Unity and unification epistemology.

The *Shuratic* Process

Verses 49-53 of the Chapter, *Shura* - Consultation of *Qur'an*, point not restrictively to the polity of *Shura* as a political institution. Rather, the process of consultation, that is interactions, is configured here as a universal one. It is seen to carry with it the Divine originary core, which alone becomes the determinant of all flows of knowledge derived from the Stock of Knowledge, mentioned in earlier chapters. The flows emerge and unify in the realm referred to by the *Qur'an* as *Lauh Mahfuz* (Perfect and Complete Knowledge = Stock of Knowledge). The flows of knowledge derived from the Divine Stock is then transmitted through the development of laws and interpretations (*Ahkam*). This is made possible by the example of the life of the Prophet Muhammad, who is seen here as the anthropic centricity of Divine revelation. The creative process of knowledge evolution from 'behind the veil' (i.e. bestowed on all men), or through sudden inspiration (i.e. bestowed on the true lovers of truth), or by sending an apostle (i.e. Prophet Muhammad). Finally, this process is completed by continuity from *Lauh Mahfuz* to the universe and back to Divine Stock again as flows interact, integrate, evolve and cumulate. The ultimate culmination of such flows is the return to *Lauh Mahfuz* in hereafter (*Akhira*). Both of these temporal processes are explained by the verse, "Oh, verily, with God is the beginning and the end of all things?" The circular causation and continuity model in the plane of Stock and flow of knowledge is thus fundamentally of *Qur'anic* essence.

The consultation process, as the title of the *Qur'anic* Chapter points to, is the universally interactive-integrative-evolutionary process encompassing both the human and the natural orders. Interrelations become intrinsic cause-effect phenomena in such consultations. In the human world, such interrelationships span across self, family, community, polity, social, economic, national and international orders. In the natural world, they span particle interactions, energy generation, inter-systemic interactions and mathematical relations explaining being and form. In every one of such entry points of knowledge comprehension, the anthropic presence is necessary to interpret (i.e. *Ahkam* formation) and to evolve from the Divine core (creative process). This is the universal concept of *Ijtehad* (authoritative Islamic research) and *Ijma* (consensus) or agreement causing inter- and intra-systemic integrations.

Finally, the concept of *Shura* now transcends the narrow meaning bestowed on it as an Islamic political form. This was how usually the meaning of *Shura* was understood by so many in Muslim history. The *Shura* describes by universal consultation, a divinely perfected process of knowledge formation, evolution, affirmation, balance, certainty, purpose and well-being. All these together form the creative order pronounced by *Qur'an*. Thus I come up with the term, *Shuratic* Process, to summarize the knowledge forming creativity in the midst of all interactions, integration and evolution that span the universe. The concept of universe itself is now the domain of pervasive and most embryonic interactions, integration, evolution and continuity by cause-effect, and made possible by the Stock-flow interrelationships given by the *Qur'an*.

It is outside the scope of this chapter to expound the details of the creative process and the nature of the universe in its anthropic centricity (Breuer 1991). We will just pass by invoking the idea of Justice as Balance, and of Creation as the realization of Justice in the midst of purpose, goodness, certainty and well-being. The implication then is, that the universe as defined above in terms of extended and evolutionary forms of interrelationships, is characterized by unification epistemology as a substantively well-defined precept of reality. Perceptions arising from plurality of forms in occidental order, are now assigned to the space of indetermination and error. The two orders so ingrained in reality form mathematical complementation of each other. The order of Justice is then seen to move in continuous counter-determination of falsehood, and confirms itself in such a universe. Evolutionary knowledge-induced equilibria form the trajectories of the *Qur'anic* creative order. A *process* is then defined by the bundle of evolutionary knowledge flows converging to an integrative order caused by systemic interactions and evolving therefrom. The essence of *Shura* as consultation or interactions in this meta-universe, remains inherent in this process.

In the *Shuratic* Process, just as flows of knowledge are derived from the Stock as unification epistemology, so also all cognitive forms are determined by the impact of flows of knowledge (Dodd & White 1980, Skinner 1957). In this way, energy for instance, is seen as the incremental generation of knowledge in a series of interrelations between the sequential reproduction of knowledge realized by interactions. Bodies or entities in this description of energy production, become instruments of measurement, since knowledge itself cannot be measured. It can simply be assigned ordinal values by agents in the interactive process. Hence, electric energy is described by geometric configurations that are knowledge-induced during interactions. Subsequently, such material points generate fresh flows of knowledge by the force of creative realization of balance, purpose, goodness, certainty and well-being.

THE PRINCIPLE OF UNIVERSAL COMPLEMENTARITY UNDERLYING UNIFICATION EPISTEMOLOGY

The methodology underlying interactions, integration and evolution in the circular continuity and causation model of unified reality, describing in this way a *process*, is termed here as the Principle of Universal Complementarity. It is opposed to the pervasive neoclassical method-ology of marginalist substitution (Choudhury 1996). Complementarity necessitates co-determination of resource allocation vertically and hori-zontally by agent-specific interactive decision-making, and axiologically by transformation of resources into mutually complementing ones rather than as competing ones. Ony in the case of the 'bad' is it necessary to replace it - not 'substitute' it, as in the neoclassical sense. The exception exists when the 'bad' itself is transformed into a good in the process. An example here is the conversion of garbage waste into an energy source or of the final discarding of lethal gases from the reproductive alternative, if necessary.

Complementarity as axiomatic-theoretic premise of scientific know-ledge reduces the internal and external cost of resource allocation. It bestows the outlook of a secure natural and human ecological environment. Thus the core of moral and ethical dimension is ingrained in complementarity principle. It is at the core of the interactive-integrative-evolutionary nature of *Shuratic* Process, by virtue of the epistemological invocation. Thereafter, the same axiomatic-theoretic comprehension finds its impact on behaviour, preferences, types of institutions and in the continuing universal interrelationships by cause and effect. Nothing thus remains insulated and independent from the moral core. Besides, since such a moral core is not rationalistic in origin but rational only as an emergent cognitive form, temporarily realized and then evolved into subsequent knowledge flows, therefore, it must be derived from a unique text.

In unification epistemology this unique text is the Unity of God as presented in the text of the *Qur'an* and in the fountain-head of Complete Knowledge, *Lauh Mahfuz*. Its realization is brought about by all types of inter- and intra-systemic discursions with the anthropic presence, for reaching universal unification. This is indeed how Ibn Al-Arabi explained Islamic epistemology. Chittick writes in this regard as translation of Al-Arabi's **Al-Futuhat -Al-Makiyyah** (the Makkan Revelations) (Chittick 1989):

> Two ways lead to knowledge of God. There is no third way. The person who declares God's Unity in some other way follows authority in his declaration.
>
> The first way is the way of unveiling. It is an incontrovertible knowledge which is actualized through unveiling and which man finds in himself....The second way is the way of reflection and reasoning (*istidlal*) through rational demonstration (*burhan aqli*). This way is lower than the first way, since he who bases his consideration upon proof can be visited by obfuscations which detract from his proof, and only with difficulty can he remove them.

The concept of Justice as Balance was taken up by Al-Farabi (Bayrakli 1992), who treated Justice as the originary balance of relationship between mind, soul and the cognitive order. In this he related the cosmic origin of the universe, the relationship between biological and psychological preferences, the role of education and the emanation of balance between cultural change and ethical conduct. Yet Farabi's theory of Justice as Balance was deeply Hellenic, for his concept of balance depended upon a compromise between ethics and desire. It was thus a relative concept, unlike the nature of Justice in the *Qur'an*, where it forms an immutable attribute of Divine Unity.

The concept of history given by Ibn Khaldun meant a structurally ordered sequence of socio-economic, cultural and ethical changes following human preferences to hedonic roots of consumption, production and desire. Consequently, Ibn Khaldun related historical processes to economic and political changes impinging upon man's changing social and cultural preferences. His reference to *Qur'anic* world view of civilizational dynamics was not in focus in *Al-Muqaddimah* (Mahdi 1964, Rozenthal 1958). Thus, Ibn Khaldun may be said to have written a spatial history of Middle Eastern culture of his time. His was not a treatise in the *Qur'anic* philosophy of history.

Ghazzali and Shatibi wrote profusely on the topic of epistemology and public purpose. But these writings proved to be forerunners of latter days utilitarianism and liberalism.

In Ghazzali we find an externalization of individual ethical perfection as the source of *Shari'ah* (Al-Ghazzali 1982). In this sense, social preferences became a lateral aggregation of individual preferences. Ethical perfection implied the type of view that was held by Aristotle in **Nicomachean Ethics** and later on by the utilitarian philosophers in their concept of interpersonal utility summation.

In Shatibi we find a much more profound concept of the public purpose (*Al-Maslaha*) and an articulation of the objective of *Shari'ah* to be the attainment of the public purpose (Al-Shatibi undated, Masud

61

1984). The view of *Maslaha* if left to a mechanistic interpretation of well-being with the concept of material happiness, as was construed by Aristotle, could lead to the kind of relationship that public purpose has in the utilitarian satisfaction of social preferences in liberal philosophy. On grounds of these problems, Imam Malik is known to have contested the unconditional acceptance of the *Maslaha* concept in terms of defining well-being and thus in relating it as an instrument of development of *Shari'ah* (Choudhury 1993b).

In view of the above discussions of occidental and early Muslim Hellenic writings, it can be inferred that a truly Islamic socio-scientific order comprising integrated science, technology and society, one that can take its epistemological references directly from the *Qur'an* and the authentic *Sunnah*, is yet to be realized.

The Prophet's experience in *Sidaratul Muntaha* (tree or region of Perfect Knowledge mentioned in the *Qur'an*) became the foundation of Madinah Charter and the Islamic State. The latter acquired its discursive, i.e. constitutional expression on the functional arrangement of life. In this way, the epistemological origin of these Islamic foundations alone must remain the immutable structural permanence of Islam (Asad 1984).

WHAT IS THE CONCEPT OF *QUR'ANIC* HISTORICISM?

The concept of historicism in light of the knowledge-centred universe presented by *Qur'an* means the end of plurality and dualism. It means the realization of a natural and not forced process of convergence to inter-actively integrated and evolutionary systems. As the systems learn by the Stock-flow interrelationships in this universe, the emergent creative evolutions determine life, structure, institutions, thought and experience. History then is neither repetitive nor sequential over time. It is rather a process of change from which we learn by the cause and effect inter-relationships among embedded systems marching in their creative process by inexorable reference to the Divine Core of Unity.

The process defines a natural convergence, because Certainty and Justice as Balance in such an order, are discursively determined by interpretive laws, and no systemic hegemony can exist in such interpretation. Contrarily, interpretive discursions that do not comply with *Ijtehad* are ruled out of a *Shuratic* Process or rejected by the majority. Intersystemic interactions, integrations and creative evolutions are pervasive. Hence, the absence of academic hegemony capacitates universality, through which by discursions, convergence by integration, is realized. Historicism becomes a critical study of the knowledge-inducing process in the midst of the universe that learns by continuous reference to the Divine Core of Unity.

There is thus a permanent structure of historicism according to unification epistemology. It is the structure of Justice as Balance, and of Creation as the knowledge-induced *process* of realizing purpose, goodness, certainty and felicity (well-being). The structure is permanent also because it remains unique and irreducible in the limit of unification analytics at the expense of that costly plurality, which breeds subjectivity and differentiations by individuation. Finally, structuralism is permanent in *Qur'anic* historicism because there exists one-to-one correspondence between the universal Principle of Just Ends embodied in knowledge flows and the emerging cognitive forms. This provides an inexorably universal convergence to Unity and unification. The evolutionary dynamics of this entire process describe the *Qur'anic* concept of historicism (Mousalli 1990).

Post-structuralism conveyed by *Qur'anic* historicism is the unified world view of the universe and all its sub-systems - in the micro- and macro-universes. This order is both discursively realized and analytically derived by scientific connection with an indispensable moral core. This comprises the totality of its epistemology, experience and applications. The bounds of rational inquiry are thus considered as a cognitive subset in the greater meaning of the unified universe. Knowledge outgrows cognition. Therefore, the knowledge-centred universe greatly outgrows the material world of rationalistic inquiry. Foundationalism is therefore not sacrificed in the *Qur'anic* concept of historicism, while discursions, complementarity, interactions, integration and creative evolution by cause and effect, remain fundamental features of unification epistemology.

Between the permanence of foundationalism as a structural order and the discursive feature of evolutionary knowledge dynamics, arises a historistic *process*. This process therefore, need not be captioned as post-modernist in occidental terminology. The 'new epistemology' always was in the natural and human worlds. Its difference in the post-modernist era is that it gives rise to renewed consciousness in the midst of a fresh anthropic awakening, most importantly among the thoughtful. This is how the *Qur'anic* world view emerges in this post-modern age.

A FUNCTIONAL PRESENTATION OF *SHURATIC* PROCESS

1. From Polity to Market: 'Action'

In the above-mentioned way, the interactive system generates its first part of the total relationship (Choudhury 1990). This relationship commences from a given primacy of flow to its topological (a specific kind of mathematical structure) mapping 'onto' cognitive forms (Maddox 1970). An example of such an action is the interpretation of textual laws and references in polity for purposes of guiding and informing the market agents. In the Islamic sense, the polity would be the *Shura* and the textual laws would be the Islamic Laws, *Shari'ah*. The interpretation and delivery of *Shari'ah* to the market system in this case is known as *Ahkam* formation. *Ahkam* is the outcome of vigorous interactions among decision makers in *Shura* (polity). These interactions and *Ahkam* are subsequently regenerated via interrelations with the ecological order (market order). Such a circular causation and continuity is at the heart of the Principle of Universal Complementarity that methodologically characterizes the unification process.

2. From Markets to Polity: 'Response'

When an 'Action' or *Ahkam* is implemented, it is followed by 'Response'. Response constitutes the augmentation of market activities and preferences of agents by means of the *Ahkam* (as knowledge flow). These market activities comprise consumption, production and distribution. The interest of market agents requires uplift of their well-being by means of social goods generated through the interrelationships among consumption, production and distribution under the impact of *Ahkam* formation. In this way, a cognitive output is realized by the impact of knowledge flows primordially premised on Stock.

The Response from market to polity appears in the form of an affirmation (or revision/rejection) of market preferences sent back to polity. The polity learns from this response either in affirmation of its previous *Ahkam* or its revision and rejection for better ones. In this way, a response from market to polity shows recreation of knowledge flows by means of attained cognitive values, which in turn, are mapped by preference changes in the market order. The assumption made here is that just as Truth must confirm Truth, so also an effective polity and *Ahkam* will generate advance of knowledge toward the confirmation of Stock, in every combination of Action and Response.

Only temporary aberrations can exist, if *Ahkam* and the real world do not correspond. Every round from Action to Response constitutes one interaction. This denotes formation of one level of knowledge. The attained level of such a knowledge flow is ordinally assigned at the end of each interaction.

3. Interactive Circularity between Polity and Market: Creative Evolution

The next part of the knowledge-centred methodology is continuity. Now knowledge flows so formed one-to-one with interactions, continue on to reinforce increasing understanding of unification epistemology. In this

65

way, knowledge flows are continuously regenerated in the interactions as both input and output over lagged time periods.

It is now possible for the interactions both between polity and markets and within polity to arrive at an agreement (majority vote) or consensus. In Islamic terminology, such a consensus is called *Ijma*. Discursions within polity (*Shura*), between the *Shura* and the market order, between micro-*Shuras*, and in the ecological order (market order), are of the nature of *Ijtehad* (discursions based on *Qur'an* and *Sunnah*).

The interactive process is described in Figure 3.1. Actions are shown to commence from the polity box. The underlying *Ahkam* in these actions impact upon and transform market preferences based on the general equilibrium relations among consumption, production and distribution. The output of this impact is delivery of social good. Responses based on social goods are received by polity. These responses denote market preferences that are now post-evaluated in polity. In this way, interactive preferences combining action and response, are generated. The cycles of interactions continue. When preferences converge, then we have a social consensus. When they do not converge, interactions must continue with due changes in the *Ahqam* until consensus/agreement is established.

The dynamic nature of interactions in polity-market knowledge-centred circularity implies, that every consensus must evolve into higher levels of consensus, except when aberrations exist, as mentioned earlier. This is the phase of creative evolution. Thus in such interactions both the polity preferences and market preferences converge in order to establish jointly interactive and consensual preferences. These preferences are temporarily attained in a given phase of development, and are improved upon by higher consensual points monotonically with the growth of knowledge flows, unless moral aberrations exist. Only joint preferences interactively generated between polity and markets matter in consensus formation, and thereby, in the continuity of the system by interactions.

Figure 3.1: The Interactive Process of Knowledge Formation

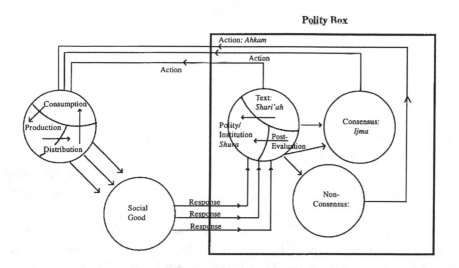

Action + Response = Interaction = Unit of Knowledge

AN APPLICATION OF THE CIRCULAR CAUSATION AND CONTINUITY MODEL OF UNIFIED REALITY IN SCIENCE, TECHNOLOGY AND SOCIETY

It now remains to be seen how the correspondence between nature and the anthropic presence of unification epistemology can be translated into experimentation. That is, in the framework of the circular causation and continuity model of unified reality the normative law (*Ahkam*) and relations are brought together to yield to inductive test (post-evaluation and subsequent continuity of process). Here is where technology becomes the field of testing for a scientific formalization as provided above in terms of the interactive preference field.

Technology is defined in the unification framework in terms of two components. First, the anthropic principle linked with scientific theory, which emanates from the premise of knowledge-values in flows, denoted by Θ-values; and secondly, in further instrumentalizing the use of cognitive values, denoted by q-values, toward experimentation. This phase in turn requires substantiation of q-values by means of Θ-values. The direction of preference field remains the same as mentioned above. There is however, a further particularization in terms of the preference field of technology, $t(\Theta)$. The total interactive preference field now comprises,

$$\{\succeq\}=\{\succeq_s\}\cap\{\succeq_t\}\cap\{\succeq_a\} = \{\succeq_q\}\cap\{\succeq_t\}.$$

Consequently, we define a technology functional by,

$$\{t(\Theta)\}=\{(q,a)[\Theta]\},$$

such that, $t=\{t(q,a)[\Theta], \text{ given } \succeq\}$.

It is the power of experimentation and the degree to which the complementarity among the preferences of the three systems works, that determines the circular causation and continuity model of unified reality now applied to the anthropic version of science and technology.

The difference between the above orientation and the occidental concept of science and technology is centred around the intra- and inter-systemic uniqueness of preferences according to unification epistemology, and this is knowledge-centred. Technology must then be appropriate with the existing and adaptive societal needs, not to be enforced as technology transfer or to be socially alienating. The neoclassical assumption of growth by substitution between sectors, resources and goods, is thus replaced by the Principle of Universal Complementarity determined by the interactive preference field as shown.

AN APPLICATION OF THE CIRCULAR CAUSATION AND CONTINUITY MODEL OF UNIFIED REALITY IN SCIENCE, TECHNOLOGY AND ORGANIZATION

We will now formalize on the linkages among science, technology and organization. First, we will explain the idea of organization in unification framework. The epistemic-ontic circular causation and continuity model of unified reality, which forms the core of the Principle of Universal Complementarity, becomes the foundation of a theory of organization in Islamic perspective. Three stages of organizational behaviour must interact and integrate among themselves to establish the above-mentioned unification and complementarity process.

First, the text of an internal deliberation by an enterprise and institution in respect to specific problems is derived by recourse to *Shari'ah* deliberations on the issue. This means that keeping the foundation of *Qur'anic* and the authentic *Sunnatic* premises in place, a micro-*Shura* or strings of such *Shuras* coordinate a series of discursions (interactions) among themselves to derive a rule (*Ahkam*) of guidance on the issue at hand. When the *Shura* is of the enterprise, it is both internal to its own interest as well as is externalized by linkages in a greater decision-making coordination with other *Shuras* of enterprises. The final hierarchy of such *Shuras* forms the grand *Shura* of science, society and economy. The grand *Shura* thus forms an institution made up of coordinated *Shuras* at the grass-root echelons. These in turn form the organizations of an Islamic socio-scientific order.

In a narrow sense of its application, the organizational *Shuras* have their own interests to pursue. Socio-economic interests are well-defined through a coordination of decision-making in strings of *Shuras*. Socio-economic interests are aimed at attaining a mix of consumption, production and distributional benefits in terms of profits, activity and well-being. Thus, the coordinated level of *Shuras* as an institution, becomes a public organization and develops appropriate policies in respect to the issues at hand, in light of the *Ahkam* emanating from the *Shari'ah* base.

In the second phase of the organizational relationship with the socio-economic order, it is expected that with the *Ahkam* in place, as actions delivered to the socio-economic order, these will generate complementarity among the targets of consumption, production and distribution. In this way, the preferences of polity, the coordinated organization or institution of grand *Shura*, are brought to bear on the socio-economic order and made to transform preferences here by recourse to knowledge formation by interactions. Now the rest of the polity/institutional-market interactions proceed as explained earlier.

The Principle of Universal Complementarity premised on the knowledge-based world view of unification epistemology across all systems, implies that science and technology curricula are to be developed in light of the interconnections among science, technology and the socio-economic world. Thus, in light of this commonness of methodology across disciplines and curricula, though not of issues and problems differently arising and being addressed in various disciplines, these disciplines get interacted by this unique methodology taken up in its most substantive terms.

We will now introduce this concept of substantive interdisciplinarity and show how this approach can be used to unify the methodology of various disciplines. It is surmised that only by such an approach can there exist a learning and unifying process between science, technology and the socio-economic world. If this interdisciplinary unification and complementarity can be attained, then the educational system will correspond with the demand of the labour market, while the labour market will in turn learn from its interactions with the educational sector. A grand educational decision-making is thus set up by interactions among the educational system, the labour market, public and private institutions and the government at large.

THE CONCEPT OF SUBSTANTIVE INTERDISCIPLINARITY IN INTERACTIVE-INTEGRATIVE-EVOLUTIONARY KNOWLEDGE FIELDS

The realization of science-technology-society interactions and integration on the basis of unification epistemology, requires substantive interdisciplinarity to prevail at the educational curriculum level. Briefly stated, substantive interdisciplinarity means integration of multidimensional problems of science, technology, society and economy and the methods by which these problems are studied in specific disciplines (Choudhury 1994c). When interdisciplinary integration is so realized, a common axiomatic premise of methodology emerges across all disciplines. The methodology deepens in the light of specific mainstream fields. Yet the problems and issues studied belong to interdisciplinary areas. There is thus a convergence of three principles in the meaning of substantive interdisciplinarity. They are namely, first, developing an interactive-integrative axiomatic premise for the disciplines. Secondly, it means deepening of methodology in the mainstream disciplines by integrating and developing the common axiomatic premise. Thirdly, it means rigorous methodological investigation of common issues and problems in the framework of interactive-integrative methodological development.

Now for example, if traditional understanding of interdisciplinarity is used to study sustainable development, this would mean economics of the environment in Economics. In Political Science it will convey the Rio-type institutional and policy development to look after environmental management. In Sociology it will mean an interactive process between ecology and society. In the natural sciences it will mean development of ways to realize environmental conservation. One can go on in this way across disciplines. The end result is a competing and non-interactive view in resource allocation among the diverse ends of serving environment, the human world and technological development.

71

In the concept of substantive interdisciplinarity, the idea of sustainable development is subsumed by that of creative sustainability. Sustainability would attend to the reorganization of ethical, natural and socio-economic relations rather than to the end point of the environment alone as the venue of the interdisciplinary approach. Environment is then seen as an instrument and not a target for bringing about these ethico-scientific elements of sustainability.

HOW CAN SUBSTANTIVE INTERDISCIPLINARITY BE OPERATIONALIZED IN SOCIETY? FOCUS ON GRASS-ROOTS

This brings us to examine the nature of interests among producers in a society that is differentiated by three kinds of consumers. These are namely, hedonic consumers with high income and wealth privileges; the middle-class consumer, with a certain degree of moderation but trying to emulate the on-going nature of demand by the hedonic consumers; the grass-roots consumer, with a moderation approach to consumption based both on income levels and an ethically conscious preference formation. The goods that can become successful in the framework of the interactive-integrative-evolutionary methodology across science, techno-logy and society are those that appeal to the grass-roots. We are then faced with an interface on the developmental front between science, technology and markets that mutually benefit from their conjoint services to the grass-roots. This brings about the rationale of a grass-roots approach to development without sacrificing economic growth (Ekins 1992).

Since complementarity is a function of interactions among the agents, the socio-economic variables, mechanisms and processes in question, and because interactions also generate by cause and effect a flow of knowledge in these factors, therefore, both the index of well-being and the constraints as costs of attaining interactive relations, become uniquely augmented by the knowledge values generated in these systems. Extensively global interactions emerge as a result.

72

The Principle of Universal Complementarity used across courses, disciplines and systems in the framework of unification epistemology, would now be taken up at the curriculum development level. We have recommended that such a course development must be at three levels with further intensification at these levels. The first level of introductory courses will integrate the philosophy of sciences in the framework of the interactive-integrative-evolutionary essence of unification epistemology. This is equivalent to applying the Principle of Universal Complementarity at the conceptual level. The sciences would then encompass the whole of natural sciences, social sciences, applied sciences, medicine, engineering, Islamic studies, general studies and education. At the second and third levels, higher methodological focus would be placed in the study of the integrative approach to the sciences. The objective of such a curriculum development would be to realize a direction of development of Islamic science premised on *Qur'anic* roots and to show how the sciences, technology, society and economy can be interactively studied together by means of appropriate academic programs. The concept of substantive interdisciplinarity is now seen to be both a pedagogical and a scientific reality that is inherent in all socio-scientific systems.

CONCLUSION

The arguments presented in this chapter lead us to conclude, that the challenge to Muslims in the post-modern age that is evolving with so many inner questionings, discontent and contradictions in occidental philosophy of science and society, is to return to a serious acceptance of *Qur'anic* epistemology. This is the root of Islamic knowledge that views the world in the framework of what we substantively explained as unification epistemology and which takes up its socio-scientific formulation in the circular causation and continuity model of unified reality - the *Shuratic* Process.

73

We found that the occidental order is incapable of advancing any further in its structurally embedded concept of dualism, plurality, individuation, hegemony, systemic differentiation and subjective perceptions. Consequently, the sciences of the natural and human order find themselves trapped in these same characteristics of ethical debility. The source of the problem is both methodological and institutional. These are deeply and inextricably rooted in occidentalism, because of the historical legitimation that has taken place in these directions. Such a system involves the entirety of preferences, science, technology, society, economics and politics of the Western world. All of these are primordially premised in Hellenic roots. Here rationalism becomes cause and effect of individualistic or hegemonic ethics. Individualism breeds pluralism and dualism in extended domains.

The earlier Muslim scholastics copied Hellenic thought and tried to put into effect a Hellenized study of principal *Qur'anic* concepts, such as of Justice, social contractarianism, scientific deduction and induction and their methodological formalization. Later on the Muslim world fell prey to colonial Eurocentricity; and in current times it has blindly accepted the petrified state of total intellectual and political subjugation (*Taqlid*).

Post-modernist Islamic emergence of thought and institutions in the sciences, technology and society thus necessitates a strict return to the authentically *Qur'anic* epistemological roots (*Tajdid*). In this sense we inferred that the ideal material state of Islamic order exemplified by the *Qur'an* and *Sunnah* (Prophetic traditions) has not yet been truly attained and is a matter of ultimate reality.

We have provided some directions as to how such a transformation process can be launched, and how the circular causation and continuity model of unified reality can become the meta-theory of scientific, social, economic and political theories in the post-modern Islamic world. This is equally a domain of knowledge for *all* nations as well.

CHAPTER 4

THE POLITICAL ECONOMY OF REFORMATION

Masudul Alam Choudhury & Abdul Fatah Che Hamat*

The objective of this chapter is to delineate some of the emerging trends in politico-economic thinking from the point of view of what in the post-structuralist literature of social change has come to be known as post-modernity. Post-structuralism embraces the doctrine of a deconstructionist philosophy applied as much to economic theory and institutions as to science, society and politics. Deconstructionist philosophy is an approach toward acquiring an atomistic view of the inner structure of social reality. Hence, its constructive pattern is based on aggregation from the level of the micro-systems and the dissociation of the monolithic structure into its micro-elements.

Consequently, we argue that such a picture on post-modernist approach to economic reasoning invokes nothing different from a utilitarian aggregation of independent decisions. Contrarily, when hegemony exists, then there is aggregation by convergence to the underlying hegemonic preferences. From the critical examination of post-modernist trends in economic theory emerges the Islamic world view for addressing the issue of Islamic political economy.

* Dr Abdul Fatah Che Hamat is Lecturer and Head of the Economics Division at the School of Social Sciences, Universiti Sains Malaysia, Penang, Malaysia. This paper was jointly presented at the International Economics Association Conference, Tunis, Tunisia, December 1995.

THE INHERENT INCONSISTENCY BETWEEN ECONOMIC
THEORY AND ECONOMIC REALITY

After the classical approach to political economy and the rise of neoclassical institutionalism surrounding contested market behaviour, there exists rarely any alternative way of viewing the relationship between markets and institutions. In a recent article, Bowles writes (1991, pp. 11-16), "The argument for social regulation of markets is transparent where either the agents or the enforcement process is endogenous. Where markets shape the capacities, values, and desires of the exchanging parties the standard normative case supporting market allocation (that it results in a Pareto-efficient outcome) collapses, for it rests on the assumption of exogenously given preferences." A reading of economic thought points out that essentially if a Kuhnian type paradigm shift caused by remarkably different ways of reasoning scientific phenomena, has taken place in economic history, then this has been with the Classical, Marxist and Keynesian schools. Thereafter, significant economic evolution can be associated with these prototypes. Of these latter days development are Hegelian and Schumpeterian development dynamics, both of which have entered Marxist doctrine and Myrdal's mixed economic order with institutionalism in it.

1. Hegelian-Marxist Dialectics

In Hegelian-Marxist dialectical process we find a regress of the mind into the limitless domain of Reason in search of Freedom. But while Hegel aspired to derive historiography in the premise of *a priori* rationalism like Kant, Marx turned it around to relate ontic origins of historiography to economism. In Marxist dialectical materialism therefore, Hegelian epistemology becomes economistic empiricism. Berman points out that in the pedagogical explanation of economic history undertaken by Marx, there was the attempt on extrapolating world history from the history of Western culture. This approach not only marginalized the otherwise great contribution of other civilizations to world history, but also made Marx's reading of history a narrow one (Berman 1989). Hegel too was locked in his belief of reproduction of the historical process of rationalistic evolution based on Germanic civilization. He writes in his **Philosophy of History** (Hegel 1956), "We have now arrived at the third period of the German World, and thus enters upon the period of Spirit conscious that it is free, inasmuch as it wills the True, the Eternal - that which is in and for itself Universal."

Thus, in Hegelian-Marxism we find two independent approaches contesting with each other as explanations of history. These are independent in the sense that it is impossible to transit from the deductive reasoning of history according to Hegel to the inductive reasoning of Marx and vice versa. In economic historicism, this divide between the purely epistemic (Kantian or Hegelian) and the purely ontic (Marxian or Humean) sides of interpreting reality, has become the sole cause of pluralism represented by methodological individualism and inconsistency between economic theory and reality. Such an inconsistency is shown in the pervasive nature of incomplete markets, which neoclassical economics and its prototypes are inadequate to treat due to the apolitical nature of these theories in the midst of their marginalist doctrines. Thus, once again to borrow from Bowles, (1991, pp. 11-16). "In many (such) contested exchanges either excess demand or excess supply will persist even in competitive equilibrium. To put it technically, these markets do not clear, and there is no pressure for supply to equal demand, no matter how competitive the market is."

The divide between Marxism and Hegelian dialectics, between Kant and Hume, and generally between the purely *a priori* conditions of rationalism and the empirical conditions of the ontic order, pervades all of occidental concept of historicism. This is not to say that attempts to unify the two parts have not existed. Indeed in recent times such attempts have become the core of scientific endeavour in all branches. In Hegelian-Marxism too we find an aspiration for the dialectical process of circularity between the epistemic and the ontic, and historical change to modernity is defined by the emergence of the dialectical progress (Howard 1985, Resnick & Wolf 1987). But apart from a mere aspiration, there persists an irreconcilable methodological gap in the entire occidental order. This persistent divide is caused by the problems equally arising from the 'finiteness' of world processes entrenched in Marxist economism as in Hume and Heidegger, and from the 'infinite' nature of open-ended system that defies a positivistic determination of systemic unification in Hegel as in Kant.

In post-modernist order, the impossibility of Hegelian-Marxism can be identified by the empirical reality of a discordant break between the responses of the purely epistemic and the purely ontic. This is exemplified by the contemporary proofs of increasing unrealism that Marxist notions of a marketless and exchangeless economic order in a highly developed socialist arrangement, tried to bequeath to posterity. On the other hand, the deconstructionist and structuralist approach of post-modernity must methodologically question the validity of the concept of modernity in Marx's dialectical process. Such a concept of modernity is represented by the dialectical process yielding absence of markets with prices as reflection of exchange value.

Today, what we are observing in the Russian transformation scene instead, is a process of convergence to global capitalism. Such a convergence process has a globally profound effect on the future of economic historicism, which Hegelian-Marxism cannot explain by its dialectics. Yet global capitalism carries with it an equally hegemonic convergent blueprint of society, markets, politics, institutions, culture, deterrence and social justice. Thus, while Hegelian-Marxist dialectical rationalism becomes historically discontinuous, so also the emergence of global capitalism is an unreal signature of the human spirit despite the cognizance of importance to markets and institutions.

2. Schumpeterian Developmental Dialectics

At this point of our discourse the explanation of the capitalist process according to Schumpeter needs to be examined (Schumpeter 1934). The moral dimension was considered by Schumpeter as part of market order, not in alienation with it. Thus the market system has a profound role to play in establishing ethics and through this in determining global change in Schumpeterian developmental dialectics. Capital came to be explained in terms of technological change by innovations and entrepreneurship. Both of these were seen as systems of relationships rather than as physical endowments acquired and preserved by the privileged few. Such systemic relationships were seen to form in the midst of organizations. This capital relationship took the meaning of capitalism as the organization that develops ever changing sequences of relations between the modes of production and the sharing of capital endowments (Holton 1992, Taylor 1967).

One notes that the particularly different treatment of the dialectical process proffered by Schumpeter rested upon his focus on the moral relevance of markets and its possibilities in the midst of knowledge diffusion. This knowledge diffusion acquired the nature of technological change under economic innovation. The moral relevance of markets was realized by the organization of collective decision-making, which came to be known as capitalism. Schumpeter's concept of holding capital as a system of organizational relationships was a moral configuration of what was otherwise inherently an amoral perspective in Marxism, for capital was associated with surplus value. But there is a greater difference in the moral perspective of a market-organization related explanation of development in Schumpeter. This is the view that ethics and morality becoming dialectical forces in the determination of capital as system of relations enforceable by organization, become endogenous processes of Schumpeterian developmental dynamics, enterpreneurship and techno-logical change. Such a perspective is quite different from the neoclassical apolitical treatment of markets.

Economic historicism in Schumpeter is essentially the cause and effect of the extensive relationship between enterpreneurship and techno-logical change. Both are realized by the ethical perspective of capital being relational in political economy. But problems arise in Schumpe-terian dynamics by the open-ended episteme of organizational behaviour. While defining the importance of ethics in markets, Schumpeter did not attempt to explain the epistemology of what must comprise a set of rules of conduct. Must this be textual in nature derived from a tradition of universally accepted primal laws or must it be left to pluralistic determination by the human praxis? The first of these is an impossibility, for occidental scholars have forever divorced God from markets at the turn of the eighteenth century Enlightenment, never to return to it. In the second case, the ascent of the praxis is once again into the Kantian and Hegelian rationalistic realms. The problems of methodological pluralism that so arise, thereafter confuse the meaning of organization formed by interactions and consensus, except as attained by dominant power in the system.

3. Schumpeter and Drucker on the Issue of Knowledge

Schumpeter's views of organization and technological change have been taken up by Drucker in recent times to expound his ideas on the post-capitalist knowledge order. But knowledge to Drucker is the end result of a relational process that underlies human capital development. He writes (Drucker 1993), "What makes the market superior is precisely that it organizes economic activity around *information*." Yet Drucker's concept of information capitalism has nothing to do with economic epistemology. Consequently, even his claim of a new economics post-Keynes and post-neoclassicism, does not yield the foundations of any alternative knowledge-centred theorizing (Drucker 1989). Contrarily however, economic history points to the fact that the turn of every major juncture of thought was preceded by a new epistemological outlook. In the absence of such shifts, one must condescend to the inevitable conclusion that the continuation of the same *a priori* and *a posteriori* ontologies, differentiated between themselves as deductive and inductive methods of inquiry, respectively, comprise the core problematique in the unification of economic knowledge.

THE NATURE OF POLITICAL ECONOMY IN MODERNIST THOUGHT

Modernity in the Hegelian, Marxian and Schumpeterian worlds reflects the nature of continuous evolution from an infinite sequence of primal forms towards a creative order. The prospects sought are liberation and freedom - not from the grips of subjectivity that random evolution brings along with it. Instead, the concept of freedom here means openness in the flight of rationalism. This makes the rationalistic mind alone as the supreme formulator of destinies and the mover of change. Thus, only cogent thoughts that can be protected by powerful survival conditions, which Nietsche and Darwin considered to be the dominant reality of existence, emerge as acceptable ones. The process of change is then described in the historicity of this dominance. Marx saw this in capitalism, but could not explain it in a functional way by means of socialist transformation, for the epistemological root of Marxist thinking is dimmed by its empiricist content (Staniland 1985). Hegel lost it in his miscontrued idea of Freedom when this was equated with Germanic civilization. Everything that happened to history after that was a convergence to the Germanic world in Hegel's view, just as capitalism, power, productivity and progress were equated with Protestant Ethics by Weber. In Schumpeter we find the continuous destruction of the present, as markets and technologies combine to evolve newer states of nature. This too is a Darwinian concept of economic evolution used here to explain the open-ended feature of embedded individualism, randomness, dominance and movement in capitalist transformation (Sullivan 1989).

FROM MODERNITY TO POST-MODERNITY IN POLITICAL ECONOMY

From the above discussion, modernity is seen to be a philosophy that takes a Rostowian stages perspective to change and growth, but underlines these with the evolutionary philosophy of the entire order. The consequence is then a convergence of individuals, groups, markets, institutions and the global order to the conditions of power and perceptions, pluralism and differentiations that capitalism enforces.

Post-modernity is a deconstructionist philosophy to liberate the tragedy of man from the aggrandising spirit of dominance by what Fukuyama called the 'megalothymia', or the very large (Fukuyama 1992). The result of dismantling the megalothymia is the rise of the individual as the powerful. Atomism becomes the return of the individual spirit. It is a convergence toward a continuing random, subjective, pluralistic and individuated order. It is now caused and enforced by what Fukuyama calls as 'isothymia'.

With the rise of the individual in the isothymotic convergence comes the relevance of micro-level preferences - of all kinds - gender, family, population, belligerence, environment, agent-agent relations. In each of these cases the rise of the individual deconstructs both the nature of the megalothymia as well as the desynthesizing language games of revealed texts (Choudhury 1994, Abu-Rabi 1990). The consequence is that gender is now not premised on the realization of an interactive convergence

82

within this group. Rather it finds expression in the definition of individu-ation within powerful groups.

The family as a social unit is seen not as a cohesive group based on gender-agent interactions but rather as a relationship whose welfare is tied to determinations arising in the market order. Becker describes the state of marital contract as follows (Becker 1989): The utility-maximizing rational choice perspective implies that a person would divorce if the utility expected from remaining married is below the utility expected from divorce, where the latter is affected by the prospects of remarriage. Human values that enter the larger decision-making framework of the family and then impinge upon economic preferences, are either reduced to technical details or assumed to be exogenous to the family as an otherwise powerfully interactive unit of the social order. Thus the family as self-seeking unit of decision makers is an example of methodological individualism and exogeneity of ethics and values in occidental economic thought.

1. Wither Economic Historicism in Post-Modernity?

The absence of an epistemological shift and the consequential inability to unify economic knowledge between the *a priori* or theoretical domains of primal relation, and the *a posteriori* or the positivistic domains including institutions and empirical facts, remain the central problem of economic history. In post-modernist context, this historiographical problem compounds by the deconstructionist and post-structuralist methods used. The compound problem manifests itself as a final fragmentation of collective decision-making into methodological individualism. On the other hand, there exists no viable method to aggregate micro-decisions to the institutional level, or to define a logical micro-macro interface. Likewise, on the side of institutions there is no connection between microeconomic and macroeconomic policies. For example, price level of macroeconomics is of a different nature from microeconomic price. Macroeconomics is not a study of aggregate behaviour and there is no decision-making inherent in it.

Thus a profound confusion over deconstructionist method is engendered by the distinct two-sided approaches. These are namely, the problem of aggregation to the collective from individuated forms, and the problem of deconstructing a collective into individuated components. This dual problem is what Rousseau recognized as he wrote (Rousseau trans. Cranston 1968), "It is said that Japanese mountebanks can cut up a child under the eyes of spectators, throw the different parts into the air, and then make the child come down, alive and all of a piece. This is more or less the trick that our political theorists perform - after dismembering the social body with a sleight of hand worthy of the fairground, they put the pieces together again anyhow." Such an aggregation problem is also to be found in utilitarianism, which in recent times has become the theoretical grounding of new institutionalism using additive social welfare functions with exogenous ethical perceptors as anthropic enforcers of the moral law (Hammond 1987).

2. Gunnar Myrdal's Social Causation Model of Development

Myrdal wanted to break away from this crass concept of institutionalism as being devoid of organizational substance. In his perspective of institutionalism, Myrdal presented a social causation model (Myrdal 1953, Lombardini 1989). This concept comes close to Schumpeterian methodology toward integrating relations across society and economy and thus in defining the developmental process. Yet Myrdal's concept of the mixed economy suffers from the aggregation problem that we have just seen. When polity is active, market interference and X-inefficiency increase. When markets become active, this causes tradeoffs with social prerogatives. At best a mixed economy can be seen as a process of

84

correcting incomplete contracts. Such contracts cannot be enforceable in either the institutional or market orders. Thus, such market incompleteness causes transaction costs, which cause pervasive economic disequilibrium. The end result is either a non-consensual organization or one where consensus is enforced by hegemonic convergence.

The historical element of social causation emerges from the deconstructionist mechanism built in the individuating relations of markets and polity. The consequences of such individualism are extensive. Individuation transmits similar behaviour to institutions as to markets. This point is well proven by the theory of public choice applied to a neoclassical utilitarian treatment of political cycles (Minford & Peel 1983). Schumpeterian kind of moral relevance of markets then becomes non-functional. Much of post-modernist aspirations to ethics and morality, aesthetics and social reconstruction, become vacuous in the future prospect of economic theory and institutionalism.

APPLICATION OF DECONSTRUCTIONIST METHODOLOGY TO SOME SOCIO-ECONOMIC ISSUES: SOCIAL JUSTICE, ENTITLEMENT AND ORGANIZATION

The deconstructionist meaning of polity-market interrelationships with the rage of individualism following this order, defeats the purpose of objectivity that deconstructionism would otherwise like to attain. Consequently, many of the social goods become distorted in meaning and substance.

1. Rawls and Nozick on the Question of Justice and Entitlement

A good example here is the theory of entitlement provided by Nozick, which clamours for a return to the pure holding of bundles in the state of nature without his 'morally abhorring' intervention of governments and

85

institutions (Nozick 1974, Steiner 1989). On the other hand, we note the market distortionary approach to distributive equity by Rawls. Here the domain of social contract is seen to start from a state of complete equality in a monadic state of the Original Position. The non-relational character of Original Position is similar to the static full-information assumption of neoclassical economics. The subsequent states of Rawls' Difference Principle are like the intergenerational second-best distortionary conditions of neoclassical school (Rawls 1971).

2. Hayek on the Question of Social Justice and Organization

Deconstructionism in every form is found to be a continuation of the old character of neoclassicism bringing it closer to a classical *laissez faire* norm. Indeed, new classicism announced by Hayek in his theory of market catallaxy and his conclusion on the functional *non-sequiter* nature of social justice in free market transformation points to such an ethically benign order (Hayek 1976, 1967; Ferry & Renault 1992).

The post-modernist historical context of Hayek's ideas on markets and social institutions is seen to be embedded in the concept of autonomy of ethical values from the market order. Indeed, Hayek like Hegel, views the historical process as the continuous progress of economic rationality expressed through market preferences. The extent of Hayek's liberalism associated with the market process makes him a protagonist of 'hyperliberalism' and hyperrationality.

Such ideas go against the economic historicism of Schumpeter and Polanyi. The rise of money is seen by Hayek as a contravention of market transactions mobilized by economic institutions. In the earlier economic historians, most importantly Polanyi and recently in the concept of moral economy given by Popkin (Polanyi 1944, Popkin 1979), one finds that informal exchange in goods and services in the absence of money, performed an important task of market transactions. Thus, cultural and social values had a primal role to play in the transactions of these earlier markets. From these transactions arose the contravention of money as a medium of exchange and store of value. Money is then seen in economic history to be an instrument rather than a fundamental factor of market order.

Hayek's onslaught against social justice in the market order is a confirmation of the capitalist order over the plight of a more organized self-consciousness. It affirms the ethically benign nature of markets and transactions that remains inherent in capitalist world-system. In this milieu, institutions too became ethically benign. Thus, the neo-liberal content severed capitalism from its Schumpeterian roots and instead placed individualism into it, that was of the nature of an utilitarian collective. Social justice ceased in Hayek to form the otherwise indispensable *sui generis* of *all* socio-economic thinking, behaviour and activities in a way that could be mobilized by a special consideration on polity-market interactions. We will take up this alternative outlook later in this chapter.

Hayek's concept of social justice and markets was also anti-Rawls and pro-Nozick. He shared some of the essence of new institutionalism in its neoclassical mould. Central social issues such as of entitlement, property rights and redistribution, were foreign to Hayek's new classicism. Thus, the exogenous nature of ethical values to be found in new institutionalism, social choice theory and public choice theory taken up in the neoclassical methodology, constitutes the nature of Hayek's institutions in the midst of market catallaxy.

Hayck is also responsible for turning a historistic concept of economic evolutionism into economism. He writes (Hayek 1976, p. 112): It is of course true that within the overall framework of the Great Society there exist numerous networks of other relations that are in no sense economic. But this does not alter the fact that it is the market order which makes peaceful reconciliation of the divergent purposes possible - and possible by a process which rebounds to the benefit of all.

WALLERSTEIN ON WORLD-SYSTEM AND POWER DYNAMICS

Wallerstein too has shown that England during the eighteenth century industrial revolution gained immensely from its expanding population size (Wallerstein 1989). This brought into existence the proletariat, which financed cheap labour and large markets with elastic demand. The capital saving innovations helped capitalists to gain from the informal sector of households and the cheap labour provided by a new culture of economic activity in the milieu of economic growth and social revolution. The proletariat thus contributed greatly to the English and French industrial revolutions. This owed much to the cultural and non-competitive nature of work at the level of the proletariat. On the other hand, the capitalist world-system managed to suppress popular organization. Wallerstein writes in this regard, "They (changes in the world capitalist system) represented its (world capitalist system) further consolidation and entrenchment. The popular forces were suppressed, and their potential in fact constrained by the political transformations." (Edited.)

Wallerstein's concept of world-system comprises a closed order endowed by its own inner culture and power relations. The difference among many such world-systems is their relative sizes. Those that are large and domineering become like empire type world-systems. In this sense of world-system there is an obvious individuation by partitioning between systems that do not integrate by exchange of relations. Thus a partitioning of economic history by means of various world-systems becomes a pluralistic approach either to endorse or to explain the positivistic case of methodological individualism gaining its high ground under neo-liberalism and capitalism. Such a critique of capitalism and democracy as supportive instruments of liberalism is also to be found in Ferry and Renault's explanation of the ideas of market oriented permissions in the concept of entitlements (Ferry & Renault 1992).

ECONOMIC FUTURES AT THE ADVENT AND
END OF POST-MODERNITY

The above discussions lead us to believe that post-modernist deconstructionism is simply a pluralistic device for asserting the structuralist and
functionalist approaches to be found in Hegelian, Marxian and Schumpeterian dynamics of social change. It comes at a time when the world-
system is required to legitimate the power-driven capitalist transformation that is taking place in the aftermath of an unnatural figment of
modernity that found expression in Hegelian-Marxist and Schumpeterian
dialectics.

The roots of post-modernist awakening in its deconstructionist
characteristics are also found in the pluralistic domains that survive in the
type of subjectivity derived from dualism and perception. Deconstructionist process leads to atomism of the mind and self. Foucault laments
on this condition of the individual as the tragedy of man (Foucault 1972).
Inter-systemic unification and knowledge formation unifying various
systems are thus rendered impossible. Along with such deconstructionism
comes the impossibility for ethics, be this in globalization, sustainable
development, human development or new institutionalism. Finally, if the
old epistemological order has become the continuing new by invoking
Greek thought in modernity and post-modernity, the central questions
remain as follows: Is atomism, individualism and pluralism the essence
of sciences, life and thought? Does the natural order belong otherwise to
an essentially interactive-integrative order of historicity, which even
though pervasive in nature, is suppressed by the order of atomism? The
answers either in the affirmative or negative to these questions will
invoke the essence of reality.

The concept of World View is substantively defined in this chapter.
In its unification epistemological core and its universally interactive-
integrative-evolutionary methodological fold, the concept of World View

89

necessarily negates atomism, pluralism and subjectivity. Deconstructionism must therefore be rejected as a viable methodology for discovering reality. It must simply remain as a subjective weapon of man in his march towards the tragedy of man himself.

In this way, the physical environment too becomes a domain of conflict between the underlying social issues of development and the efficiency issue of preserving the stock of resources for future economic production and for deriving consumption-based economic welfare. This is the view of the environment as a good or a service that is rendered a distributive usage intertemporally. Future generations become targets of environment-related social welfare by means of delivering the environment as a means of productive and consumptive capacity. Thus much of the ecological essence of physical environment that could target the latter for the realization of ways and means of establishing accord between the modes of production and consumption, between institutional and group preferences, is lost. Goods and services are simply traded in the pure market system with or without institutional controls. In the latter case, their prices get distorted and a conflict ensues between the economic passion of capitalist ownership and social demands. One displaces the other in this conflict. At the end what emerges in a methodological fold reflecting individualism and self-interest, is the neoclassical marginalist substitution of resources between these competing ends. Finally, as growth and development are linked in this order by most structural development and adjustment policies and programs, the short-run adjustment costs of lost resources, unemployment and increased poverty, result. There is no guarantee from the side of market order that such adjustment costs can ever be written off. A good example is lost human resources with long-run automated unemployment caused by technological change. Human ecology, the study of relationships between the human and physical environment with social implications, is full of such examples.

ENVIRONMENT AS A RELATIONAL SYSTEM:
ALTERNATIVE TO DECONSTRUCTIONIST APPROACH

The resource of environment suffers in its objective concept from the misleading identity of how it is treated. In other words we pose the question: Is environment a good or a service? If the nature of physical environment is any of these, it gets rendered to consumptive hedonism. It experiences efficiency-equity distortions as the conflict between polity and market proceeds over the control of environment as such a good/service or a resource. At the end, deconstructionist methodology converges to the individualistic perspective of neoclassicism. If environment is to be treated as an ecological common, then deconstructionist methodology must yield to the primal concept of environment and ecology as a system of monotonically positive interactions between the social and economic goals. The ecological order with human dimensions is a field of cognitive realizations caused and affected by interactive preferences.

The ecological order with interactions between physical and human forms represents an understanding and application of laws emanating from an epistemology that unifies relationship between and among the human world and the universe. Within this unifying epistemology, bits of ethically endogenized general equilibrium sub-systems perpetually develop into more extended systems. In other words, temporary general equilibrium sub-systems in the small assume grander forms in the large, as knowledge proceeds to evolve. Therefrom, the ethical nature of socio-economic comprehension and its application proceed as cause and effect interrelationships. Such evolving knowledge-induced or interactive relations progressively well-define the global concept of ecology and environment (Choudhury 1995).

How does the post-modernist methodology of deconstructionism appear in the light of such a conception of environment and ecology? To

91

investigate this we show how modernity and post-modernity both become dysfunctional in addressing the ethics-centred focus of development.

The issue at point transcends from the particular treatment of environment and ecology as relational commons to a generalized treatment of all experiences of thought in a morally prevalent universe. Here the methodology of deconstructionism is seriously questioned by its inherent plurality of beings, multitudes of subjective forms, all necessitating convergence by dominance for attaining functionalism and structure. Institutions and science suffer from the same type of methodological individualism in their axiomatic core. Ethics is then misconstrued as an individualistically perceptual, and hence, subjective notion of reality. The mosaic of social cohesion is ruptured as atomism deepens more of individualism, subjectivity and plurality. Inter- and intra-systemic differentiations intensify. The neoclassical order of the past and the atomism, individualism, ethical subjectivity of Ghaia, are re-established in post-modernity. Only the focus of the agent has changed from 'megalothymia' to 'isothymia'.

In the 'transformation' process from modernity to post-modernity, the instruments of nihilism over paternalism, pluralism over collectivity, reflect the context of methodological individualism in the entire occidental scientific, political, economic and social orders. This strong inference follows from the fact that a transformation of preferences and the deconstruction of institutional preferences is found to take place in the midst of this self-same individualism. Epistemologies, the search for meta-theory and notions of socio-scientific relations, are now all being subsumed in this individuation process. The consequence, when referred to the problem of environment and ecology, is a hedonic notion of consumption and production in the changed preferences of individuated form yielding aesthetic but not a moral understanding of ethics.

The concept of sustainability is then a readjustment process of understanding a conscious use of the environment as an intergenerational common good. It does not yield to the understanding of environment and ecology as a domain of ethics-centred relations between economic and social forces while retaining the great relevance of markets. This is to say that we are looking into the new set of environmental-ecological relational world view for a moral transformation of the economic and scientific methodology, experience and historicism. We are thus pre-scribing an ethics-centred regenerative socio-scientific process to replace the ethically neutral neoclassical continuity in post-modernity.

THE UNIVERSE AS A RELATIONAL DOMAIN

The universe in the *Qur'anic* order is not taken to be additive, as was the case of deconstructionist methodology of post-modernity. Rather, the concept of the universe is that of a relational domain of inter-systemic forms in the small and in the large scale orders. They are all continuously and dynamically interacting, integrating and evolving on the premise of the unification epistemology. The concept of the universe in which Truth pervades and beings take forms, interrelate, change and indefinitely conserve themselves, is one of causation, continuity and unification.

This precept of the universe markedly differentiates from the Hegelian-Marxist concept of the universe as an Idea. It also differentiates from Ibn Khaldun's idea of convergent pluralistic syndromes of cultures, for this tantamounts simply to a version of latter days utilitarianism and of the additive utility concept found pervasively in neoclassicism, liberalism and now deconstructionism.

The *Qur'anic* precept of the universe and its pervasively interacting-integrating sub-systems within a primordially unified universe, is also not the concept of mental forms governing reality that has been given by Iqbal, Hubner, Reichenbach and Foucault (Iqbal 1934, Hubner 1983, Reichenbach 1958). In all of these we find that either a Greek perception of ethical serenity defeats the human reach for any functional use of the

93

concept of Freedom (Iqbal); or the open-ended *a priori* realm of reason rejects self-referencing by means of the Divine Agent. A tacit recognition is thus made regarding the impossibility of attaining knowledge in the order of rationalism (Foucault's lament on the tragedy of man and Hubner's search for 'systems ensemble').

The understanding of the *Qur'anic* precept of the universe was definitely lacking in the medieval Muslim Cosmological Schools, for their approach centred around Hellenic notions of atomism and metaphysics (Nasr 1978). They did not emanate from a *Qur'anic* premise that could subsequently gain discursive and analytical power. We therefore do not find in the Muslim legacy of the sciences, with the exception of a Unity-based explanation of Number Theory by Al-Kindi and the theory of knowledge by Al-Ghazzali, Fakhruddin Al-Razi and Imam Shatibi, too many other Islamic thinkers who have originally based their work on *Qur'anic* socio-scientific theory. Even when such a research project was launched by Ibn Al-Arabi and Al-Ghazzali, we do not find an analytical possibility to develop science from their theories of knowledge (Chittick 1989, Karim undated, Ma'sumi 1974, Shatibi undated).

We have called the universally unifying premise of the *Qur'an* as unification epistemology. Let us then investigate how this epistemology can be applied to a new construction of ecological awareness different from the post-modernist approach.

THE ALTERNATIVE ETHICO-ECONOMIC APPROACH IN ECOLOGICAL ECONOMICS

Ethical neutrality in neoclassical economics is caused either by the effect of market consequentialism on exogenously ethical policies or by the inability for ethical preferences to integrate with market process. Contrarily, the approach to the study of environment-ecology as a relational domain, makes this to be knowledge-induced. This knowledge induction comes about in two ways. First, there is the inherent knowledge of the physical order. But this needs anthropic presence to tap and use the embodied knowledge. Thus the correspondence between physically endowed knowledge and the anthropic comprehension of the same, generates two-way discursions. Discursions emanate from the anthropic understanding of physical reality in the light of the endowed Precept of Unity. Secondly, this process intensifies in discursions among the anthropic agents themselves. Discursions as the central means of discovering knowledge, make the unification epistemology or the unifying essence of this episteme, as both the cause and effect in a circular causation and continuity model of unified reality premised on that epistemology. This presents an altogether new approach from the deconstructionist nature of reborn neoclassicism in post-modernity. It presents instead, an ethico-economic study of environment-ecology as a relational system.

THE NATURE OF ETHICS IN UNIFICATION EPISTEMOLOGY: PRINCIPLE OF ETHICAL ENDOGENEITY

The nature and substance of ethics in the cause-effect circular causation and continuity model of unified reality must be one that endogenizes ethics in all decision-making systems. Here not merely agent-agent specific interrelationships but also conceptions of the physical environment are induced by the unique view of a universally relational order. The environment by our definition of such an agent-cosmic anthropic interrelationship and its development into the epistemology underlying such interrelationships, fits directly the perspective of such a universally interactive order.

1. The Concept of Ethical Endogeneity in Political Economy

First, by ethical endogeneity we mean the formation and continuity by

95

cause and effect of interactive preferences between and among anthropic agents and the socio-scientific world. The first set of preferences generates a movement toward knowledge formation leading thus to consensus. The second set of preferences generates a natural way of deriving, comprehending and applying a unification epistemology to the physical world in relation to its human effects and vice versa.

Instead of purely market equilibrium prices of neoclassical economics, we have now prices emanating from interactions endemic to agent-agent specific decision-making. This would involve conscious processes encompassing a large number of considerations. Important ones are to realize the nature and quantity of goods to be produced and sold, the nature of technology to be adopted, economic cooperation in production and consumption. Such an interactive decision-making assumes the existence of underlying processes that simulate the issue at hand between polity and the market order. Consequently, interactive preferences between the two kinds of agents arise. These are brought about by dynamic changes in consumer preferences, production menus, and hence, in modes of income distribution. Interactive preferences represent knowledge formation in the polity-market (ecology) interrelationships. They establish continuity and circularity in the polity-market (ecology) interrelationships.

2. An Ethico-Economic Reformulation of the Ecological Problem

With the above introduction to interactive and integrating preference fields embedded in the ecological order, we now undertake the following simple formulation:

Consider the following chain of circular causation and continuity relations:

$$\Omega \to_g \theta_0 \to_{f0} x_0 \to_{f1} \theta_1 \to_{f2} x_1 \to \dots \tag{4.1}$$

That is, $\theta_0 \subseteq g(\Omega)$; $x_0 = f_0(\theta_0) \subseteq f_0(g(\Omega))$; $\theta_1 = f_1(x_0) \subseteq f_1(f_0(g(\Omega)))$, etc.

Therefore, $(\theta_0, \theta_1, \theta_2, ...) \subseteq \Omega$, by means of the compound transformation, $f_0 of_1 of_2 o...$ Likewise, $\cap_s \theta_s \subseteq \Omega$. Besides, the compound functional (shown by o), such as, $f_0 of_1 of_2 o...$ defines continuity and interconnectedness in the movements of θ-values. This in turn defines the completeness of the space of θ-values. Finally, the possibility of all types of discursions in Ω must qualify the complementation of θ-values, say $\theta^{\sim}$-values, to be included in Ω. Hence, $\theta \cap \theta^{\sim} = \Phi \in \Omega$. Therefore, θ-values and their complete space, Ω, form topological spaces. Furthermore, since completeness results, therefore a norm must exist. With these conditions, Ω and its class of subsets, $\{\theta\}$, form a Banach topology (Maddox 1970).

Next let us examine the cognitive forms of the x-values formed by previously inducing θ-values. It is noted that cognitive values are temporal causations of θ-values in Ω. Hence, (θ, x)-tuplets form a topological space in Ω. Any functional of (θ, x) in the topological space is then a simulatively related tuplet, such as, $W=W(\theta, x)$, where, $x=f(x', \theta')$; $\theta=h(x', \theta')$. θ', x' are recursive values of θ-values and x-values, respectively, as shown in the chain (4.1). $f(.)$, $h(.)$ are appropriate evolutionary functionals relating to (θ, x)-tuplets.

We will now characterize θ-values as flows of knowledge and Ω as Stock (unification epistemology) of Knowledge. Reality is thus premised in Ω alone. Ethical relevance of the ecological order shown in the chain (4.1) of universal and evolutionary interrelationships, is thus actualized by the topology of Ω alone and uniquely so.

The uniqueness property is established by the unification world view and not by a perceptual nature of Ω. Otherwise, differentiations in Ω would render the premise of learning to the type of individuation that characterizes the neoclassical order.

The circularly continuous and interactive nature of θ-values primordially derived from Ω by means of the mapping g - that is, a 'text' of ethical reference which is universally applicable (e.g. global ethics) - proves that knowledge becomes both the input and output of the recursive cause-effect system in the domain of Ω. On the other hand, for θ-values we note that interactions and evolutionary epistemology in the system necessitate that interactive preferences, $\{\succeq_a\} \cap \{\succeq_b\}$, between agents a and b, must iterate to a convergent θ-value. This value subsequently launches new rounds of (x,θ)-values and their functionals. We then derive dynamically moving consensual (or by majority votes) interactions. This is the phenomena of interaction-integration in such a cause-effect circularly continuous and evolutionary systems of knowledge-induced forms.

We then have, $\lim(t \to N_r)[\{\succeq_a\}_t \cap \{\succeq_b\}_t] = \{\succeq_{Nr}\}$ as the convergent preference between agents over N_r number of interactions t. Now there exists (θ,x)-tuplet corresponding to $\{\succeq_{Nr}\}$. For this to occur there must exist a functional, say $f=f(\theta,x)$. All of these values emanate from the completeness property of a topological space of (θ,x)-tuplets, their recursive values and functionals. Hence we have identified $\{\succeq_{Nr}\}$ with the formation of a flow of knowledge. We denote this by θ-value. It is in turn related with x, x', θ' values.

In the neoclassical system, $\{\succeq_{Nr}\}=\Phi$. Consequently, there can neither exist interrelationships nor continuity between and among θ-values and x-values. This is a logical consequence of marginalist substitution, which results in ethical neutrality and ethical exogeneity in the neoclassical order.

In the ecological order explained by chain (4.1), the essence of interactions, continuity and evolution in knowledge values, establishes the principle of ethical endogeneity. Such an ethico-economic order and its ecological implications completely replace the marginalist substitution idea of neoclassical economics. Subsequently, the assumptions of a process benign nature of equilibrium, optimality and full-information qualifying economic rationality, are all abandoned in the principle of ethical endogeneity. This replacement of neoclassical assumptions is not simply local but a global one in the ecological order by virtue of its relational concept.

To examine these implications of the endogenous relationship between ethics and economics in their ecological context, we now study model (4.1) alongwith the chain (4.1) as follows:

$$\Omega \rightarrow_g \theta_0 \rightarrow_{f0} x_0 \rightarrow_{f1} \theta_1 \rightarrow_{f2} x_2 \rightarrow \dots\dots\dots\dots\dots\dots\dots$$

$$
\begin{array}{lll}
\downarrow & \downarrow & \downarrow \\
(f_0(g(\theta_0))) & f_2(f_1(f_0(g(\theta)))) & f_s(f_{s-1}\dots(g(\theta))\dots) \\
= W_0(\theta_0,x_0) & = W_1(\theta_0,\theta_1,x_0,x_1) & = W_s(\theta_0,\dots,\theta_{s-1},x_0,\dots,x_{s-1})
\end{array}
\quad \dots(4.2)
$$

The 'arguments' in these functionals show the sequence of evolution of the (θ,x)-vectors over interactions, continuity and evolution in the ecological system. In general we can write the simulative objective criterion:

$$
\left.
\begin{array}{l}
\text{Simulate } \{\theta,x\} \; W(\theta,x) \\
\text{subject to, } x=f(\theta,x') \\
\theta = h(\theta',x),
\end{array}
\right\} \quad \dots(4.3)
$$

where, (θ,x)-tuplets and their functionals as shown, are defined for the range of interactions in the domain, $\lim(t \rightarrow N_r)[\{\succeq_a\}_t \cap \{\succeq_b\}_t] = \{\succeq_{Nr}\}$. The last expression implies that $W(.)$ is influenced by N_r and not by the number of agents. Thus by cumulation of a nexus of evolutionary epistemologies in the ecological system, we can further qualify the objective criterion as follows:

$$W* = \int_\theta \int_x W(\theta,x)d\theta dx. \quad \dots (4.4)$$

Finally, in the same ecological order with ethical endogeneity in it, the relations in the cosmic environment with anthropic presence in it, is established by observing the x-values as cognitive forms emerging out of the cosmic environment by discovery. Hence, cognitive forms in such an ecological order of global interrelations are simply knowledge-induced ontic forms of the circular causation and continuity model of unified reality.

99

HISTORICAL EVIDENCE ON ISLAMIC ECONOMIC TRANSFORMATION: THE CASE OF MALAYSIA

There is a good deal of positive evidence for the human ecological transformation that can be created by the Islamic basis of financing and development, particularly at the grass-roots. For example in Malaysia ever since the inception of Islamic financial institutions and their instruments to finance shareholding and ownership among the poor target groups, a massive amount of financial resources has been mobilized. Here are some statistics in that regard (Bank Islam Malaysia 1994, Government of Malaysia 1991).

It is important to note here the depth of attractiveness that the Islamic financial instruments have generated to bring about an ethical value-centred transformation along with economic profitability in the Malaysian 'ethicized' market transformation. There exists cause to be hopeful about the realization of economic growth with distribution and a civil caring Malaysian society by the year 2020. Such a transformation on the basis of both economic prosperity and development of values, grounds the Malaysian Vision 2020.

The central message of the Islamic financial instruments is to operate on profit-sharing, equity-participation, shareholding cooperative investments, while eliminating the interest rate gradually. The attractiveness of such instruments is caused both by the economic interests of ownership among the poor target groups and by Islamic value orientation. However, certain kinds and denominations of such grass-roots shares can also be held by the well-to-do to cooperatively finance joint ventures for the common benefit of both the poor and the well-to-do.

Amanah Saham Nasional as these shares are called, comprised a total share value of M$5,200 million with an accumulated investment of M$11,000 million by the end of 1990. The number of Bumiputera (Malay poor target groups) shareholders stood at 2.5 million, which comprised

46 per cent of the total number, 5.4 million of eligible (underprivileged) Bumiputeras.

Interest rates on savings hovered between 3.50 per cent and 6.00 per cent annually, between 1985 and 1990, respectively. As opposed to these rates, Islamic Bank Malaysia paid monthly rates of profits to depositers amounting to 9.43 per cent on 60-months deposits and 7.25 per cent on 12-months deposits during this time period.

In 1985 alone Islamic Bank Malaysia as a Group had current savings, investment and other deposits of customers of M$410,224,204. This comprised 4.18 per cent of total national savings. Shareholders' funds stood at M$422,650,150 (Bank Islam Malaysia Berhad 1994). In 1994, total liabilities, shareholders' funds and *Takaful* or insurance funds (= total assets) amounted to approximately M$3.046 billion for the Islamic Bank Malaysia Group. This marked a 51.63 per cent increase over the 1993 value; and an average annual increase of 62.18 per cent between 1985 and 1995. Net profits in 1994 was M$29.906 million. This marked a 36.34 per cent increase over the 1993 value. Dividend rate was 8 per cent in 1994.

The Malaysian New Economic Policy which is now replaced by the New Development Policy, aimed at the alleviation of poverty. These schemes were designed to correct the social imbalance that existed widely for some time between the rich and poor in Malaysia. The result has been impressive, as Malaysia today becomes an exemplary country in the world to have virtually eliminated abject absolute poverty, although relative poverty between the various states remains. The historical Malaysian economic record based on Islamic financial markets has shown a positive impact on the human ecological transformation in terms of development and ownership at the grass-roots.

There however, still remains the need for alleviating rampant relative poverty. In some states, such as, Kelantan, Sabah and Sarawak absolute poverty exists.

CONCLUSION

In this chapter we have highlighted on the importance for the Muslim world to organize itself as an Islamic political economy. The idea of economy, society and polity functioning in isolated domains of their own and competing with each other, would not help the much needed interactive, integrative and evolutionary process toward realizing the *Ummah*, or the conscious world nation of Islam. In this chapter the message of the entire book continues. It is to pursue Muslim reformation in the midst of a geo-political, economic and socio-scientific transformation premised on the epistemology and application of the *Shuratic* Process.

The advance of occidental societies is deeply premised in its dualistic independence between the purely *a priori* and purely *a posteriori* parts of an otherwise unified reality. From such epistemological origins are derived the occidental prescriptions of behaviour, institution, state and science. Nothing is left untouched in this epistemological entirety. Thus, there is no immanent neutrality in science as in political economy, from this distinctly occidental essence. Occidentalism is primordially derived from Hellenic thought compounded with extreme rationalism and individuation of self. Society and state, economy and markets, globalization and international relations, all form themselves within this perception of functional reality. Such a foundationalism gains profound pervasiveness in the occidental order, giving it legitimacy by dominance. This is how methodological individualism is explained scientifically by neoclassicism. The models simply change structure from the individual to institutions, to state and to the global order. Across the advance from modernity to post-modernity, the underlying neoclassical methodology and its emerging forms are found to continue, simply with a change of agent-specific focus. The focus now deepens toward individualism.

At the epistemological level this carries with it a perceptual, non-integrating, non-interactive, subjective and random flight of the intel-

102

lection process to the extent that individuation creates plurality of forms. Dualism is extended to pluralism in this order. In the midst of these differentiations, convergence is possible by means of two factors. These are, Eurocentric dominance representing power and a common epistemology determining all forms and behaviour of occidental pursuasion.

We have discussed this transference of the unique neoclassical methodology of individualism in both modernity and post-modernity by taking the example of sustainability as a form of world view. We have shown that sustainability and ecology cannot be liberated from the hedonic passions of the consumer and producer in a consequentialist market economy. Here ethics remain neutral to all forms of neoclassicism in modernity and post-modernity. The issue of sustainability cannot be addressed in the absence of an ethics-centred meta-theory of life, thought and experience.

This search brings us to the only other alternative to occidental order - the Islamic world view as premised on its unification epistemology. Thus, unification epistemology emanating directly from the *Qur'an*, is shown to be of the essence of a unique process of historicism that is dynamic in principles. Events are descriptive of this principle of conflict between Truth and Falsehood. In this order, *Qur'anic* historicism remains unbounded by space and time, finding pervasive applications as descriptive confirmations of the principle. Knowledge now becomes the thoroughly endowing element of this order. It moves the world into the evolutionary process of knowing by cause and effect. We thus introduced the circular causation and continuity model of unified reality to explain the universal order of the *Qur'an* in the midst of its unification epistemology.

The theme of ecology and environment as relational domains in the context of a unifying knowledge forming process, is once again taken up and studied. What is true of the address made to environment, ecology and sustainability (Viederman 1993), is equally true of the universal entirety and its sub-systems. Thus, while post-modernity remains a

103

continuity of modernity, both being premised on their occidental culture of individuation and rationalism, the *Qur'anic* world view presents the universe as a relational and integral form. These relations are learned by textual reference to unification epistemology using discursive methodology. In this, ethics become endogenous explanation of regenerative forms.

CHAPTER 5

THE INSTITUTIONAL BASIS OF REFORMATION: ORGANIZATIONAL THEORY OF THE FIRM

Our principal objective in this chapter is to critically examine an organizational theory of the firm in received economic theory and then to develop such a theory in light of the *process* model of Islamic political economy. This organizational process is termed the *Shuratic* Process. It will be substantively explained in terms of global interactions, meaning strong and pervasive interactions across systems, and on which organizational theory will be shown to be premised (Smith 1992). Finally, from the above two vantage points of this chapter, we will develop limited number of applications (because of limitation of space) of the *Shuratic* Process toward formulating the firm's objective criterion, its problem of resource allocation, pricing and equilibrium. We will then also discuss the nature of market interactions amidst which the firm is situated using the *Shuratic* Process as an interactive knowledge-forming process.

A CRITICAL REVIEW OF PROBLEMS IN THE THEORY OF THE FIRM

The principal elements of the theory of the firm in received economic theory involve a constrained maximizing objective criterion from which are derived the pricing relations of the firm's output and the optimal pricing relations for factors of production in the firm's production function. The technology of production is externally endowed. Also the preferences of consumers in relation to the production menu or technology of production remain exogenously prescribed. The optimal criteria are often taken to be the profit function, the cost function, the revenue function and the production function. The concept of optimality here leads to a conjoint existence of equilibrium (equilibria), which may or may not be of the stable type locally or globally (Henderson & Quandt 1971).

Alternative concepts of equilibrium have been prescribed in the literature. The simplest kinds are static equilibria of the Pareto optimal type attained from the classical Lagrangian optimization problem. In the case of dynamic equilibria, optimal control theory has been used to determine the conditions under which objective economic criteria attain their optimal values by control of state and control variables that are time-dependent (Intrilligator 1971). In such cases, when even the co-efficients of the model become time-dependent, stochastic control theory is used for estimation purposes and the coefficients are assumed to have Bayesian probability distribution (Pontryagin et al. 1962).

Recent work in the existence of economic equilibrium takes us into moving and unstable equilibrium conditions. Here Lyapounov conditions for the existence of equilibrium uses differential equations applied to excess demand functions to find whether limiting values of prices exist towards attaining zero excess demand (Hahn 1963). We also have moving equilibria that are of the nature of temporary equilibrium caused by past and future shocks on expected time-dependent equilibria. Temporary equilibria theorists argue that the state of the economy to be sequentially interrelated at any time, must be functions of the information function that generate moving expectational equilibria. These historically moving expectational equilibria then determine the current state variables and which then determine future state variables (Grandmont 1989).

Intertemporal equilibria have played a key role in the decision-making process involving future contingency states of the economy that impinge upon state variables (socio-economic variables). As examples, models of stock market behaviour are modelled by including perturbations of information flows that affect price movements and traded quantities. The problem of intertemporal resource allocation of the firm on which is based the characterization of opportunity cost of alternatives leads to intertemporal equilibria with strong implications on the determination of discount rates with contingency conditions (Hirshleifer 1970). These contingency-related discount rates that ration future resource allocations have important relations with the consumption theory of interest in received economic theory.

1. Equilibrium at the Core of the Economy

The theorem on the core of an economy is a well-known notion on the existence of certain classes of equilibria for a private ownership economy that cannot be improved upon in spite of coalitions among agents (Hildenbrand 1989). The core of the economy is a groundwork toward the mathematization of the economics of perfect competition wherein agent-agent cooperation is totally replaced by atomistic competition as a necessary property of such a core that disciplines all its agents to be self-seeking optimizing ones. The theorems of competitive equilibria are trivially satisfied for the core of the economy. These are namely, that all competitive equilibria form a subset of the core of the economy; that a competitive equilibrium is Pareto-optimal; that because no coalitions are possible in the core, therefore, a core is also in a permanent state of Pareto-optimality (Debreu 1970).

2. Walrasian Equilibrium

A Walrasian equilibrium is also closely related with the core and competitive equilibrium economies. Here the search for the independence and decentralization of the price variables leads to the existence of optimal plans made by self-seeking agents. Such decentralized prices for commodities and resources finally clear the multimarkets (Walras 1954).

It is also noted in the Walrasian case that the existence of equilibrium necessitates the number of equations of equilibria in multimarkets (demand=supply) to be less than the number of variables (usually by one). This additional variable is assigned an exogenous value, such as the monetary *numeraire*, to solve the multimarket equilibria equations in the Walrasian general equilibrium sense (Mansfield 1985, Quirk & Saposnik 1968).

In these solutions of the equilibrium values, stable equilibria exist locally if there are prices and quantities that cause the limiting zero value of the excess demand functions to lie within an infinitesimally small neighbourhood of these variables. That convergent vector is the equilibrium value. Contrarily, when the neighbourhood is the whole of the positive orthant, that is the convergence can take place anywhere in this space, the equilibrium is said to be globally stable. Finally, within a subset of the positive orthant with a bounded value in price and quantity vectors, the equilibrium is said to be semi-stable (Morishima 1964).

While it is not possible to exhaust the literature on economic equilibrium in this chapter, what is important to note from the above coverage of the concept of economic equilibrium are the following inferences: First, the concept of general equilibria in the microeconomic sense and in the sense of Walrasian type economy-wide treatment, is built upon the exogenous characteristics of self-seeking preferences, adaptive information flows and market clearance. Second, the economy and the agents both share the same optimization-equilibrium characteristics, and one is the dual of the other. Consequently, even by expanding the base of the micro-agents through number, interactions, information flow and technological change, no particular structural change occurs in the economy-wide sense that could alter the organizational characteristics of the agents. Third there is no substantive relationship between time and information flows in these systems, one that could generate a theory of economic time in terms of the information inputs. The two are treated sequentially, although in economic realism uncertainties on information flows defy the sequentially adaptative nature of information over time. The cause and effect of the actual sequential independence of information on time and the need for establishing a theory of economic time in terms of information flows, is the central premise of the difference between an exogenous treatment of preferences, time, technology and changes in the state variables in received economics (principally of neoclassical genre) and of an endogenous treatment of such variables in alternative frames (Reinhardt 1987).

In all therefore, what we have in received economic theory of the firm is an axiomatically behavioural treatment of optimizing economic agents. This displaces an organizational theory of the firm in economic theory albeit with a limited number of exceptions.

FROM THE CONCEPT OF EQUILIBRIUM TO THAT OF ORGANIZATION AND PROCESS IN ECONOMIC THEORY OF THE FIRM

1. Shackle's Concepts of Equilibrium and Time in the Context of Organization Theory

We have now understood the idea of economic equilibrium both with regards to the economy and the firm in the midst of the markets, as a state of efficient conditions for the firm's pricing that yield optimal values (maximum or minimum) for the firm's output, cost, revenue, profit and intertemporal resource allocation (Samuelson 1970). An equilibrium is thus codetermined with an optimum. In this context of optimality-equilibrium relationship, the explanatory nature of changes in decision-making, preferences and environmental impacts, are all marginalized to zero in order to attain the end state of the equilibrium and optimality. Shackle incisively saw the inadequacies of the equilibrium approach towards solving the real economic questions, for in his view equilibrium is a solution to which human beings and societies are not instruments. Equilibrium solutions are invisible laboratory experimentations of a reasoned imagination that establishes consensus out of assumed behaviour preassigned to agents. In organizational theory this mathematical limitation of equilibrium arises from two causes. The mathematical logic and instrumentation of economics has depended for too long on the assumed nicety of behaviour, rather than on the reality of discovering new ways of explaining change through the interactions of agents taken up in the field of knowledge-centred timal events. The direction of causation here is quite different from the timal determination of event-related sequences. Reason is taken as an adaptive behaviour of economic agents responding to a systemic predictablity of events in which knowledge has been controlled (Shackle 1972).

Besides, the instrumentation of such limited mathematical imagination has resulted in crystalizing data out of axiomatic notions rather than human presence. The data of economic agents thus turn out to be extended categories of power benign relations. This absence of the anthropic presence in economic theory makes such a theory of a non-interacting nature across other human domains of experience. Consequently, a substantive theory of organization cannot be found in received economic theory. Marglin comments that the production theory of the firm cannot answer one of the central issues of organizational theory, namely the possible interactions between workers and capitalists. Neoclassical production theory of the firm is thus epistemologically premised on the strict dichotomy between labour and capital (Marglin 1974).

On the issue of organization Shackle writes (Shackle 1972 p. 150, edited): "Walras accordingly spoke of *tatonements* and Edgeworth of re-contract. Both of these terms mean that sets of prices would be tried out until a set was found which taken together with the quantities that individuals would buy and sell at those prices, offer to each person that particular exchange of goods for goods he most prefers. When we

examine this suggestion, we see that it is no more than a formal acknowledgement of a problem, the problem of how (by what institutional
arrangement, by what organization of affairs) the equilibrium prices are
to be discovered. Repeated trial and error, while the market stands in
suspense awaiting the outcome, is not a practical resort. The number of
distinct trials, even if confined to discrete steps of price and quantity,
would be so immense that the necessary 'market day' would extend
beyond human lifetimes."

Shackle's treatment of time as an integral part of the treatment of
knowledge embedded in human and societal fields of experiences
grounded on incessant choices, is a cornerstone to an understanding of
the role that knowledge primordially plays in organizational behaviour.
According to such a theory, knowledge is seen to exist in a permanent
and continuous state of change, flux and extensions. Some of these
knowledges are known and some unknown. Hence the knowledge fields
of human experience comprise Shackle's Scheme of Things as they are.
Time on the other hand is sequential measurement of events as they
occur. If such events are equated with time as in the relativistic principle
of equivalence of event and time, then time must be a created organism
of knowledge. Thus, state variables in organizational behaviour must
derive from the occurrence of knowledge through interactions, which in
turn must determine the concept of events and this must then stand for a
transformation of events into time. In other words, a commodity is an
economically meaningful thing only if it has a value through knowledge
induction on the part of the consumer and supplier. Otherwise, a
commodity that exists in time without value is not of any social and
economic significance. The absence of interactions between that value-
less entity albeit in real time, does not create an event and hence knowledge. The absence of such an event is thus both a cause and an effect
premised on the primordiality of interactions between an entity and its
environment in a global sense. Interactions are cause-effect consequences

of knowledge. In the absence of such interactions, and hence of event and thus of time to measure such an event, there can be no organizational behaviour.

2. Concept of Organization According to Arrow

What then is an organization? First let us invoke Arrow's definition of this concept. Arrow defines (Arrow 1971): "An organization is a group of individuals seeking to achieve some common goals, or, in different language, to maximize an objective function. Each member has objectives of his own, in general not coincident with those of the organization....Finally some but not all observations about the workings of the organization and about the external world are communicated from one member to another."

In spite of the important work by Arrow on organization, it must be construed technically that the implication of the conjoint notions of optimality and equilibrium are embedded in Arrow's definition of organization. Consequently, without repetition here, our discussions above must reject such a definition of organization as being responsive to the knowledge-induced environment, such as of Shackle, that defies the notion of equilibrium-optimality relation in a knowledgeless world. On these same grounds we have Whittaker's comment on Arrow's concept of organization (Whittaker 1987, p. 574): The most obvious point to make about Arrow's discussion of organizations ... is that it conveys merely a broad vision rather than a specific theory. The speculation is on the grand scale, with few clues as to how the general perspectives can be applied to concrete cases and issues, let alone the formulation of precise refutable hypothesis.

In this respect Shackle's ideas of epistemics and economic theory differ considerably from those of Ludwig von Mises. Hayek is only a marginal exception to Ludwig von Mises.

3. A Critique of Shackle's and Arrow's Approaches to Organization Theory

On the other hand, the question remains: Can we deduce a positive theory of organization from Shackle's views on epistemics and economics, in spite of the insightful inferences to be gained therefrom respecting an incisive critique of economic theory of optimality-equilibrium relations? Shackle's **Epistemics and Economics** brings out these issues, just as Arrow's **Limits of Organization** invokes a competitive equilibrium formulation of organization, but none of these proffer an answer on the positive side as to how the normative issue of interactions, continuity of knowledge and experience and their relations to time, events and state variables, can be translated into a positive theory of economic organizations. In other words, our problem arises from the silence of these theories in answering the following question: Can these theories establish the existence, plausibility and application of interrelationships (i.e. cause-effect circularity) of the following type?

Primal Knowledge (Unique Reality) → Knowledge (Reason, Event, Experience) ⇌ (time, state variables) ⇌ New Knowledge (Reason, Event, Experience) ⇌ new (time, state variables) ⇌ ....→ Cumulation to Primal Knowledge (Unique Reality).

In this relationship, ⇌ denotes circular continuity of cause and effect, one feeding into the other through the pervasive chain of interactions and knowledge formation.

Clearly, Arrow's limited domain of economism under perfect competition marginalizes all continuous knowledge-based interactions among wider domains. Shackle's reason premise is open-ended and no answer is proffered on the question of Primal Knowledge (Unique Reality). His concepts of reason and time in the domain of epistemology

113

are irreconcilable. He writes (Shackle pp. 26-7): "We cannot claim Knowledge, so long as we acknowledge Novelty. Novelty is the transformation of existing knowledge, its reinterpretation; in some degree its *denial and refutation*." Further on, "Time is the denial of the omnipotence of reason."

The utmost comprehension of these systems in the light of the cause-effect relationship given above can be limited to the domain, $S_1 = \{$Knowledge (Reason, Event, Experience) $\rightleftarrows$ New Knowledge$\}$, disjoint of $S_2 = \{$time, state variables) $\rightarrow$ new (time, state variables)$\}$. Thus a cause and effect cannot be discerned in Shackle's system as also in Arrow's toward establishing the above cause-effect circular causation and continuity on the basis of knowledge premised in Unique Reality.

We will bring to bear on this Unique Reality the Unity of God and then explain the dynamics of organization and processual change when we come to the section on Islamic organizational behaviour applied to decision-making in the firm.

HERBERT SIMON'S ORGANIZATIONAL THEORY OF THE FIRM

For now then our search for any alternative available theory of organization in received economic theory continues. We turn now to Herbert Simon's theories of the firm and socio-economic interactions (Simon 1957, Simon 1987). Herbert Simon is well known for his concept of bounded rationality and 'satisfycing' behaviour of the firm. He has proffered two kinds of organizational theory, one at the level of the firm and the other as a decision-making theory of the firm. This is how Simon explains these two levels of his organizational theory (Simon 1952-53).

The F-theory of the firm treats the entrepreneur as a rational and optimizing agent to whose preferences all other participants in the firm, such as labour and consumers, adapt benignly. Optimization and equilibrium behaviour are thus part and parcel of the F-theory. Organizational

114

theory as a decision-making aspect of the firm is seen as a system of interactions among agents and entrepreneurs. The participants are seen to be induced to contribute to the enterprise through a system of perks.

In the O-theory, information does remain optimal. Hence, three behavioural possibilities are mentioned with respect to satisfycing behaviour in Simon's O-theory (Simon 1955). These are, first the information set may be optimal as in received economic theory. Then the economic agent is rational and the O-theory is identical to F-theory. Second, the information set may be less than the objectified set of the rational agent. This too is the case of monopolistic competition and oligopoly. Third, there is a further restriction of the information set due to incomplete knowledge. The last case describes satisfycing behaviour as the agent tries to improve upon this limited knowledge space by interacting internally and externally. The consequence of satisfycing behaviour is that the state variables also take up multiple possibilities when limited information influence decisions, causing mutliple possibilities on the space of state variables.

Social interactions arise in Herbert Simon's social processes by means of interrelationships among the following variables as shown here (Simon 1957): R_1: Interactions (I) → Cohesion (C); R_2: C → Diversity (D); R_3: D → C; R_4: C → I; R_5: I → D. But from his concept of causal relations (Simon 1952-53), while there would exist a causation (S_1) from R_1 to R_2; S_2 from R_3 to R_4, yet S_1 and S_2 are independent in themselves. Likewise, R_5 is an independent causal relation in itself. Simon's concept of causation is based on disjointly asymmetrical relations. In this way, the induction of knowledge in such models of man and in satisfycing and bounded rationality behaviour of agents, is of a peculiar type. It implicates a unidirectional observational capacity, which earlier we found to be linked with the sequential relationship given by economic theory to time and state variables by means of adaptive relationships on information flows that characterize future state variables. The meaning of interactions in these models is then seen to be feedbacks between state variables by means of iterations. On the other hand, the interactions that must primordially be realized in the knowledge variables endowed to various systems, are not made to determine causation as a two-way possibility. Simon thus develops his idea of interactive sentences (relations) from atomistic ones, hence making the agents independent among themselves.

For this reason we find that in Simon's dynamic equations on 'intensity of interactions among members' of an organization, 'the level of friendliness among the members', 'the amount of activity carried on by members within the group', and 'the amount of activity imposed on the group by the external environment', global interactions are not possible. Friendliness becomes a function of internal activity and a level of friendliness, independently of interactions, while external environment is treated exogenously.

At the end of the line, we are again unable to invoke received economic and social theory to define the idea of substantive interactions as a knowledge-forming process that integrates and evolves systemic interrelationships. The absence of a causal relation between knowledge, event and the cognitive result of these in time, limits the treatment of interactions to adaptive iterations among state variables in the absence of a meaning of causation that is circular and not one-directional.

THE CONCEPT OF PROCESS DERIVED FROM THE CONCEPT OF ORGANIZATION

From the theory of the organization we can derive the meaning of Process. In all of received economic and social theory, a process is a rule-based field of interactions that monitors the systems toward their integrative goals. A process as a dynamic phenomena also means that such a causation is indefinitely repeated over time and learning. When the direction of causation remains one-directional and thus asymmetrical over systems, a process must necessarily imply an adaptive behaviour under controlled conditions that functionally map certain information flows on state variables to make these predictable. By our arguments given above, such a one-directional evolution of a process is qualified by all the assumptions of economic rationality, bounded rationality and optimality-equilibrium relations that we have taken up.

LESSONS LEARNED ON ORGANIZATIONAL THEORY IN RECEIVED ECONOMIC THEORY: TOWARD REDEFINING THE CONCEPT OF PROCESS

The inability of received economic theory in answering the questions of process and organizational theory is noted to be due to the failure of such doctrines in establishing an interactive-integrative and evolutionary circular causation and continuity world view between knowledge and the world and to explain socio-economic reality including the treatment of the firm, in the midst of this world view. Consequently, the absence of such a circular causation and continuity model in mainstream economic doctrines causes these doctrines to be unable to treat time as a relational output of knowledge. This means that real time cannot be the primal determiner of events. Rather it is knowledge that first forms an event and this causes time to occur simultaneously to event. In this way, time and state variables become determined consequences of event. The state variable is the event and its simultaneity is time. For this epistemological reason the expression $x(t)$ for time-dependent state variable is replaced by the variable $x(t(\Theta))$, where Θ denotes the knowledge variables. $t(\Theta)$ denotes primordiality of Θ on time.

In organizational theory this would mean that two types of dynamics transform the system. First it is decision-making and the resultant planning in appropriate time. Both of these provide a value to $x(t(\Theta))$. Since no action and interaction can be undertaken in the absence of decision-making, i.e. knowledge formation, therefore, the existence of a state variable becomes meaningless. Hence there is no relevance of time for such events. When knowledge is primordially invoked, time is seen as the mapping of the knowledge-based topological space into the real line (in the case of receptacle time) or into another measurable topological space (topological time=unknown events that still interact with reality) (Maddox 1970).

Such a knowledge-centred world view that assigns state variables simultaneously to time is essential in establishing the various attributes of the circular causation and continuity model. Besides, the substantive meaning of *process* as systems of interactions leading to integration and further evolution of the knowledge space, can only be acquired if causation is described as forward and backward mappings. For this reason even the theory of economic processes offered by Georgescu-Roegen turns out to be an evolutionary theory with strong Darwinian roots (Georgescu-Roegen 1981). Such a theory of economic process that treats evolution as a means of intensifying differentiation among conflicting prototypes in the process of evolutionary, is far from being a model of interactions that leads to integration and evolution and then repeats this same process.

Redefining Process

Now $\Theta \to_f \{x\} \cap \{t\} = x(t(\Theta)) \to_g \Theta' \to$ etc. $\{\Theta'\}$ are new springs of knowledge-forming interactive-integrative and evolutionary chains. A process is now defined by the field of interactions and evolution as described by the above chain of relations. Thus a process represented by, $P = \{(g \circ f)[t(\Theta, \Theta')]\}$, where f and g are mappings of Θ into the real space or another topological space. o denotes compounding of the mappings to describe the interactions, integration and evolution. The mathematical

118

intersection, $\cap$, denotes simultaneity of event and time (also organizational consensus, integration) in the formation of x(t), which by the primacy of Θ, becomes x(t(Θ)).

AN EXAMPLE IN THE ORGANIZATIONAL THEORY OF THE FIRM

To understand further the nature of process in organizational theory of the firm we turn to the following mappings: (1) t → x, giving x=x(t); likewise, Θ=Θ(t) independently (received organizational relations). Thus a relationship such as, x=x(Θ,t), treats Θ and t as independent variables influencing the state variable, x. (2) Θ →$_f$ {x(t(Θ))} → Θ' → etc. We will use (1) in the following problem of the firm (Simon 1952-53):

According to the demands of equilibrium-optimality of the firms, C(Q(t)) = w(t).L(t) + r(t).K(t) = p(t).Q(t). Since one of the objectives of the firm is to hold costs at a minimum level, say C*, therefore, C*= C(Q(t)), implies that Q(t) must have reached a maximum, say Q*. Consequently, revenue is also maximized at this level of cost.

1 Participant	2 Inducement	3 Contributions
entrepreneur	sales revenue (p(t).Q(t))	production cost (C(Q(t))
employee	wage (w(t))	labour L(t)
capitalists	rents (r(t))	capital K(t)
customer	goods Q(t)	selling price p(t)

These results also imply that there is substitution between capital and labour caused either by the wage bill, w(t).L(t) increasing (decreasing) to compensate for cost of capital, r(t).K(t) decreasing (increasing). But these can happen if w(t) and L(t) move in opposite directions in the demand for labour function. Likewise, r(t) and K(t) would move in opposite direc-

119

tions. Besides, there are gross factor substitutions replacing global complementarity between labour and capital. Even if technology is induced in the production function, this causes the level of substitution simply to shift while leaving the structure of substitution and related decision-making unchanged. The effect of time variable on the state variables $(t \rightarrow x(t))$ does not change the conflicting nature of organizational relationships between capital and labour in spite of technological change in the production function.

Next write,

$$C(Q(\Theta,t)) = w(\Theta,t).L(\Theta,t) + r(\Theta,t).K(\Theta,t) = p(\Theta,t).Q(\Theta,t),$$

by the output exhaustion theorem of microeconomics. Since $\Theta = \Theta(t)$ is adaptive for purposes of bounded rationality at the worst, therefore, any inefficiencies arising from a suspected non-optimal nature of C(.) and revenue, R(.), will cause conflicts among the agents. This will call forth reallocation of the costs among factors of production and the consumer. Such a state of optimization of C(.) and R(.) once again leads into the same results as discussed above. These produce the re-contracting points mentioned by Edgeworth where each shifting point inside the Edgeworth-Bowley Box may then be considered as an allocation caused by shifting production possibility curve and production isoquants under the impact of technological change denoted by the values of Θ.

The above two cases result in the inertness of the Θ variables in the resource allocation problem of the firms, because of the nature of decision-making and hence marginal substitution as organizational behaviour of the firm both under perfect and incomplete information. The process so embedded in the firm's organizational behaviour is a permanently conflicting duality comprising the following relations: (A_1:entrepreneur $\rightleftarrows$ labour)$\cup$(A_2=entrepreneur $\rightleftarrows$ capital), with $A_1 \cap A_2 = \Phi$. Furthermore, since the consumer is either a worker or a capitalist, therefore, the same disjoint relationship is extended to the consumer as well. This is a further strong implication of the fact, that if general economic equilibrium of the neoclassical type exits, then the independence of consumer preferences in this state also causes independence among firms' production menus.

THE CONCEPTS OF PROCESS AND ORGANIZATION IN ISLAMIC PERSPECTIVES

1. Introducing the Concept of Process in Islamic Perspectives

Having failed to discern a substantive theory of process and organization in all of mainstream economic doctrines, we are led to search it elsewhere. Our principal goal is to find a viable meaning of process and the construction of an organizational theory in the midst of a circular causation and continuity world view. Within this model we are to establish the methodology of generating state variables such as $x(t(\Theta))$, in terms of knowledge parameters, Θ. We are also simultaneously to claim that this same methodology replaces the marginal substitution principle of neoclassical economics by what we will term as the Principle of Universal Complementarity (Choudhury 1994a). This concept was also introduced earlier. We are also simultaneously to claim the establishment of endogeneity of Θ-values in the entire socio-economic complex within which the firm makes its decisions governing its organizational behaviour.

These are the goals that now bring us to the development of a theory of the firm as an organization in Islamic politico-economic perspectives. We must begin by viewing the firm as an organism that produces social goods with market values and for individual, human and ecological welfare all at once. This means that there would be strong interactions among all agents that interrelate across economic, social, political and other segments of human activity. While it is impossible to begin in this extensive manner, it is still possible to extend interrelationships from lesser to greater levels of such interactions, i.e. attaining $\{\Theta\}$-values. Note that monotonicity of $\{\Theta\}$-values is not assumed. Besides, the same

121

kind of dynamics will apply to 'de-knowledge' values in their own plane of action.

The unifying of these systems into cohesive wholes is the act of integration, i.e. commonality of knowledge values denoted by $\Theta^*(N) = \lim(i \to N)\{\Theta\}$, over interactions $i=1,2,..,N$. $N \in \mathbb{N}$ (natural numbers) or $\mathbb{R}$ (real number system) or in T (topological space). In this way interactions lead to integration. Finally, from the attained limiting values N we discover newer vistas of continuity in the knowledge plane as implied here. Thus interactions lead to integration and these lead to evolutions. A process is thus formed in interactions-integration-evolution. Such processes are pervasive in knowledge space.

2. Introducing the Concept of Organization in Islamic Perspectives

The above being a delineation of process, what then is the organizational behaviour in this? An organization is a realization of a space of state variables induced by Θ-values, that is, in vector notations, $\mathbf{x}=\mathbf{x}(\mathbf{t}(\Theta))$, is an organization. Such an organization is formed in the midst of the process that was denoted as,

$$P = \{\Theta \to_f \mathbf{x}(\mathbf{t}(\Theta)) \to_g \Theta' \to \text{etc.}\} = \{(g \circ f)[\Theta,\Theta']\}.$$

In this form, an organization is a stage of realization of a process when the knowledge-based interactions-integration-evolution types of relations are established among the agents and parameters of the systems covered by such interactions.

3. The Nature of Islamic Firm

In the above complex of relationships, a firm ceases to be an isolated organism governed by self-seeking optimization goal. Nor is the firm simply producing private goods for a hedonistic market. Instead, it is an organism that develops and survives in the midst of an organization taken with an extended social process. The output of the firm is a social good in the sense that it serves this interactive-integrative-evolutionary character of social purpose in accordance with the determination of the Θ-values from primordial roots of ethics and morals. Because of the interactive nature of the firm in the social systems, the ethics and morals invoked in the production and delivery of social goods must be trans-systemic and universal. The uniformity of such universal values necessitates the premise of knowledge to be unique. On the contrary, if as in the case of Shackle who we examined earlier, the Θ-values remain undetermined on any primordial source of universal values, then they become identical with pluralisic reason and rationalism. Such Θ-values can then be identified with the praxis of human reason upon which Ludwig von Mises wrote his economic epistemology (von Mises 1976).

When the firm is seen as a social embryo amidst strong interactions, the state-policy variable vector, $x(t(\Theta))$, is further extended by important Islamic instruments, such as, the elimination of interest called *Riba*, the elimination of waste called *Israf*, the establishing of mandatory wealth taxes for the needy, called *Zakah*, along with the institution of profit-loss sharing called *Mudarabah-Musharakah*. Detailed treatment of these instruments in the context of a general equilibrium in Islamic politico-economic perspectives is given elsewhere (Choudhury 1992, 1993a).

INTRODUCING UNIFICATION EPISTEMOLOGY TO THE ISLAMIC FIRM

The premise of the unique generic epistemology of universal values that unifies all systems into integrative wholes out of interactions and that bring about further knowledge-induced evolutionary creativity out of affirmed well-being and diversities, must itself be of the most unified and irreducible nature. Otherwise, the mappings such as f and g that we have shown earlier, will emanate from differentiated premises and produce conflicts among goals and systems. This we cannot accept in such con-

123

sensual wholes. All our earlier observations relating to received economic doctrines will then return.

In the *Qur'an* this premise of the unified and most irreducible epistemology of universal values is termed as *Tawhid*, the Unity of God. This primordial premise is the endless creative core (*Qur'an*, Chapter LIX, v. 22-24). On the basis of this epistemology, a circular causation and continuity model of unified reality is constructed that explains all systems as unifying wholes out of their intrinsic interactive, integrative and knowledge-induced evolutionary attributes. This interactive-integrative-evolutionary character of the emergent process and organizational behaviour from the primal epistemology of *Tawhid*, is referred to here as unification epistemology. The difference between *Tawhid* as the primal epistemology and derived unification epistemology from *Tawhid*, is like that of a Precept and a Field (Choudhury 1991). A Precept forms the epiphenomena of the project of Divine Unity. The Field establishes its empirical and explanatory domain of Divine Unity.

In the *Qur'an* the Field is referred to as creation (*Khalq*) that is incessantly described by the Signs of God (*Ayath Allah*) (*Qur'an*, Chapter III, v. 190.). Thus the perpetual primacy of *Tawhid* on the created order, creating diversities of new Signs, is referred to in the *Qur'an* as the creation that is forever renewed (*Khalq in-Jadid*) (*Qur'an*, Chapter L, v. 15). This process of continuous renewal is also termed as *Khalqa Summa Yueid* (*Qur'an*, Chapter XVII, v. 64). In this order, the creative diversity of the Divine Laws acting upon the Field of creation, is referred to in the *Qur'an* as the 'Goodly Tree' that produces 'fruits at all times, by the leave of its Lord'. Likewise there is the natural opposite to this parable in the example of the 'Evil Tree' that has no stability (*Qur'an* Chapter XIV, v. 24-27).

One notes the permanent endogeneity of the *Tawhidi* creative process on knowledge, but the Precept of Unity remains the only exogenous *a priori* reality whose link with the world is real, although corporeal forms cannot fathom *Allah* (hence *Allah's* singular exogeneity in the order of creation). Such a world view of Unity is contrary to Kant's *a priori* ontology and Hume's *a posteriori* ontology (Friedrich 1971, Hume [1739] 1992). The ontology of Divine presence in every spec of creation is mentioned in the *Qur'an* as the Command of Being: "Verily, when He intends a thing, His Command is 'Be', and it is!" (Chapter XXVI v. 82-83). We must further equate the domain of this Absolute, Complete and Unchanging Knowledge, which we will therefore call as the Stock of Knowledge, with the uncreated quintessence of the *Qur'an* (Referred to as *Lauh Mahfuz*) (Chapter LXXV v. 21-22).

Yet the domain of knowledge in the Field remains as the unifying force of systems. Because of the intrinsic nature of interactions, integration and creative evolution into higher planes of knowledge, such a domain of knowledge must be in the perpetual state of flows deriving from the Stock and finally cumulating to the Stock again (phenomenon of *Akhira*=hereafter). This is the relational concept of creation of which the *Qur'an* says, it emanates from Divine Will and then returns to the Divine Stock by learning through degrees (Chapter XLII v. 53). The creative process explaining the divinely ordained evolutionary process is contained in the entirety of the *Qur'anic* Chapter LXXXVII.

Finally, the emanation from the Stock to the flows of knowledge, followed thereafter by the human understanding of creation and its creative evolution in diversities of meaning, is summarized in the *Qur'an* in terms of the five attributes: justice, purpose, certainty, well-being and renewal.

THE *SHURATIC* PROCESS REVISITED

The process that is based on these attributes that continuously qualify all state and knowledge variables in all systems and causes inter- and intra-systemic unification according to the unification epistemology, is described in the *Qur'an*. (Chapter XLII v. 49-53.) We call this as the *Shuratic* Process, being derived from the generic title of the Chapter, *Shura*, Consultation.

125

It is obvious from the above derivation of the *Shuratic* Process that its essence is knowledge based. Consultation in this sense means the interactions deriving from and generating into fresh knowledge flows that then guide the world of cognitive forms. It is also seen that neither this relationally creative concept of the *Shura* nor the meaning of *Shari'ah* as presented here, is restricted to political and socio-economic phenomena. Rather, by the extensive field of interactions and the unifying nature of the *Qur'anic* knowledge-based world view, these concepts comprehend the entire creative order as they come to be unravelled by continuous chains of *Ahkam* formulations and circular renewals of the creative order (Choudhury 1995a).

It is also important to note the cumulative essence of the *Shuratic* Process. Since the Field of Unity (of Divine Signs= *Ayath Allah*) comprises confirmations of Divine Unity in the meaning of the Precept of Unity, its ultimate value must comprehend the Stock. That is, the Field must cumulate to the Precept or Stock. This can only take place in the *Qur'anic* terminal domain called *Akhira*.

1. The Concept of Equilibrium in *Shuratic* Process

There is an important message here that must be understood with regards to the concept of process. While each finite process occurring in the domain of Knowledge flows is an open-ended one, the total process from Ω to A (=*Akhira*) is a closed one. The *Shuratic* Process thus attains multiple knowledge-induced dynamic equilibria that can be unique only locally, but must be diverse globally. Optimization is thus impossible in the dynamic sense of the flows. It is replaced by the method of simulation or topological mappings across knowledge-induced systems. Global equilibrium is constructed by multiple loci of short-run equilibria. The optimality-equilibrium perspectives of received economic theory is thus eliminated in the *Shuratic* Process.

Figure 5.1: The *Shuratic* Process

The Exogenous Primordial of God as Creator:

P

The Emanation of the Divine Laws for the Creative Order
= *Tawhidi* Epistemology, Stock of Knowledge

R

Ω

← <u>Attribute of Justice and Balance</u>

O

↓

C

← <u>Attribute of Purpose</u>

E

Creative Flows: Evolution of *Shari'ah*
(*Qur'anic* Laws Applied to the World by Effort and Interpretive

S

Rules called *Ahkam*)
$\{\Theta\}$

S

↓ ← <u>Attribute of Certainty</u>

1

Guidance: The Knowledge-Induced State Variables
$\{x(t(\Theta))\}$

R

↓ ← <u>Attribute of Well-Being</u>

E

Return of Creation to the Primal *Tawhidi* Roots and Origin:

N

Completion and Continuity of the Creative Process
$\{x(t(\Theta))\} \rightarrow \{\Theta'\} \rightarrow \{x'(t(\Theta))\} \rightarrow etc.$

E

← <u>Attribute of Renewal</u>

W

—————————————————————————↑

A

showing the endogeneity of Θ-values; →
showing the exogeneity of Ω impacting
on the creative evolution.

L

127

Yet the super-global order, that is $\Omega \rightarrow A$, is closed, making the originary *Tawhidi* Stock to be 'attained' in the topology of A. Thus the total creative order according to the *Qur'an* remains in Equilibrium (Choudhury 1995b).

We have here a theorem that is a combination of Kakutani's Fixed Point Theorem and Rolle's Mean Value Theorem of Differential Calculus (Nikaido 1989, Leithold 1972). This theorem states that since the *Qur'anic* Universe is Complete and every subset of it continuously differentiable in the Θ-values, therefore, equilibrium points must be 'attained' in the topological space, $T=[\Omega,A]$. But since any point $a \in T$ is Θ-induced, therefore, the equilibrium is never unique, is perpetually perturbed. Such multiple equilibria are simulatively dynamic in the knowledge flows that primordially determine time.

The concept of time (t) can now be taken up in this meaning of *Tawhidi* T-topology (Maddox 1970, Choudhury 1995a). If t was an independent variable in T, then the dynamic treatment of objective functions could be solved by optimal control theory. This would imply uniquely global as well as multiple global equilibria. But now with no globally independent elements existing except Ω and A terminally, we cannot treat the objective functions in the same light as in optimal control theory.

We have now established the *Qur'anic* methodology of the process called the *Shuratic* Process. This is the view of creation in all its micro and cosmic elements, as knowledge-based interactive-integrative-evolutionary cause-effect relationships unifying all systems in degrees of knowledge flows, when these are derived and guided according to the Most Unified Knowledge Premise, that is *Tawhid*. Because of these attributes of the *Shuratic* Process, the general methodology underlying it is referred to here as the circular causation and continuity model of Unified Reality. Its structure is as follows (Choudhury 1993b):

$\Omega \rightarrow [\{\Theta_1\} \rightarrow_{f1} \{x_1(t(\Theta_1))\}] = P_1 \rightarrow [\{\Theta_2\} \rightarrow_{f2} \{x_2(t(\Theta_2))\}] = P_2 \rightarrow ..P_\infty \rightarrow A.$
The subscripts i=1,2,.. denote processes and [ ]'s denote completed knowledge-induced processes. The vector values (indicated by bolds) of the knowledge-induced state values and the flow values of knowledge signify that these are generalized n tuples formed by systemic inter-actions-integration and evolution.

2. The Concept of Organization Derived from the *Shuratic* Process

We will now invoke this methodology and the *Shuratic* Process to define the corresponding concept of organization. The concept of organization in the knowledge-induced sense is conveyed by the inter- and intra-systemically determined n-tuples of values, $\{x(t(\Theta))\}$. A number of attributes of such an organization can now be noted: An organization represents strong interactions inter- and intra-systems. It is guided by rules called *Ahkam* derived from knowledge flows premised in Ω (or equivalently in A). Such *Ahkam* are also determined by the endogenous nature of policy variables, plans, programs, instruments, all taken up with the Θ-augmented $x(.)$ variables. The dynamics of the organization are determined by such interactions that lead to consensus and then to creative evolution into higher planes of Θ-values and thus generate $x(.)$ values, etc. The *Shuratic* Process is thereby, a compounded relationship of such organizational menus. Since the *Shuratic* Process can be diverse in nature, so also the organizational menus can be diverse and mutiple in nature.

But since a process and hence organizational menu are intrinsically formed by knowledge-based systemic interactions, therefore, the plans, programs, policies and menus of an Islamic organization are guided by universally complementary menus. This inference follows directly from the *Qur'an*, wherein apart from the only two disjoint realities, namely Truth and Falsehood, there is pervasive complementarity within these categories (*Qur'an* Chapter XIII, v. 3-4; Chapter LI, v. 8-11). Diversity is the result of complementarities in the domain of Truth (*Qur'an* Chapter IV, v. 24-27). The concept of universal complementarity means the capacity of complementary extensions across systems and issues as the flows of knowledge expand from lesser to higher degrees of manifestations of the principal attributes in the *Tawhidi* core that we have seen, namely the vector, (justice, purpose, certainty, well-being, renewal). Hence, in between the perfect disjointness of Truth and Falsehood, there may exist temporarily undetermined regions of organizational menus, called *Mubah* (indeterminate between permissible and forbidden). But all *Mubah* are temporary phenomena, subject to final well-determination with the evolution of Θ-values.

THE ISLAMIC FIRM'S MENUS DERIVED FROM THE *SHURATIC* PROCESS AND ORGANIZATION

The Islamic firm is an organization as defined above in the midst of the socio-economic complex of market, economy, society and polity. The agents of the firm being individuals who are consensually integrated together through interactions among and outside themselves, are endowed with endogenous preferences based on the menus of social goods to choose. Likewise, they have their choices of technology and menus of production in which factors of production (capital and labour) are globally complementary to each other. The pricing of the firm's product is interactively determined in the market system, and the market system itself is subject to interactive demand and supply menus. The firm's resource allocation is dynamically determined by means of organizational interactions among factors and institutional arrangements that enable this to happen.

The circular causation and continuity model of unified reality shows that the inputs and outputs of the Islamic process and organization are simply knowledge flows, which then give meaning to goods and services and to the dynamic structure. Thus due to the globally simulative nature of knowledge flows, the Islamic firm's objective criterion is to simulate - not to maximize - its profitability function, subject to a social well-being function and the resource allocation relations among endowments and factors. The allocational and decision-making perspectives that impact upon the firm's menu are determined by the complex of plans, programs and instruments that activate the process and the organization. An alternative social objective would be to simulate the social well-being function subject to the profitability relation and the endowment and resource constraints.

The Islamic firm's production menu is thus a technology for producing social goods as guided by *Ahkam*, subject to the Principle of Universal Complementarity among factors and social agents. The social well-being function is determined by the mutual knowledge-inducing state and policy variables that bring about consumer and social benefits as well as profitability of the firm. The concepts of profitability and efficiency are thus substantively different from the ones we come across in the neoclassical theory of the firm.

On the pricing side, while markets are relied upon, such markets themselves are subjected to the extension of the knowledge-forming interactive process. Such markets under the guidance of *Shari'ah* and social regulations, such as the *Hisbah* (social regulatory institution of markets in classical Islamic period), are transformed by the underlying interactive preferences of agents, output menus, instruments and institutions, into ethicized markets (Chapter 4 in this book). Yet it is to be noted that the *Hisbah* was not meant to unduly interrupt due market process. Its function was simply guidance when socially needed. Ibn Taimiyyah when formulating his theory of *Hishah* kept in view the strict ruling of the Prophet Muhammad sayings and practices not to tamper with the market process unduly, except to establish fairness.

OBJECTIVE CRITERION OF THE ISLAMIC FIRM AS AN ORGANIZATION

The firm's objective is now written down as follows:

Simulate $\{\Theta\}$ $\pi(L(t(\Theta)),K(t(\Theta)) = [Q(t(\Theta)) - C(t(\Theta))]$

$= p(t(\Theta)).F(L(\Theta),K(\Theta),t(\Theta)) - w(t(\Theta)).L(t(\Theta)) - r(t(\Theta)).K(t(\Theta))$

subject to, $W = W(r(t(\Theta)),w(t(\Theta)),L(t(\Theta)),K(t(\Theta)),p(t(\Theta)),Q(t(\Theta)))$,

$\Theta = \Theta(r(t(\Theta)),w(t(\Theta)),L(t(\Theta)),K(t(\Theta)),p(t(\Theta)),Q(t(\Theta)))$.

This criterion function shows the feedback that must take place between state variables and renewal of knowledge formation in the circular causation and continuity model. Finally, systemic unification would require interactions leading to consensus (integration) followed by knowledge-induced evolution (renewal). This phenomenon is implied by, $\{\Theta\}\in\{\cap_j\succeq_j;$ attributes=$\mathbf{a}\} \subset \Omega$. In this problem a continuous version of the functions and variables is used instead of the iterative version showing feedback. The assumptions of the model are two: First, there is a monotonic circular causation and continuity effects between Θ-values and state variables and policy variables. Second, Θ being derived from the unification epistemology (Ω), it affects all systemic unification in the Islamic political economy.

The symbols of the above expressions are herewith defined:

L(.) denotes labour qualified by its relationship with the learning process signified by the knowledge variable, $\{\Theta\}$. Since Θ-values are formed through interactions leading to consensus (integration) and then evolution, therefore, the learning process for labour is taken up in this milieu of change.

K(.) likewise denotes the stock of capital.

w(.) denotes the wage rate. Once again wages are determined interactively, integratively and in evolutionary fashion over time with the progress of Θ-values. This is the result of the cooperative nature of the Islamic firm as an organization.

r(.) is the price of real capital which likewise depends upon t(Θ).

p(.) is the price of the social goods, which are likewise determined for both consumer well-being and the profitability of the firm.

Q(.) denotes the quantity of social goods produced by the firm's menu, F(.).

Thus organizational behaviour is formed by interactive preferences $\succeq_j$ among the j agents (systems), j=1,2,..n. The consensus (integration shown by $\cap_j$) attained through such interactions is due to the learning process based on the attributes, **a**=(just balance, purpose, certainty, well-being, renewal). {Θ} values thereby include the plans, programs and policies that are continuously qualified by **a**. In this way, coercion in the organization is replaced by learning and knowledge exchange from one level to a higher level of Θ. It is easy to see now that Θ, **a**, $\cap_j\succeq_j$, and the state variable plus policy variables, $\mathbf{x}(t(\Theta))$, all complement each other. This is possible because the function of Ω is to unify these parameters and variables through the unification principle of Θ-values over cycles of interactions, integrations and renewals.

The Islamic firm's objective function is essentially a knowledge-induced dynamic problem in simulation over iterations of Θ-values, and hence over interactions, integration and evolution. The static case of the above problem can happen if and only if Θ is not evolutionary. This is the case either of the momentary short run or a relapse into neoclassical analysis.

The dynamic Lagrangian function, $L(t(\Theta))$, for the Islamic firm's objective function is,

$L(t(\Theta))=p.F(L,K)-wL-rK+\lambda(W(r,w,p,L,K,Q)+\Theta(r,w,p,L,K,Q),$

$Q=F(L,K),$

where, each of the variables is a function of Θ through $t(\Theta)$.

Now by differentiating with a particular value of Θ, we obtain,

$dL/d\Theta=Q.dp/d\Theta + p[(\partial Q/\partial L)dL/d\Theta + (\partial Q/\partial K)dK/d\Theta] -Ldw/d\Theta - w.dL/d\Theta -K.dr/d\Theta - r.dK/d\Theta + \lambda[\{(\partial W/\partial r)+(\partial\Theta/\partial r)\}dr/d\Theta +$

$\{(\partial W/\partial w)+(\partial\Theta/\partial w)\}dw/d\Theta$ + $\{(\partial W/\partial p)+(\partial\Theta/\partial p)\}dp/d\Theta$ +
$\{(\partial W/\partial L)+(\partial\Theta/\partial L)\}dL/d\Theta$ + $\{(\partial W/\partial K)+(\partial\Theta/\partial K)\}dK/d\Theta$ +
$\{(\partial W/\partial Q)+(\partial\Theta/\partial Q)\}dQ/d\Theta \geq 0.$

The non-negative condition is due to the monotonic effect of Θ on L(.) and the knowledge-inducing effect on the utilization of L in production.

Thereby,

$(dp/d\Theta)(Q+(\partial W/\partial p)+(\partial\Theta/\partial p))\geq(dL/d\Theta)[w-p.(\partial Q/\partial L)-(\partial W/\partial L)-\partial\Theta/\partial L)]$
$+(dK/d\Theta)[r-p(\partial Q/\partial K)-(\partial W/\partial K)-(\partial\Theta/\partial K)]$
$+(dw/d\Theta)[L-(\partial W/\partial w)-(\partial\Theta/\partial w)]+(dr/d\Theta)[K-(\partial W/\partial r)-(\partial\Theta/\partial r)].$

This result is due to the monotonic effect of Θ-values on the state variables and the knowledge-renewal effect on Θ.

By the monotonicity of the variables on Θ-values and complementarity among the variables via the Θ-effect, we would have, $dL/d\Theta>0$, $dK/d\Theta>0$, $dw/d\Theta>0$, $dr/d\Theta>0$. But we do not know the precise sign of the coefficients of these derivatives. We can effectively argue that the signs will be the same for all these coefficients, whatever these are.

If $w \geq (\partial/\partial L)(p.Q-W-\Theta)\geq0$, this would mean that labour is being compensated more by increasing returns to revenue than by contributions to social well-being. Although the firm is contributing to social well-being, its contributions toward its own profitability is proportionately greater. Now by the complementarity among the factors, $r\geq(\partial/\partial K)(p.Q-W-\Theta)\geq0$, means that capital too is being compensated proportionately more by increasing returns to revenue than by social well-being contributed by the same firm.

Consequently it is expected that, $L\geq(\partial(W+\Theta)/\partial w)>0$ and $K\geq\partial(W+\Theta)/\partial r>0$. That is, either $L/(\partial(W+\Theta)/\partial w) \geq K/(\partial(W+\Theta)/\partial r)$ or $K/(\partial(W+\Theta)/\partial r) \geq L/(\partial(W+\Theta)/\partial w)$.

These results mean that although labour and capital complement each other, it is not required for the well-being of either of these to be equal to each other, compensation being measured in terms of factor payments. This is true even in the midst of knowledge formation and renewal. All

134

that matters is that the evolution of knowledge values through interactions and consensus among labour and capital should bring about mutual well-being.

The above results are summarized as follows:

$$(w/\imath)\geq[(\partial/\partial L)(p.Q-W-\Theta)/(\partial/\partial K)(p.Q-W-\Theta),$$

and then $L/K\geq[(\partial(W+\Theta)/\partial w)/(\partial(W+\Theta)/\partial r)],$

in the case of increasing returns to knowledge formation in capital-labour relations being more favourable to labour.

Likewise, $(w/r)\leq[(\partial/\partial L)(p.Q-W-\Theta)/(\partial/\partial K)(p.Q-W-\Theta),$

$L/K\leq[(\partial(W+\Theta)/\partial w)/(\partial(W+\Theta)/\partial r)].$

This implies that increasing returns to knowledge formation in capital-labour relations is found to be more favourable to capital, albeit both factors being benefited mutually in their social well-being.

Values for L now depend upon multiple configurations for the state variables according to the above-mentioned relations. Equity rather than equality is taken as the scale of distributive justice in the eyes of *Shari'ah*. The *Qur'an* is clear on this point (Chapter XXIV v. 39). "Verily my Lord enlarges and restricts the sustenance to such of His servants as He pleases: and nothing do ye spend in the least in His Cause but He replaces it: for He is the Best of those who grant sustenance."

SIMULTANEITY OF ECONOMIC EFFICIENCY AND DISTRIBUTIVE EQUITY IN THE ISLAMIC FIRM'S PRODUCTION MENU

When the above-mentioned conditions of distributive equity are combined with the fact that they are associated with increasing returns to scale in both augmented capital and labour by means of Θ-values, as shown above, we then obtain the important result: Economic efficiency and distributive equity coexist in the Islamic resource allocation problem. Here only the power of the knowledge variables causes the factor payments to be in accordance with an efficiency that is gained under

135

participation and mutual well-being. Hence complementarity between economic efficiency and distributive equity is attained by means of the presence of Θ-values. Besides, we note that all of the above results are independent of price level to the firm. Thus, $dp/d\Theta$ can take all possible signs in the midst of product and factor complementarities (also by means of product diversification).

Since time is a monotonic function of Θ-values on the real line, as mentioned earlier, therefore, the results derived here are general with respect to intertemporal allocation of resources. But we suggest for purposes of a discrete problem, the iterative simulation of $L(t(\Theta))$ as given above. Methods of estimating stochastic processes will help here (Dhrymes 1970; Turnovsky 1995).

THE ISLAMIC FIRM'S PRODUCTION MENU IN RELATION TO ORGANIZATIONAL BEHAVIOUR

We will now go on to show that mutual well-being with the firm as an embryonic organization in the social system, is established through participatory organization. The presence of Θ-values and their circular causation and continuity in relation with the state variables in the presence of the **a**-attributes and interactive preferences, conveys the fact that organizational behaviour is an important aspect of decision-making in the theory of the firm in Islamic perspectives. Various instruments of organization in the Islamic firm are well known: participation between capitalists and labour (profit-sharing called *Mudarabah*) and among themselves (*Mudarabah-Musharakah*). The important aspect to remember here is that such participation by no means conveys sleeping relationships. In the knowledge model of the firm we have presented, such a participation is always under agent-agent cooperation. This is a point that is found to be largely absent in the Islamic profit-sharing literature (Siddiqi 1985; Chapra 1985), and must therefore be brought at the centrepiece of the instruments, policies, plans and programs of the Islamic firm as an embryonic entity in Islamic political economy. Obviously, this idea of cooperation extends beyond the internal agents of the firm to Islamic political economy and conforms with our understanding of the *Shuratic Process*.

It is not my intention here to cover the topic on *Mudarabah* and *Musharakah*, which has been extensively treated in the Islamic literature. Instead I will delineate some of the instruments and policies that must emerge from the **a**-attributes toward forming consensus $\{\cap_j \succeq_j\}$, $j=1,2,..,n$ agents or systems, and thus lead to the formation and renewal of Θ-values (evolutionary process).

I now reformulate the organizational problem of the firm given by Herbert Simon, which was examined earlier, in Figure 5.2. One notes from Figure 5.2 that the connecting variable across all of the agents relating to the firm's production menu is participation, and hence cooperation taken up in a politico-economic sense. When taken up in this extensive sense, this concept of participation is extended beyond *Mudarabah* and *Musharakah* of the firm's internal decision to agents in the political economy. Cooperation in this extensive domain simultaneously causes stability through risk-diversification, product-diversification and economic-diversification and causes both political and economic entitlements among all agents. These conditions imply the attributes of balance, purpose, certainty and well-being.

The knowledge-induced economy of scale in the production menu of the firm, causes increasing social goods and profitability to occur in the midst of equity-efficiency simultaneity. These conditions imply the attributes of balance, purpose, well-being, certainty and productive evolution. Extensive complementarity through interactions (participation) causes mutual well-being without factor marginalization. This condition implies the attribute of purpose, well-being and certainty. The extensive institutional interactions imply policy endogeneity in relation to the state

137

variables. Technological factors as part of the institutional factor also bring about similar induction in the firm's production. These conditions induce balance, purpose, certainty, well-being and evolution. Thus in all, the attributes are reflected in the global complementarity among the state variables (Q,L,K,w,r,p) and the policy variables (economic cooperation, distribution, social goods, stabilization, information flow and social control=*Hisbah*).

The Role of Divine Attributes in Contrasting Paradigms

It remains to be seen whether the above attributes can be derived from sources other than *Tawhidi* epistemology to establish the uniqueness of the Islamic organizational theory of the firm. Clearly, in all of mainstream economics including the central issue of capital-labour conflict found in Marx's labour theory of value in his theory of exploitation of labour and in all kinds of Darwinian natural selection processes, the assumption of marginalist substitution is central. By means of the marginalist substitution principle is defined the idea of economic efficiency and stability. Consequently, on the basis of its very epistemology, all such systems marginalize themselves in generating the kinds of attributes we have shown to emanate from the *Qur'an*. The essence of cooperation as interactions leading to integration (consensus and hence temporary equilibria) and thereafter to knowledge renewals (creative evolution) and perpetual evolution of the circular causation and continuity processes, totally replaces the idea of the marginalist firm.

Thus the connecting variable among all the agents and their attributes given in Figure 5.2 being participation, i.e. cooperation, means the enaction of the *Shuratic* Process as explained in terms of its epistemological extensiveness. This epistemology established the circular causation and continuity world view of unified reality premised on unification of systems (agents, variables, policies, instruments, plans) by

138

Figure 5.2: Organizational Theory of the Islamic Firm

Participants	Inducements	Contributions
entrepreneur	sales revenue, economy of scale based on equity-efficiency, participation to attain risk and product diversification.	production cost
labour	wage, participation employment, entitlement	service of labour
capital	rents, participation utilization, entitlement	service of capital
social agents (other firms)	social well-being, participation,	cooperation goodwill
institutions (internal & external)	information flow, participation, planning policies, programs, technology, (social control=*Hisbah*)	cooperation social well-being
consumer	well-being participation	stable prices, goodwill

means of knowledge flows. Such an epistemology makes 'a' as the attributes and their derivation unique to the *Tawhidi* roots in the organization theory of the Islamic firm. Global complementarity and economic cooperation now become the knowledge flows in the organizational theory of the Islamic firm. One notes however, that such flows are developed by active human participation and not by the Smithian Invisible Hand Principle. Hence, there exists a visible anthropic relationship in creating knowledge out of interactions-integration-evolution. This real human action is shown by, $[\{\cap_j \succeq_j; \text{attributes} = \mathbf{a}\} \rightarrow \{\Theta\}] \subset \Omega$.

RELATIONSHIP BETWEEN WAGES AND PROFIT-SHARING IN THE ISLAMIC FIRM

One last point to be understood here is the relationship between wages and profit-sharing in an Islamic firm that evolves into more cooperative stages under knowledge induction. Wage rate is a value associated with the marginal productivity of labour, which in turn is a phenomenon of marginalist substitution, in spite of technological change in the neoclassical production function. On the other hand, wages and rents are codetermined by factor complementarity in the Islamic production menu. As the firm transforms from a less cooperative enterprise to a more cooperative one, present wages must be channelled into retained earnings to generate profit-sharing. Besides, since no perfect Islamic state of economic and social arrangements is being claimed in the organizational theory of the firm, therefore, some amount of wage earnings must always exist in the firm. But the transformation process from a wage-earning labour to profit-sharing contracts in the more cooperative firm would mean that the profit-share is being generated by recycling wages and rents into retained earning to form higher profits (Choudhury & Malik 1992, pp. 184-92).

140

SIMULATIVE EQUILIBRIUM CONCEPT FOR THE ISLAMIC FIRM

The above results in the organizational theory of the Islamic firms can now be represented in terms of the knowledge-induced dynamic equilibrium concept. In Figure 5.3a of Figure 5.3, we show that global complementarity among agents and factors in the case of knowledge evolution will yield curves of the types $Oe_{11}e_{12}...$ between L and Q; $Oe_{21}e_{22}...$ between K and Q; $Oe_{31}e_{32}...$ K and r; $Oe_{41}e_{42}...$ between L and w. These e-points are the knowledge renewal points where simultaneously new factor-augmenting technological inductions come about. These points denote the evolutionary equilibria. The positive shapes of the curves indicate systemic complementarity. The correspondences $e_{11}e_{21}e_{31}e_{41}$ span out to other levels as shown in Figure 5.3a, due to the impact of evolving Θ-values.

Organizational theory of the Islamic firm is made up of the knowledge-induced equilibrium points in the state and policy variables represented by points in the polity-state set, such as, $\{e_{ji}\} \in S_{ji}$, i=1,2,..., j=1,2,3,4, shown in Figure 5.3b. We have shown such strong interactions in the simple case of two sets only, S_1 and S_2, with vectors $\{e_1(\Theta)\} \in S_1$, $\{e_2(\Theta)\} \in S_2$.

All agents (systems, state and policy variables) have knowledges to share with each other. The knowledge variables, $\{\Theta_{ji}\}$ induces $\{e_{ji}\}$. Hence $\{e_{ji}(\Theta_{ji})\}$ are knowledge-induced state and policy variables for agents j=1,2,3,4 over interactions i=1,2,... Note now that because of monotonicity between e-values and Θ-values, $\cap_j S_{ji}$ will increase in dimensionality as $\cap\{\Theta_{ji}\}$ increases in dimensionality. The result is a feedback expansion of $\cap_j S_{ji}$ as i takes up increasing values in i=1,2,... Thus the two-way arrows indicate knowledge-induced evolution over iterated e-values, as intersections (i=1,2,..) and integrations are formed ($\cap_j$). These in turn are functions of the attributes **a**=(justice balance, purpose, certainty, well-being, recreation).

It can be further noted that the process of diversification that is linked with complementarity, will cause j to increase. Now a greater densification of the knowledge sets and consequently, of the knowledge-induced state-polity sets, will increase the force of interactions and consensus (unanimity or majority voting), and thus cause rich evolutions, such as diversity of thought and technological change. Such an agent-specific consensus is known in the *Shuratic* terminology as *Ijma* and *Qiyas*. The interactions are known as *Ijtehad* and renewal is the *Qur'anic* relational and creative order (Muslehuddin undated). In this chapter, these same Islamic legal terminologies have been extended to incorporate a breadth of meaning conveyed by the *Qur'anic* universality of the *Shuratic* Process.

CONCLUSION

We now conclude this chapter. Market transformation of Muslim countries in a globalizing age needs a fresh look at the underlying concepts of economic transactions. The demand for ethicized markets in Islamic setting leads to a theory of the Islamic firm seen essentially as an organization theory. The firm is now seen as an organization with visible human contracts and interactions, and not the result of optimal processes of invisible hands and hedonistic markets. The anthropic essence in the processual perspective of organizational theory of the Islamic firm is a substantive issue centred on the knowledge-based world view of the *Shuratic* Process.

The organizational theory of the Islamic firm is thus developed in comparative perspectives from the *Qur'anic* epistemological premise of Unity of God and the unification epistemology, in ways as this epistemology can be applied to issues relating to the firm as an embryonic social entity amidst strong and global interactions in the political economy. The circular causation and continuity model of unified reality is

Figure 5.3: Case of Knowledge-Based Interactions-Integration-Evolution in the Organizational Theory of the Islamic Firm.

Figure 5.3a

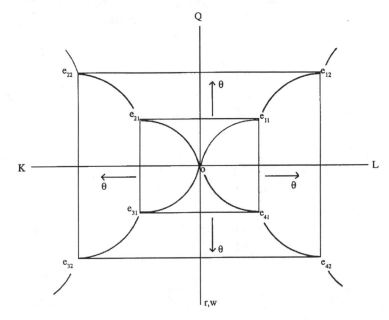

Figure 5.3b

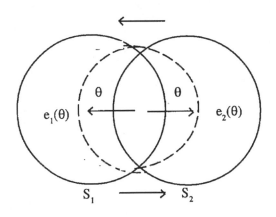

thus established to explain these unification perspectives of the organizational theory of the firm. We find that this is an area that has deep academic import and strong empirical strengths, as the theory addresses non-optimal situations and dynamic equilibrium situations of the real world socio-economic phenomena.

Our focus in this chapter was on introducing the methodology of the interactive, integrative and evolutionary models of knowledge-based processes of the Islamic firm. We have thus not focused on the price determination problem and the impact of knowledge induction on intertemporal allocation of resources. For analytical treatment of pricing issue, the reader may refer to the author's work elsewhere (Choudhury 1994b). To cover our scope in the chapter we have dealt with the organizational problem of the firm and have tried to show how the organizational theory of the Islamic firm differs from a similar problem in received economic theory and what it is alternatively.

CHAPTER 6

REFORMING THE CAPITAL MARKET: ISLAMIC CONCEPT OF MONEY

To introduce the idea of money in Islamic political economy we ask the following questions at the outset: Is money a financial contravention or a commodity in economic activity? If money is a financial contravention to promote economic activity, then what is the real output against which money must be measured and valued? If money is a commodity, then what is the real price of money? In all of these cases, what are the functions of money? Answers to these questions will suffice to explain the meaning of money in Islamic political economy. In this chapter we will introduce and explain the meaning of money in Islamic political economy in light of the knowledge-based interactive methodology that we have throughout developed.

VARIOUS TREATMENTS OF MONEY IN THE LITERATURE

The treatment of the concept of money as a financial contravention to value the basic function of exchange in the real sector, is not new in the literature. Aristotle thought of money as a contravention with no real value, but he abhorred wealth albeit the necessary evil that men possess in acquiring wealth (Barker 1959). Thus, although Aristotle saw the unethical element of the rate of interest in the generation of wealth, he maintained its necessity for the human economy. Money in the context of these facts, turns out to be a financial contravention driven by the rate of interest for the purpose of accumulating wealth.

Hume and Fisher saw in money the concept of bullion that is transacted through trade. If a commodity had value, that is because it was made expensively and then traded for cheaper things through international trade (Fisher 1911). This mercantilist concept of money as bullions was a fallacy that Hume pointed out (Hume 1752), for if expensive goods were produced at home through the supply of an increased quantity of money and then traded for cheaper goods from abroad, that meant an export of money capital while raising prices at home. The mercantilist bullions theory of money was the result of delinking money from the productive roots of economic activity.

Marx saw the use of money as a contravention that remains independent of economic activity. He argued that if a given quantity of money (M) was made to transact a certain amount of goods (T), say in trade, then the unit price is given by, $p=M/T$. Now the lesser is the number of goods, the less is the circulation of that quantity of money. Hence p would increase. On the other hand, the higher is the quantity of money that is created independently of the level of economic activity (T), then this too will create price increase (Mandell 1971). Finally, if M was low in quantity and was independent of T, then T would be generated by other means, such as, barter and book-entry means of transactions. This method was practised by the Soviet Gosplan for a long time (Zimbalist et al. 1984).

If M is related with T, so that functionally, $T=T(M)$, then lower M would mean lower $T(M)$ and vice versa. p would now remain stable but at the social cost of prosperity. Finally, if both M and $T(M)$ were high, then too p could remain stable. But now the mere contravention of money must be abandoned.

The treatment of money as a commodity is to be found in the classical school with its rebirth in new classicism today. Thus Adam Smith, Hume to Marx and later on Walras and Hayek, and today Friedman, all see money as a financial contravention and not as a commodity. The meaning

146

of money as financial contravention is that of money affecting the level of economic activity, to be thus evaluated in terms of the return to real capital serviced by money.

With the neoclassicists and Keynes, the quantity theory of money came to be challenged by the commodity concept of money. This meant a return to yet another view on the commodity concept of money from that held by the bullion theory of money in the mercantilist school. To the neoclassicists, money represented a dated exchange intertemporally, just like any commodity. Hence, there must be a price as value for money as dated commodities.

To Keynes, money as commodity is interpreted by the way in which it is held. Hence, a transaction demand for money meant the use of money in alternative items for immediate use. This kind of activity did not qualify money to be held as commodity *per se*. Rather, the real outputs transacted by money provided the commodity substitutes for money (Tobin 1958). In the precautionary and speculative demand for money functions, the commodity nature of money is reflected by the perception of the holder on what money does. The speculative idea of money now serves a certain psychology that was assumed by Keynes to characterize uncertainty. There was a sense of sacrifice in intertemporal allocative character given to money as commodity. Such a characteristic was also neoclassical in essence. Money as commodity that is held as traded exchange intertemporally, carries a subjective price with it. This price of money is called the rate of interest.

Only when money is held as a commodity directly and not valued in terms of the real goods that it serves, and only if money is a financial contravention independent of real economic activity that it serves, then this financial aggregate comes to be held subjectively. Interest rate now becomes a subjective price for money held as commodity with subjective pricing. In recent quantity theory of money, the combination of money as both transactions of financial securities and real goods, makes the theory of money relapse into accepting interest rate as a price for such dated exchange of money as commodity (Friedman 1989).

Contrarily, if it was thus possible logically to eliminate the connection between the nature of money and its subjective pricing when held as a commodity or a contravention over time, then the rate of interest would become a wasteful cost. It would cease to be accepted in economic transactions. All valuations of goods would then be reduced to real economic activity. Intertemporal treatment of goods in exchange would proceed in the light of real goods in exchange. What transacters would eventually come to hold is not money but goods. Money would then lose its functions of commodity-like exchange value. It would reflect simply a store of value imputed primarily by the exchange value of the real goods transacted by means of money. In this light then, capital markets, financial institutions, international transactions and monetary currencies, would all be treated in terms of real sector activities. Money would cease to be a commodity but will continue to be a financial contravention that is functionally determined by the level of real economic activity, actual or expected (Choudhury 1991).

MONEY IN ISLAMIC POLITICAL ECONOMY

Islamic political economy is the study of knowledge-induced interactions among economic participants, society, institutions and ideas, once the interactive-integrative-evolutionary nature of the unification process emanating from the epistemology of Divine Unity, is upheld. In this light therefore, money must be seen as the result of a series of interactions in real sector activities that primordially create a thing of real economic value. Thereafter, this value reflects the configuration of money as currency in the system. The real bills would then mark the store of value of real goods exchanged in the absence of speculation (Laidler 1990).

To formalize, let Θ denote knowledge flow that in turn creates time

148

t as a reflection of simultaneity between event and time. Thereby, Θ determines t, and t then determines socio-economic values denoted by the vector $\mathbf{X}(t(\Theta))$. Now since all possible combinations of Θ in the domain of interaction-integration-evolution equivalently generates all similar combinations of $\mathbf{X}(t(\Theta))$ values and in similar domains, therefore, $V_1 = \cup(\cap(t(\Theta))) \rightarrow_s \cup(\cap(\mathbf{X}(t(\Theta))))$. Here, $\cup$ denotes the mathematical union, and $\cap$ denotes the mathematical intersection of the knowledge sets shown. Thus, $s(\cup(\cap(t(\Theta))))$ as a mapping of a domain must belong to the 'onto' domain, $\cup(\cap(\mathbf{X}(t(\Theta))))=V_2$, say. The assumption of monotonicity between s(.) and V_2, and hence between V_1 and V_2, is automatically made. The topological space in the sense of such domains is the vectorial tuplet, (V_1, V_2). The monotonic functional defined on this topological space is, $S(V_1(t(\Theta)), V_2(t(\Theta)))$. The important difference between S and the concept of social welfare function used in neoclassical economics, is the existence of universal complementarity among V_1 and V_2 through the effect of Θ on time and systems. In neoclassical economic theory there must ultimately be gross substitution between V_1 and V_2, although partial complementarities may exist. One representation of $S(V_1, V_2)$ is, $S = \Pi[M(g, \Theta)]$, where now we take $V_2 = M(g, \Theta)$ as money defined by its evaluation parameter g in terms of knowledge value Θ over time t.

Now we have a way of examining the recursive nature of money in the Islamic political economy. $M(t(\Theta))$ is the result of knowledge values, Θ, that are formed by institutional-economy-markets and agent-specific interactions. Since interactions are real events in space-time, therefore, money must be a functional product of such real events. The use of speculation for purposes of valuation cannot any more be acceptable in this knowledge-based interactive order. The very fact that interactions produce knowledge and integration produces consensus means that uncertainty is reduced within such a diversified and complementing political economy.

SIMULATION WITH MONEY IN ISLAMIC POLITICAL ECONOMY

The recursive nature of the interactive-integrative-evolutionary system of Islamic political economy leads to the following simulation problem involving money:

Simulate(Θ) $\Pi[M(g,\Theta)]$

subject to, $M+(\Theta+) = f_1(M(\Theta))$,

$$\Theta+= f_2(\Theta).$$

The variables with + indicate forward recursive values. Although simulation over Θ-values does not assume monotonicity of such values, yet the relationship between M and Θ and various combinations of these, is strictly monotonic. This means that the growth parameter, g must be a monotonic function of Θ-values. Now since Θ-values are generated by interactions, an example of which is participation in real economic activity, therefore, g, must be a measure of profitability, growth rate of output and prices of commodities in actual transactions in the real economy. Money in the Islamic political economy is thereby a contravention and not a commodity. But it is a contravention strictly for imputing the value created by real sector activity. The growth of money-value as such a contravention, is imparted by the growth rate of the real goods sector, profitability rate, rate of changes in prices. All of these are reflected in $g(\Theta)$.

THE NATURE OF INTEREST RATE IN MONETARY VALUATION

The question we now want to examine is whether the same kinds of growth effect can be given to money by the rate of interest as by $g(\Theta)$? Let us proffer an answer from the Keynesian side. In the Keynesian economic system, an increase in interest rate as a policy variable set by the central bank, is accompanied by a decrease in money demand and money supply. With this monetary contraction, the immediate effect is a decline in national income, investment and employment. Increased interest rate gives incentive to savers at the expense of resource mobilization into real investment immediately. There is a waiting time before savings can once again be so mobilized. During this waiting time, productivity is lost and along with it, holding of money as savings translate into inequitable resource allocation in favour of those who are privileged to earn and save in these high unemployment regimes. Interest rate thus becomes a price for holding on to savings as liquidity and withdrawing funds from productive economic activity. This cost increases with deferment in time.

Examining the money relation from the side of the quantity theory of money, we note the fundamental equation, $MV=PT$. Thus, $M=k.P$, where, $k=T/V$, is assumed to remain fairly constant. This implies that an identity exists, making the relationship between P and $\hat{M}$ two-directional. The result is a lack of well-defined causal relationship between these variables and the resulting absence of a deductive theory of money and prices. Money in financial and economic transactions now exists as an *a posteriori* empirical fact.

Barro's market clearance model links up the market for commodities to the money market (Barro 1993). But since real incomes remain unchanged in a given menu of production, so Barro's commodity market model determines the equilibrium level of interest rate and output. When these are substituted in the equation for the demand for money, money market clearance takes place at equilibrium levels of price and quantity of money. The linkage created between the two markets is therefore, through the inverse movements between price level and interest rate. Now interest rate once again becomes a subjective valuation factor rather than a real valuation of market exchange. Barro's market clearance model does not provide a rationale as to how the interest rate leads to and emerges from the clearance between the two markets, except that it feeds in from the side of commodity market into the money equation. In the commodity market interest rate is the creation of an intertemporal valuation of perceived though not real scarcity.

From all of the above perceptions on the rate of interest in conjunction with money and prices, we obtain the following relations:

	M	E	Q	P	Q/P	I	S	r	U(i,X)
i increasing	--	-	-	+	-	-	+	-	i,X substitute

with t (time) increasing

i: interest rate (nominal or real);   I: investment;
M: quantity of money;   S: saving;
E: employment;   r: profitability rate;
Q: output;   U(i,X): utility function
P: prices;   in terms of i and X as
Q/P: real output;   substitutes;
X=(M, E, Q, P, Q/P, I, S, r)   - negative
    -- undetermined

VALUATION OF MONEY IN ISLAMIC POLITICAL ECONOMY

Next we will examine the topic of valuation of money in Islamic political economy. The relationship between the real rate of profitability, $g(\Theta)$ in terms of the knowledge variable Θ, and in relation to quantity of money to be determined by and to support real economic activity, showed that such a rate is caused by a wide range of participatory functions. Thus, money ceases to have an independent existence of its own either as an aggregate or as a time-valuation of commodity. Only real economic activities count. Money appears as a financial contravention to support these activities and to be created in turn by the volume of demand for such activities. The last point is that of recursive simulation in the way we have formulated this.

Now Θ determines price level, $p(\Theta)$, which determines values of $g(\Theta)$, which determines $X(\Theta)$, and which then determines $M(\Theta)$. In turn through the recursive simulation problem, $M(\Theta)$ determines $X(\Theta)$, and thereby, by the reorigination of knowledge variables, new Θ-values emerge. This circular causation between $M(\Theta)$ and $X(\Theta)$ through the effect of Θ-values, continues.

The recursive problem and the relationships between M and X are now as follows. In the Islamic political economy, the interrelationships between money and real economic activity are given by,

$$M = F(X(\Theta),\Theta),$$

subject to a series of derived relationships between any one of the X-variables and the remaining ones in X; and the recursive equations, $M+ = f(M(\Theta))$; $\Theta+ = g(\Theta)$, the symbol + denotes forward recursive values. It is clearly seen that through these recursive equations, all variables in the derived equations of the X-variables are recursively determined. The simulation of M-X relationship here points to the cause-effect feedbacks between money and the real economy.

The M-X relationship is now through the cumulative effect of $g(\Theta)$, instead of being through i. The effects are as follows:

	M	E	Q	P	Q/P	I	S	r	$S(g(\Theta),X(\Theta))$
$g(\Theta)$	+	+	+	+	+	+	+	+	complementary between g,X, as explained earlier.

Θ is monotonically related with $X(\Theta)$ but not so with time t, as knowledge values can change in all directions over time. The created nature of t by means of Θ is simply to establish the observational capability of the X-values over time. Hence, $X=X(t(\Theta))$.

The positive relationship between $g(\Theta)$ and S is afforded by the reinterpretation of saving as an increased amount of resources channelled into productive investments without undue waiting time. The price level P is then non-inflationary, because since the growth effect of M is determined by g, the latter must also determine the growth of prices in the midst of the commodity-money feedback linkages. Hence, M/P approximates to Q/P. That is, Q/M remains stable. This means that the productivity relationship is sustained in the midst of the quantity of money. Now in any of these variables, if the effect of Θ is not uniform, then the stability relationship would not hold, since g of money would be different from the r of Q and profitability. As Θ increases over series of economic epochs, there is a tendency to attain $g(\Theta)$ instantaneously in any phase.

DEFINITION OF MONEY IN ISLAMIC POLITICAL ECONOMY

Where then lies the difference of such a definition of money centred around endogeneity of real sector activities from the exogenous nature of money in economic systems given by Keynesian theory or by the quantity theory of money? We will explain these differences by examining the comparative meanings of monetary equilibrium in Islamic political economy and other systems.

First we will look at the usual monetary equilibrium with interest rate (i) and money (M) relations in demand and supply. The intersection of money demand (Md) and supply supply (Ms) determines the equilibrium interest rate and quantity of money. But at the same time, there comes about corresponding equilibrium levels of X(t) and M(t) relations. We have approximated X(t) by the price variable only, P(t).

In Figure 6.1, these simultaneous equilibria are shown by points like E_1 corresponding with e_1. But as decreased interest rate policy shifts Md to Md', so also the following shifts are realized: Ms to Ms'; Xd to Xd'; Xs to Xs'. Now E_1 shifts to E_2; e_1 shifts to e_2. This is the picture expected in the Islamic concept of endogenous monetary relations with real economic activity. It also signifies an economy in the process of transition to an Islamic political economy with declining i.

154

In Figure 6.1, with the growth in real sector activity X(t), shown by X_D to X_D^* and X_s to X_s^*, price level P(t) increases. This causes increase in currency demand as endogenous money demand M(t). The monetary equilibrium points shift from e_1 to e_2.'

In the Keynesian case for example, only a decrease in interest rate from i_1 to i_2, can cause a shift of money demand curve from M_D' to M_D'', and money supply curve from M_s' to M_s''. The reverse is the case when interest rate increases. Consequently, the real sector is adversely affected by an increase in interest rate causing a decline in the quantity of money and hence in GDP. Furthermore, as i increases in the presence of declining GDP, because of a turn around in the business cycle, price level remains high. Hence real growth is adversely affected.

Figure 6.1: Simultaneous Equilibria in the Money and Goods Relationship

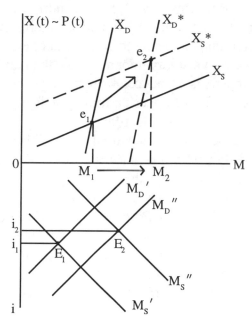

Next we show in Figure 6.2, that as i increases (i_1 to i_2), the production menu is adversely affected. Increased cost of investment and the consequent increase in prices due to scarcity, will both cause inflationary pressures arising from the cost-push side. The effect will be a decline in the quantity of money (M to M') available for spending. Whereas, we note in Figure 6.1, that increasing prices driven by productivity gains will establish a direct relationship between M(t) and P(t) with declining i.

Thus there is an inconsistency between the relationship of M(t) to P(t) caused by an increase in P(t) as a monetary phenomenon and by productivity gains. The presence of active interest rate policy being endemic to both the Keynesian and quantity theory of money, as we have noted above, now gives opposing signals for the strictly endogenous monetary relations in the Islamic political economy. In Islamic theory money and monetary aggregates are therefore endogenous in nature and provide a spending-related concept linked with real economic activity. Likewise too, as we have pointed out earlier, such a concept turns money into a financial contravention that can have no independent exchange value but simply a store value with stability imparted from the real goods markets.

The stability property is introduced from the side of Q/M relationship. Through the uniform effect of prices on money and output, price stability is attained and is linked with productivity.

The endogenous theory of money in Islamic political economy brings us to examine the following problem (Desai 1989). Note that each of the variables is a function of $t(\Theta)$, which we do not show. The rate of change of the quantity of money, m is given by,

$$m=(1/M)(dM/dt)=\sum(1/F)(\partial F/\partial x)(dx/dt)=\sum q(x).dx/dt,$$

where, x is an element of X; $q(x)=(1/F)(\partial F/\partial x)$ denotes the contribution of the x-element to the growth in the quantity of money in real economic activity. We furthermore note that each of the q(x) is recursively interrelated among the x-elements through feedbacks. Thus, the above measure for m is recursively solved by means of interactions among the derived relations of any x in terms of the other x-elements of $X(t)$. The institutional meaning of such a relation is that creation of any socio-economic value and hence of money, is now automatically determined endogenously in the economy. Such an endogeneity is importantly conveyed by the anthropic presence of decision-making as in the *Shuratic* Process.

In Figure 6.2, interest rates and price levels move in the same direction as monetary authorities exercise strict money supply policy (M_s' tends to M_s'', as i_1 increases to i_2). With higher rates of interest, the transaction demand for money falls, while the holding of money in speculative assets increases. Thus a consequent withdrawal in the form of savings increases. Now M_D' shifts to M_D'', and the aggregate supply effect of decreased GNP can now increase price levels, particularly along the vertical long-run aggregate supply curve.

Figure 6.2: Interest Rate, Price Level and Monetary Relationships

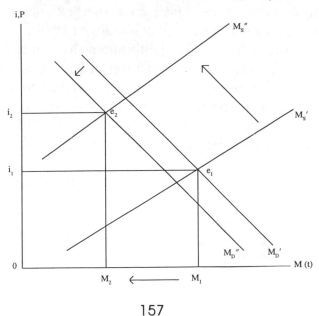

RELATIONSHIP BETWEEN MONEY AND INVESTMENT

One of the important elements of X(t) is investment demand, I. We know for the business cycle that in hyper-inflationary peaks, I and P tend to be inversely related, making the economy swing back to full-employment equilibrium. How are we to explain the I-P relationship in an Islamic economy?

We note that increases in M and I can be at a cost if there is a slack in the expected one-to-one feedback between Θ-values and M,I values. There is nothing to ascertain that such a one-to-one interrelationship will always exist. Because the politico-economic system goes through interactions into temporary integration (convergence of Θ-values) followed by continuity of the process (i.e. evolution of Θ-values), therefore, there are phases of limit points for Θ-values. In the limit of Θ tending to Θ^*, over given sets of interactions and convergence of organizational rules, temporary equilibrium values (M^*,I^*,P^*) come about. However, these are replaced by subsequent new values as new knowledge-induced dynamics continue. That is, (M^*,I^*,P^*,Θ^*) is an instantaneous point of local equilibrium in any particular phase of interactions-integration. But in the global sense there are no unique equilibria (Grandmont 1989).

In Figure 6.1, such multiple equilibrium paths between (M,P,Θ) are shown by (e_1e_2), (e_2e_3) etc. These are reproduced in Figure 6.3. The nodes of emergence to new Θ-values at temporary (instantaneous) equilibrium points like e_2, e_3, etc. are permanently perturbed points. Now by an equivalence between event (Θ) and time (t) the multiple equilibria changes are also charted over time while we are charting them over assignments of Θ-values.

Hence there are permanently increasing relationship between M,I,P as lone as Θ is increasing globally. Within this global change, only instantaneous equilibrium values are attained. In the global sense multiple (M,I,P,Θ) values exist. Such a result is consistent with the simulation problem given earlier (Choudhury 1992).

158

Figure 6.3: Knowledge-Induced Evolutionary Equilibria

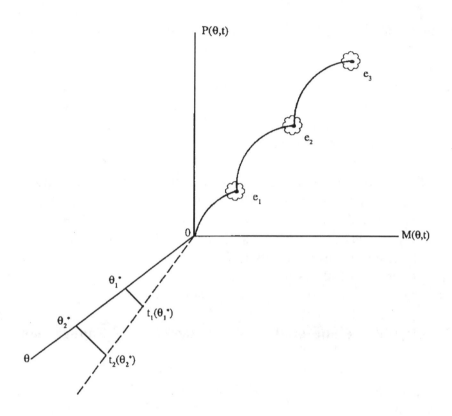

Here time variable t is shown as a linear map of Θ-values. Thus as $\Theta \rightarrow \Theta_1^*$, so also $t \rightarrow t_1(\Theta_1^*)$. Subsequently, the quantity of money as an endogenous variable dependent on time and hence on Θ-values, converges as follows: $M \rightarrow M^*$. Likewise, the price level converges as $P \rightarrow P^*$. The temporary equilibrium points for $P(\Theta,t)$ and $M(\Theta,t)$ are given by e_1, e_2, e_3. The region around these points shows perturbed evolution of new equilibria.

THE USE OF RESERVE RATIO IN MONETARY POLICY IN ISLAMIC POLITICAL ECONOMY

How can we explain the relationship between the reserve ratio and the inter-bank loans with increasing demand for liquidity for investment? We note here that since inter-bank loans will increase in the face of increased demand for investment, therefore the reserve ratio (say r') will decline. Now, a change in money supply, dM will be related to the increase in inter-bank deposits (signifying demand for liquidity), dD, by the following multiplier relation: $dM=dD/r'$. dM is inversely related with r'; i increases as r' declines with increased demand for liquidity for investment.

Let B_1 and B_2 be two banks engaged in inter-bank loans. Under transactions on a profit-sharing contract in an investment venture, let g_1 denote the return to B_1, which then forms asset for B_1. Let g_2 denote the return to B_2, which then forms a liability to B_1. Likewise, g_2 forms a return to B_1 and g_1 forms a liability to B_2. The balance sheet of the two banks will appear as follows in Table 6.1:

Table 6.1: Balance Sheets of Banks in the Case of Endogenous Money

Balance Sheet for B_1
initial deposit = \$1
r'=0
retention=$1.g_1$
loaned=investment
in joint venture=$1.g_2$

Balance Sheet for B_2
initial deposit = 0
new deposit=$1.g_2$
retention=$1.g_2.g_3$
loan=$1.g_2-1.g_2.g_3=1.g_2{}^2$

Thus new money in the economy equals the amount of investment capital $1.g_2$. In this way, in a multiple bank loan case under joint venture, the total new money or investment capital in the economy from $1 of initial spending equals,

$$g_2+g_2^2 + g_2^4 + g_2^8 +....= g_2(1+(g_2/(1-g_2^2))).$$

The total amount of spending, Sp, which must be matched by endogenous money, is then given by,

$$Sp=\$1 + g_2 + g_2^2 + g_2^4 + g_2^8 +... = g_2 + (1-g_2^2)^{-1} = (1+g_2-g_2^3)/(1-g_2^2).$$

To a linear approximation, Sp = new money = $1 + g_2$. Likewise, for $M of initial spending as endogenous money, the total money creation or new spending equals $M(1+g_2)$. Since g_2 is determined by the growth of the real sector output, hence, money is created in exact equivalence with this growth rate.

Inflation can then be impossible in such a monetary arrangement. As a matter of fact, if money supply was lower than the ex-post demand for spending, there would exist an upward pressure due to scarcity. That is, the ratio, (value of transactions, X)/M, would show a higher value for a smaller unit of money, causing inflation due to demand pull type, until the value of money increased to equal the value of transactions. A similar inflationary effect would result due to monetary causes if there was an excess supply of money, until the transactions increased to match the quantity of money. Endogenous money is thus a source of economic stabilization.

TRANSACTIONS WITH CURRENCY BASED ENDOGENOUS MONEY

To complete our discussion of money in Islamic political economy we will merely hint upon the operational aspect of currency related endogenous money here. Banks become partners in joint and profit-sharing, equity-participating ventures with other firms and investors (Chapra 1985). Households become partners through banks in such ventures. To diversify the risk and preserve an attractive return with low risk, banks as intermediaries act as both managers and allocaters of currencies toward projects that arise in the real goods sector. Speculative projects qualified by virtue of their inadequate show of real expected prospects, are avoided. Examples of such speculative projects are futures markets, forward currency swapping, arbitrage and gambling in product designs not yet proven to be adequately feasible and those that do not comply with *Shari'ah* standards.

In a currency based endogenous system, individual account holders receive chequeable certificates with specific denominated values for liquidation in goods and services of all kinds. Such certificates are different from usual current account cheques in the sense that they are not promissory notes; otherwise the functions are the same. These certificates can be exchanged for currencies at the bank counter. Since the market marginalizes speculative ventures, the liquidation of the certificates at the bank matches with the value of transactions in the real goods sector. In this way, supply of savings in the form of currency as money is matched up with non-speculative demand for investments. The residual of the currency after use in real assets, goods and services would be re-converted at the counter in exchange for value-denominated certificates. The currency is then held as a future value of expected transactions in non-speculative outlets.

During the temporary phase of a country while transforming into an Islamic political economy, such a country would hold debt to pay off past liabilities. Such debts are settled through instruments such as debt-equity swaps activating productive activities in the real goods sector (Choudhury 1993). Here all the dynamic basic needs approach to development in an Islamic political economy fuses with monetary sector stabilization.

The change from a promissory notes system of exogenous money to the currency based endogenous money of Islamic political economy, is significantly affected by the degree of participation of various agents who in the first place would hold currencies for various activities. Such a demand for currency is in direct relationship with the agent-specific interactions among preferences that cause socio-economic transformations to come about. Thus the knowledge-based model as an interactive-integrative-evolutionary process is once again invoked to combine with the generation of endogenous money as currency in tandem with the demand for real sector activities in the absence of speculation.

CONCLUSION

A most pressing need of Muslim countries for gaining collective self-reliance and *Ummatic* transformation is the development of an Islamic capital market. Since the capital market cannot exist independently of the total transformation process, hence such a capital market must serve as both the cause and effect of *Ummatic* transformation (Akkas 1993). In this context the endogenous nature of money would play a significant role. In this chapter we have introduced such a concept of money on which the Islamic capital market transformation would have to take shape and form.

The endogenous concept of money is also the nature of money emanating directly from the extension of the *Shuratic* Process to this field of inquiry. Here then is a lesson of significant theoretical and applied value for Muslim scholars, decision makers and pioneers of change to reflect upon the concept of endogenous money for *Ummatic* transformation.

CHAPTER 7

REFORMATION IN THE MIDST OF GLOBALIZATION

Post Cold-War world is a bastion of economists, strategists and cold calculators. It is a world of vehement competition and mergers in the name of economic integration and the rise of market power, from the cradle to the grave. While the belligerence of world-wide military conflict recedes, yet the *raison d'être* behind the passion for acquisition and political stratagem, is all over being realized through the instrument of economic power. In this economic power resides institutional functions integrating dominant decisions in view of shared returns from a well-coordinated direction of change by design.

The questions then to ponder over are several in the context of this semblance of economic power: First is the seeming market process of economic expansion and integration called privatization, a process launched by the enterprises? By the same question: Is wealth being distributive, resources being shared both intra- and inter-nations in the midst of privatization? Second, to what extent is institutional interaction in the privatization process devoid of political interest? Third, if political interest remains intertwined with economic expansion and growth, how does trade, macroeconomic coordination, and the world organizations perpetuate power and strategy?

Is conflict resolution possible in the midst of such dominant power and strategy? Or is it that the global order is inexorably proceeding toward a bi-polar state, although the instruments though not the spirit of globalization, present this global transformation as a unifying one? Where then is the genesis of the problems and their resolution? Note that

I have maintained the thesis of bi-polarity in global conflicts, because of the convergence of global capitalism on the one hand and the distinctness of Islam as a world force on the other hand. This distinctness is far from a picture of multi-polarity sometimes painted.

The picture of globalization as a process of economic expansion and integration, institutional strategies towards attaining these goals, and long-term contract agreements signed internationally and regionally, is painted by the West. Its imitative representations are found in the Pacific Rim, South-East Asia, the Middle East, Eastern Europe, the Commonwealth of Independent States and Russia. All of these developments in global partnership follows the end of the Cold War. They picked up momentum with the announcement of a New World Order by George Bush and Gorbachev.

The IMF has been mobilized in Eastern Europe, Russia and the Commonwealth of Independent States. The formation of North American Free Trade Agreement is now being looked upon by the U.S. as a design to extend it to the Asian Pacific Basin by means of Asian Pacific Economic Cooperation. In the development field, World Bank's structural adjustment policies have now entrenched themselves in Official Development Assistance and have combined with IMF conditionalities to determine allowance for loans and assistance. The conclusion of the Uruguay Rounds of Trade Talks aim at globalizing future trade relations between countries premised on the Bretton Woods surge for transformation in the external sector and in development matters (General Agreements of Tariffs and Trade 1993). The future of global trade and market order is seen as an extension of the Most Favoured Nations Clause to all nations in a uniform claim for export orientation, import penetration and open linkages among capital markets. Yet such generalization of the MFN will not be without political strings. This is well-known from the recent attempts of the U.S. Congress to deny MFN Rights to China.

166

NEO-MERCANTILISM

The above-mentioned initiatives toward globalization are seen to be both a continuance of the old Eurocentricity mercantilism of the West as well as an entrenchment of the global neoclassical model. We will take up these two parts separately.

Let us view the world balance of payments situation from a mercantilist viewpoint (Tisdell 1989). Mercantilists believed that the wealth of a nation which to them was Britain, depended upon the riches and bullions it could command. To attain this state, mercantilists promoted the development of trade mechanisms (ships); colonial taxation; selling of expensive goods while protecting the British economy against expensive imports but encouraging the import of cheap goods. Through such trade mechanisms, the following relevant kinds of balance of payment relations can be seen to explain present day neo-mercantilism: The focus of the external sector is placed on export orientation. Export in value terms is seen to be a function of nominal protection of critical goods; whereas, import of cheap raw materials, intermediate technology and commodities, is encouraged. To correct for trade deficits, government financial resources using general tax revenues, or official development resources, or in-flight of capital in high interest bearing assets, are activated (Lessard & Williamson 1987). Thus, the level of deficits determines exchange rate, interest rate and protective levels at home against the competitiveness by other nations.

Trade relations in a globalizing order show all these to exist: for the developing countries, we find a continuation of worsening terms of trade of commodities; lost sectorial competitiveness and food self-sufficiency; flight of capital; and extensive external sector volatility. On the other hand, industrialized economies are trying to protect their agricultural and manufacturing sectors against the external flow of goods, such as in textiles, automobiles in the U.S. and in general terms within EC. This is tantamount to selling expensive and buying cheap inputs of production.

167

Overall deficits in industrialized economies are being mitigated by taxation and by flight of capital from developing countries. Thus, under such a neo-mercantilist order, the drive to secure external sector balances at home under exchange rate flexibility and perfect capital mobility, causes industrialized economies to adopt monetary policies. The interest rate and exchange rate volatility of monetary policies prove to be permanently disequilibrating for the developing countries. The developing countries have been historically selling cheap and buying expensive from the industrialized economies. Thus, both export orientation and capital transactions in the overall balance of payments prove to be permanently de-equalizing.

DE-EQUALIZING GLOBAL TRADE

Such a de-equalizing situation in foreign trade is not globally eliminated, even if we hold export to equal import values regionally. For even if trading partners are well integrated regionally, trade with the rest of the world and importantly so with the West, will cause the neo-mercantilist disequilibrium. This consequence in turn, will cause global disequilibrium in the external sector. Beyond these simple economic factors of disequilibrium lies the institutional and strategic instability caused by political and macroeconomic policies formulated in the West. The developing world submits to the policy consequences of Western macroeconomic coordination. We found this to be the result of international Keynesianism of the Bretton Woods institutions promoting fictitious notions of full-employment target, monetary and fiscal disciplines in the pretext of controlling an inflationary pressure, that was caused in the first place by interest-based financial speculation, monopolistic competition and declining productivity in the industrialized countries. Thus, monetary and fiscal disciplines following Keynesian foundation of macroeconomic coordination in the West led to world-wide recessionary and stagflationary pressures during the eighties.

168

Next come the regime of export orientation, a negation of import substitution and interlinked IMF World Bank financing formulas revolving around structural adjustment and conditionalities. The neo-classical prescription became predominant in such financing and developmental formulas. Despite the oft-quoted catch-word on alleviation of poverty globally by the World Bank, the rising tide of the poor remains a staggering three billion today (United Nations 1991). Poverty is proving to be the result of failure in exchange and ownership entitlement, in spite of governments allocating social expenditures toward transfer incomes.

The structural adjustment formula financing advocates against social expenditures in favour of markets and economic efficiency. But the markets wipe out the poor in the catch-word of what has come to be known in neoclassical economics as adjustment cost or equivalently as substitution (trade-off) between economic efficiency and distributive equity. Contrary to such neoclassical consequences, entitlement and ownership as the premise for alleviating poverty, is to integrate the poor in an arrangement of world trade and development (Choudhury 1993a).

Thus if we look at the experience of poverty alleviation in the Newly Industrializing Economies, we find either extensive transfer incomes as an instrument; and this has not resulted in real productivity gains. Contrarily we find acute relative poverty, which too is a case of unequal distribution of income and wealth. The example of the first case is Malaysia; that of the second type is China and Brazil. Economic distribution is thereby, not a congruent part of neoclassicism. Allocation means putting resources to most efficient/productive use, but this is socially conflicting (Phelps 1989). Although the theory of development has always mentioned about growth with distribution, yet the methodology of marginalist substitution in neoclassical economics cannot make extensive complementarity possible. Hence economic efficiency (growth) and distributive equity remain permanently in trade-off. This is a methodological consequence of neoclassical marginalist substitution with wide institutional consequences as explained by public and social choice theories.

169

PROBLEMS OF TRADE AND DEVELOPMENT POLICIES OF THE BRETTON WOODS INSTITUTIONS

While many Newly Industrializing Countries will eventually become industrialized, this will be realized by means of foreign trade. But statistics in Table 7.1 point out for Malaysia, that foreign direct investments being in export-oriented sectors, are not deep in agricultural and agro-based industries. Consequently, under the neoclassical prescription of globalization, social expenditure remains an activity of either national governments or of official development assistance. All of these approaches are conflicting ones in the globalization scene. First, government expenditure and official development are discouraged by structural adjustment under its focus on privatization. Where such transfer incomes exist, they cause a perpetuating dependency syndrome and low factor productivities in the recipients. The poor is thereby, not integrated with world trade and development in a self-reliant way. Finally, IMF conditionality promotes government policies toward export orientation, trade liberalization and external sector balances through the process of privatization. All these work in concert with structural adjustment. Consequently, IMF conditionality is totally targeted to efficiency.

EUROCENTRIC ECONOMIC REASONING AND GLOBALIZATION PROCESS

1. Neoclassical Individualism

The above discussion on the nature of economic reasoning based in Western socio-economic models and institutions show that neither neoclassicism nor Keynesianism and their latter-day development (monetarism and rational expectations as combination of these two), can resolve the intrinsically destabilizing nature of globalization. The macroeconomic policy coordination in the West; the neoclassical macroeconomic and microeconomic roots; the Eurocentric dominance of neo-mercantilism; and the dominating nature of Western institutions led by the Bretton Woods institutions, are all interactively reinforcing toward deepening global methodological individualism (Mehmet 1990). In this order, globalization becomes a process of conflict resolution under a dominance model of economic, institutional and strategic hegemony. The same perspective repeats itself either internationally under the Euro-centric model, or regionally by a dominant regional player. Subsequently, this dominant player by its relationship with and as part of the Western model, drives the regional integration process into one global process of competition via strategies (Wallerstein 1974).

Table 7.1: Foreign Direct Investment in Agro-Based Sector in Malaysia (Percentages of Total Foreign Direct Investment)

Year	1987	1988	1989	1990	1991	1994
Industry						
Food manufacturing	9.8	11.7	3.3	1.8	1.4	0.2
Textile & related products	2.7	4.9	5.9	5.0	2.5	9.3
Rubber & related products	9.3	13.6	4.2	0.3	0.9	0.8
Beverages, tobacco, wood etc	13.1	12.3	20.8	14.2	8.6	17.8

Source: Computations from data from the source, **Economic Report 1995/96**, Ministry of Finance Malaysia, Kuala Lumpur, 1995.

2. Strategic Global Model

We will now look at this question of strategy in the globalization process. Global strategy in the framework of economic and political interests is a

171

function of economic expansion and integration on the one hand, and their desired complementarity with geo-politics, on the other. Western market power and institutionalism would like the two to coexist, so that democracy and capitalism can go hand in hand. Yet, the reality is a conflict between the two.

The methodological explanation for this rests on the delinked bi-polarity between economic and social ends, as is to be found in neoclassicism. If at all the two ends merge, then this is due to a dominant interest. In some cases, as in the Middle East, the dominant interest is now subsumed by the predominantly economic one. In the case of Iraq, Somalia and Bosnia-Herzegovina, the dominant interest is subsumed by a geo-political one. In the Muslim CIS area, the Western strategic interest is subsumed in an economic predominance. In the APEC arrangement extending to Malaysia and Indonesia, the aim of Western strategic interest is predominantly for economic control. In Turkey, the strategic interest is divided between political and economic, as the need of the situation arises. Thus for instance, on the question of Cyprus Western control over Turkey is predominantly political. On matters of greater Western economic integration in the Middle East markets particularly after PLO-Israeli pact, the interest is predominantly economic. It is highly likely, that through U.S. foreign and military policy in East and South-East Asia, the present economic interest will tilt towards a political one. This was evidenced in Bill Clinton's obvious anger on Dr Mahathir's strong and justified stand against U.S. hegemony in APEC at the Seattle APEC Conference in 1993. Similar opposition has been raised by the U.S. against Malaysia's active role in the East Asian Economic Caucus (EAEC), although this is not a forum for trade but rather for trade negotiations. This forum is different from APEC and the matter was pointed out by Dr Mahathir to the United States, Japan and Australia, but without much avail.

172

3. Summary Features of Western Globalization Model

These constant shifts and convergences in neoclassical model of politico-economic dominance are a permanent feature of a Eurocentric model of globalization. They comprise all the features we have discussed above, namely, neo-mercantilism, Eurocentricity and a strategic model that intensifies conflict. Methodologically, because of the behavioural pattern and its transmission into markets, institutions and politico-economic relations, such a globalization arrangement cannot realize conflict resolution and coexistence, except by dominance. In this model and process, markets, privatization, trade and development, all become instruments to enforce the dominant behaviour in the globalization process.

Other instruments that have been used by the West to establish its hegemony in the resource-rich developing economies are macroeconomic in nature, which we have referred to earlier. Such policies coupled with the neo-mercantilist approach to stabilize external sector imbalances with capital flows from a capitalist transformation of Eastern Europe and Russia, have caused a diversion of concessionary development resources away from the needy developing economies. Whatever export revenues are available in the face of declining terms of trade of primary goods, were directed to debt financing. Consequently, their use in generating domestic economic growth was hampered in the developing countries.

ECONOMIC PROBLEMS FOR MUSLIM COUNTRIES IN THE GLOBALIZATION PROCESS

In Table 7.2 we point out the economic adversity being faced by OIC members in general in their external sector adjustment. Since most of these countries are predominantly resource based and hence export oriented, therefore an inference we draw is the adverse effect that globalization is likely to cause in the external sector of these countries.

Table 7.2: Selected Macroeconomic External Sector Indicators for OIC Members.

	1987	1988	1989	1990
Percentage Rate of Real per capita GDP Growth	-0.7	-0.2	0.8	3.2
Rates of Inflation	20.7	22.3	21.2	14.7
Percentage Rate of Change in Exports	19.1	5.8	18.4	22.6
OIC Members Share in Total Developing Countries Debts (%)		30.1	30.5	30.8
Debt/GDP Ratio (%)	-	83.0	82.4	80.3
(Developing Countries)	[-	45.9	42.7	41.8]
Debt Service/Export Ratio (%)	-	35.4	31.0	27.5
(Developing Countries)	[-	26.7	22.2	19.8]

Source: **SESRTCIC Documents** Presented by SESRTCIC to Twenty-First Islamic Conference of Foreign Ministers (SESRTCIC, Ankara, Turkey April 1993).

The improving trend in real per capita GDP growth rate is seen to carry with it a high degree of export orientation. But dependence on foreign loan capital is significant, as economic growth is shown here to be highly debt-creating. The composition of debt in GDP is double that of the developing countries. The debt-service/export ratios being significantly higher than those for the developing countries, this is another pointer to the vulnerability of OIC members to the interest rate and exchange rate mechanisms under macro-economic coordination in the West (SESRTCIC 1993).

IMF claims in its October 1993 **World Economic Outlook**, (IMF 1993) that the debt problem of developing countries has bottomed. Yet it is suspect that such a dip in the debt levels is just part of a long-run debt-business cycle position. The debt position of developing countries in general and the OIC members in particular, being susceptible to interest rate and exchange rate mechanisms in the West, become doubly vulnerable as these countries would move to capital-intensive menus of industrialization. Thus debt-business cycles of countries subject to outward-orientation risk are expected to become volatile if these countries fail to utilize the inter-country economic complementarity from a strengthening of labour-augmenting technological change (Allen 1970).

In such a process of sectorial transformation, a number of factors will become predominant. Intra-country, there must exist a good degree of resource-based manufacturing linkage. Human resource development must intensify in such a sectorial linkage to improve skills, productivity and efficiency in both sectors. Otherwise, sectorial linkages will not exist. Other inter-country joint ventures, foreign investments and complementarities must be so exploited as to generate shifting socialization toward labour-intensive technological transformation. A condition for such a transformation is increasing population, mobility of skilled labour in diversified labour-intensive industries and in inter-communal markets.

On the side of technological change, inter-communal relations in the Muslim world would mean orientating production to available intermediate technologies to start with. This will at once be led by upgrading and evolution of the intermediate technologies into high tech. Relevant institutions to generate technological futures out of available intermediate technologies in Muslim countries with the complementary advantage focus mentioned above, is a condition for technological change. All these are necessary in order to reduce dependency on loanable capital that are found to cause large external sector disequilibrium; to generate complementary advantages directed to labour-augmented technological change; and to insulate these economies from their vulnerability to interest rate and exchange rate mechanisms of industrialized economies.

The degree of vulnerability of the OIC countries to such global consequences can be inferred from the pattern of relationship among inflation rate and exchange rate variations in these countries. It is seen from Table 7.3, that although interest rates had bottomed in industrialized economies, yet inflation rates remained considerably higher in Islamic countries than the average for Asia and Africa, by 1990. Exchange rate variations on the negative side (shown by rates of change) for export-oriented countries, such as, Turkey, Pakistan, Jordan, Egypt, Bangladesh and Algeria, have been volatile.

These trends indicate that debt-business cycle that is being shown by IMF for 1993, is a temporary relief based on instruments such as, debt-equity swaps, debt write-offs. It cannot be seen as the result of interest rate relief. This cycle is also highly vulnerable to exchange rate mechanism. Debt pressures remain unmitigated on a relative scale for the Muslim countries even in the face of export-orientation following declining exchange rates. IMF conditionality on export-orientation, trade liberalization, exchange rate float and the World Bank's structural adjustment policy prevailing upon global privatization, are clearly not stabilizing the external sector of OIC countries.

ADVERSE CONSEQUENCES OF INTEREST RATE AND EXCHANGE RATE MECHANISMS BY INDUSTRIALIZED COUNTRIES

The uncertain external sector results can be deduced by noting that in the case of interest rate and exchange rate hikes in industrialized nations, the goal of keeping inflation rates under control at home, would drive up both exchange rate and interest rates. Consequently, export would fall under this compound effect. By the same compound effect, investments would decline. On the other side, import volumes and saving would increase under this joint influence of interest rate and exchange rate effects. The increase in saving gap would be due to a shortfall in productive capacity domestically. For an export-oriented economy, the wide saving gap also adversely affects the external sector disequilibrium. Thus, the net effect of these movements is increasing debt.

It can thus be inferred that interest rate and exchange rate mechanisms (macroeconomic policy instruments) will always be held as potentially strategic weapons by the industrial nations. These are weapons that can be used by the West to attain a number of goals. First, unabsorbed savings in productive activities at home will drive out capital into Western financial institutions. This is the perennial problem of capital flight from developing countries. For the OIC countries, the capital surplus Arab countries are found to hold very large financial assets in the IMF and Eurocurrency Markets. Secondly, import penetration of industrial nations' goods is realized to the benefit of these nations. Thirdly, world resources are consequently allocated in strategic ways by the interest rate and exchange rate instruments. Fourthly, victimized nations are driven to compete among themselves for access to Northern markets (UNCTAD 1989).

In the political scene, diversion of domestic capital to overseas financial institutions in the face of a lack of productive capacity at home, breeds financial dependency, and finally, subservience and inability to get out of this dependency. Examples are of the capital surplus Arab States, whose allegiance has been acquired by the West through the financial services provided to these states. Twice in recent political history, there has been a freezing of financial assets - one of Iran; the other of Iraq, by the West.

In South-East Asia, the policy to extend MFN Clause to China by the U.S. is a means to control resource allocation through financial flows in such a way, that two objectives can be attained. First, such a trade relations and its effect on this regional allocation of resources will serve to neutralize the power of Japan over its trade surpluses with the U.S. Second, this is desired ultimately to integrate the Pacific and South-East Asia Region to APEC and NAFTA and then into the North American and South American Free Trade Pacts, followed by a further integration of all of these with the EC and Eastern Europe. This is the far look of Euro-centricity in all its design. There will be many Newly Industrializing

177

Countries who will join the camp of this mode of globalization. This will leave behind the Muslim countries poised between selecting this camp or turning to communal solidarity in trade, development and own political interests.

In the interactively developed complementary model and the inter-relationships among economic, political and social forces in the authentic model of development, such forces must be endogenous to the Islamic comity of nations. The Muslim nations therefore, have a choice. They can submit unquestionably to the globalization process that is now aimed at subsuming all nations to the neoclassical model of Eurocentricity born out of alienation and strategic interests. Or else, they can opt for a co-operative model within the *Ummah* (World Nation of Islam) and thus neutralize the Eurocentric model through a constructive, global teaching and sharing objectivity.

Table 7.3: Interest Rates in Industrialized Economies, Inflation Rates and Exchange Rates in OIC Countries

	1985	1987	1988	1989	1990
Short Term Interest Rates	8.4	-	7.2	-	9.2
Long Term Interest Rates	9.9	-	8.1	-	9.0
Inflation Rates	-	20.7	22.3	21.2	14.7
Exchange Rate Variations					
Algeria	-3.0	-18.0	-22.3	-15.1	
Bangladesh	-1.8	-2.5	-1.7	-6.6	
Egypt	-11.1	-31.7	-11.7	-7.0	
Indonesia	-22.0	-2.5	-4.8	-3.9	

Jordan	3.3	-8.8	-34.9	-14.1
Nigeria	-56.3	-11.5	-38.4	-8.4
Pakistan	-4.3	-3.4	-12.4	-5.4
Turkey	-21.3	-39.7	-33.0	-18.7

IMF, **World Economic Outlook**, Oct. 1992.
SESRTCIC, see Table 7.2.

THE RISK TO MUSLIM COUNTRIES IN THE GLOBALIZATION PROCESS

External sector instabilities have made OIC members very risk prone to foreign investments. This state is recorded by **Euromoney** and is shown in Table 7.4 for selected countries.

Table 7.4:   OIC Country Risk Rankings and Ratings

International Rank				Rating		
1991	**1990**	**1989**	**Country**	**1991**	**1990**	**1989**
26	24	29	Malaysia	76.0	75.8	68.0
32	35	39	Indonesia	57.3	65.7	62.0
37	44	37	Saudi Arabia	54.0	60.0	65.0
40	54	39	Turkey	53.1	54.0	62.0
42	50	43	U.A.E	52.7	56.0	61.0
56	57	86	Pakistan	41.3	53.0	35.0
58	93	90	Iran	40.5	33.8	33.0
42	106	44	Kuwait	37.0	28.0	59.0
80	80	75	Egypt	34.5	39.6	38.0
88	96	82	Nigeria	31.0	33.0	36.0
102	97	74	Jordan	25.7	31.0	39.0
112	102	88	Libya	22.8	28.7	34.0
130	129	101	Iraq	1.9	18.4	28.0

Source: **Euromoney**, Sept. 1991; Sept. 1990.

Except for eight OIC countries in the detailed listing, all other members rank below 50th standing in international risk ranking. Within this list, it is informative to note the rank-rating changes between Iran and Iraq. The lowest level in this, given for Iraq, is due to the aftermath of Desert Storm. It is thereby, an example of what can arise as the consequence of political disturbance caused by the West on Muslim countries. In the same light, by reallocation of preference between Iran and Iraq through a Western type strategic deterrent in this region, Iran's position has improved, although the West had caused immense injustice on Iran during the Iran-Iraq Gulf War. The same picture emerges from the changes in risk-ranking/rating for Libya. These indicators point out, that in the dominance model of Western Eurocentricity of the neoclassical type, economic deterrent can be subsumed in political interest, under a framework of Western political and military strategy.

On the other hand, evidence of Western indifference to democratic transformation in the Middle East can be seen from the almost unchanged risk-rank for Saudi Arabia, U.A.E., Egypt and a comeback for Kuwait, the financial high grounds of the Western Alliance during Gulf War 1991. All of these OIC countries turn out to be oppressively autocratic. The neoclassical model of dualism and alienation is thus found to be fully effective in the Western mode of control and in the allegiance of OIC member states to that divisive and disabling modality. This carries with it all the aspects of the globalization philosophy in the neo-mercantilist order that we have laid out earlier. These are namely, a conflict producing dominance model and a strategic interest model.

THE ISLAMIC CONCEPT OF GLOBALIZATION FOR THE MUSLIM WORLD

The next issue then to investigate is whether the dominance and stra-tegically alienating model of global control by the West and intra-communal relations among Islamic countries, is going to end under the

180

present arrangements. We have abundantly shown that globalization as a neo-mercantilist regime carried out in a Eurocentric framework, is part and parcel of the philosophy, methodological individualism and extensive institutional behaviour of the occident. Such a form cannot be displaced from occidental life. Thus, the Eurocentric framework will always be aimed at by the West in its prescription of globalization.

The remaining question to address then is whether the same kind of behaviour that has gripped the Muslim world will ever cease in favour of the only other alternative - the Islamic system of globalization. What then is the Islamic prescription of globalization?

1. The Philosophical Premise of Globalization in Islamic Perspective

The philosophy of Islamic globalization is a unique process of inter-actions and integration among all kinds of agents and system of thought, institutions and the socio-scientific order, by means of the unification epistemology of God's Unity (*Tawhid*) (Choudhury 1993b). The sub-stantive meaning of this unification epistemology is not simply a static understanding of the Unity of God. Rather, in this, Unity is seen as the dynamic process of reducing all systems to the most irreducible reality that can unify the systems by the process of integrating them through interactions on the bases of the Islamic Law (*Shari'ah*) premised on this Unity. The process of globalization in this philosophical context means the emergence, conduct and convergence of endless cycles of discursions among agents of diverse systems for greater understanding and realization of *Shariah*, while the axiom of *Tawhid* remains the immutable foundation of such dynamics.

As an example, such a precept of globalization when applied to the subject matter of human resource development, would mean development of the complementary and interactive-integrative-evolutionary world view in and across all disciplines, skills and training. This is based on an

181

epistemology that is derived from the nature of *Tawhidi* dynamics, and is subsequently, evolved through relevant instruments of the knowledge process to reinforce the *Tawhidi* episteme. In the area of human resource development, the normative essence of *Tawhidi* episteme is integrated with the positivistic essence of the methods and disciplines of learning. The normative essence is called *Fard A'yn* (obligatory knowledge). Interrelations between these move in reinforcing cycles. Thus, conflict resolution, complementarity and continuity inter- and intra-systems, become the cause and effect of such a circular process of evolutionary epistemology.

2. Institutional Aspect of Globalization in Islamic Perspective

Next we turn to the institutional aspect of such a globalization methodology (AbuSulaiyman 1991). In every Islamic system we have the embryonic textual reference to *Shari'ah*, as the interpretation of its tenets apply to the nature and problem of that system in any instance. We may call this embryonic textual reference to a *Shuratic* interpretive reference, as the polity (*Shura*). Thus, the concept of *Shura* is trans-political. It is pervasively embryonic inter- and intra- systems (*Qur'an*, Chapter *Shura*: 42, v. 51-52). The function of the embryonic *Shura* is to develop rules of life pertaining to the given problems at hand. This is called *Ahkam* formation. *Ahkam* thereby, represents a preference of polity based on the level of acquired knowledge on the understanding, interpretation and delivery of the rule. Neither the *Shura* nor the *Ahkam* can be imposed. They can only be established and reinforced by acceptance of their truth and welfare (*Islah* and *Falah*) by the whole system.

The first part of the system being polity (*Shura*), the other part is the socio-scientific order (e.g. market as a subset of ecology). This system receives the *Ahkam* as a preference of polity (*Shura*) aimed at transforming the principal activities and behaviour of the socio-economic order. The market activities of consumption, production and distribution are thus aimed at for transformation by the influence of *Ahkam*. The socio-scientific order thus delivers a social good. In this way, the preferences of polity are examined, accepted, revised or rejected by the socio-scientific order. The resulting preferences of the socio-scientific order represent interactively generated preferences between those of *Ahkam* and the socio-scientific order.

Such responses as interactive preferences from the socio-scientific order are post-evaluated as a learning process in polity (*Shura*). This response recreates knowledge in *Shura* as interactions between polity and the socio-scientific order proceed. Consensus or majority rule is established as partial or complete *Ijma (Qiyas)*, as interactions are continued circularly between polity and the socio-scientific order. The circular continuity of the *Shari'ah* and *Ahkam* through interactions and integration is thus seen to be the recreative essence of *Tawhidi* episteme via the instruments and institutions of change. The totality of the process circularly established and continued between the socio-scientific system as a universally pervasive and embryonic one, is termed here as the *Shuratic* Process.

3. Application of *Shuratic* Process to Globalization

Our third task here is to apply the *Shuratic* Process to globalization through trade and institutionalism. The textual reference to liberalized trade in goods that generate justice, truth and welfare, can be derived from the following *Qur'anic* verse (Chapter 16 v. 14):

"And He it is who has made the sea subservient [to His laws], so that you might eat fresh meat from it, and take from it gems which you may wear. And on that [very sea] one sees ships ploughing through the waves, so that you might [be able to] go forth in quest of some of His bounty, and thus have cause to be grateful [to Him]."

The interpretive domain of *Ahkam* relating to the above verse implies development of useful diversity that reflects Divine Essence. The *Qur'an* continues on in this topic (Chapter 16 v. 13):

183

"And all the [beauty of] many hues which He has created for you on earth: in this, behold, there is a message for people who [are willing to] take it to heart!"

The *Shura* in this regard is an Islamic World Trade Organization that is linked from down-to-up-to-down with indefinitely large strings of micro-*Shuras* that link upwards. The most micro-level of such *Shuras* is that of the grass-roots, whose preferences are *Shuratically* evolved by the same process and are represented at higher echelons of *Shuras*. Likewise, the *Ahkam* respecting the Islamic World Trade Organization reflects the interactive-integrative-evolutionary preference of the strings of *Shuras*. This reflects the intra-*Shuratic* process in polity.

The socio-scientific order of foreign trade in light of the attributes of balance, purpose, truth and welfare, means interactions in the ethico-economic order, between the politico-economic system and foreign trade financing through the *Ummatic* model, since the occidental model is found to remain antagonistic to the unified world view. Thus a system of instruments of liberal managed trade with requisite tariffs, is developed. Other instruments are participatory financial instruments, foreign trade financing and secondary instruments. Trade flows through complementarity, diversity, solidarity and dynamism through evolutionary linkages characteristic of technological change, are thus maximized within the *Ummah*. Residual trading is then carried out with the non-Muslim world, but still on the same *Shuratic* principles on a second-best sense.

The delivery of social good on the basis of the above *Ahkam* is expected to be collective self-reliant development, complementarity and growth arising from the *Ummatic* diversity; a natural process of commodity price determination in a market that arrests free-ridership on excess supply to the domineering West; and a process of evolutionary learning that reinforces unification epistemology as the singular premise of unified reality. While this establishes itself in the *Ummah*, it subsequently extends itself by the same open and purposeful trading principles to all the world. Such is the reinforcing response from the agents and agencies of the *Ummah* extending from the grass-roots upward and then downward (Choudhury 1991). This would result in interactive preferences between the grass-roots, the Islamic World Trade Organization, the strings of *Shuras* and the *Ummah* at large. The *Shuratic* Process is thus established and perpetuated.

The market order and its consequence on privatization in the *Shuratic* world view of globalization are now felicitous orders of balance, growth, goodness, purpose and distributive equity. These cannot be, and methodologically now are not, substitutable ends. By the *Ahkam* and the process of their realization via the Unity Precept and institutions/instruments, such ends become complementary, because the unification epistemology of *Tawhid* constitutes the unique essence of the world view. Consequently, the *Shuratic* Process model of international trade, globalization and privatization is distinct and polar to the occidental system.

STATE OF EUROCENTRICITY WITHIN THE MUSLIM WORLD SYSTEM

Is the Muslim World at present equipped in its orientation and institutions towards realizing an Islamic globalization process? We return here to the intra-communal individuation, alienation and conflicting model of Western heritage presently being copied by the Muslim world. In the midst of this, neither has there been progress nor institutional development in the Muslim world on the basis of a truly Islamic solidarity.

On examining the state of trade between OIC members, we get the picture that over the last two decades the flow of trade among OIC members as a percentage of world trade has remained at or about 8.8 percent (1985), only. On the other hand, the flow of trade from the world to member countries was also low at 7.9 percent; from industrialized countries at 7.7 percent; from developing countries at 8.0 percent (Islamic Development Bank).

185

Furthermore, in the case of Malaysia, Indonesia and Bangladesh, the flow of inter-trade, particularly in capital goods, has been dismal (Choudhury 1993c). The trade flows are particularly dismal between Malaysia and Bangladesh, Indonesia and Bangladesh, when compared to their shares with world trade. The inference to be drawn is one of competition among these countries for access to northern markets; serious shortfall in trade complementarities; absence of effort toward establishing a regionally linked Islamic economic cooperation. There has been a failure in general of institutions such as the Islamic Development Bank, Islamic Chamber of Commerce, Commodity and Merchandise; the Islamic Centre for Development and Trade; and the Standing Committee for Economic and Commercial Cooperation of the OIC, toward fostering substantial progress in Islamic Economic Integration and Islamic Common Market. The bitter conclusion of such developments in the area of trade and economic cooperation is that no sign of Islamic globalization of the *Ummah* presently exists. This otherwise could be instrumentalized through Islamic economic cooperation (Choudhury 1989).

The question to wonder about is why such a state of affairs has persisted, when the Western world and the developing countries other than the OIC countries, are fast moving toward globalization? An answer to this question was provided earlier in the fact that the Muslim countries being submerged in their own Eurocentricity, have themselves developed a world-system of such individuating and conflicting models. But beyond this explanation is the fact that almost all Muslim governments today have no Islamic legitimacy. They are not affirmed by a genuinely Islamic response from the society itself. Within these countries are those who are authoritarian, and hence a legitimation is not allowed. There are others who are democratic to an extent, but in these an elitist and not a grassroots democracy, exists. Such a democracy is used to legitimate the power of reigning regimes, just as in the case of a Western political philosophy. Contrarily, an Islamic transformation according to its globalizing force must be legitimated through the *Shuratic* Process. This

186

alone as we have seen, is the cause and effect of the philosophy, methodology, institutionalism and application of the Islamic global model.

THE WAY OUT FOR MUSLIM COUNTRIES IN THEIR OWN GLOBALIZATION PROCESS

What is then the way out of the Muslim stalemate in realizing authentically Islamic roots of globalization? First, it is to attain two structural changes together. This will comprise a thorough adoption of the prevasively embryonic *Shuratic* Process in socio-scientific thinking. Simultaneously, through grass-roots action and agitation, this *Shuratic* Process is to embrace institutional and political change. Secondly, within this institutional change must come about realization of the *Shuratic* framework of thinking, organization and action in the OIC, the Islamic Development Bank and their sister agencies. If this is not possible, alternative institutions capable of developing Islamic globalization, are to be established within a framework of grass-roots democratic change of the participatory type.

Without such a thoroughly authentic Islamic change, the Muslim countries will remain perpetually subservient to the West and will be copying that model for itself. Dominance and external sector instability will characterize any other means of economic cooperation for Muslim countries in the globalization process that is presently on. The realization of the Islamic change does not lie on imitative science and technology catching up. On the contrary, such state-sponsored educational means will further strengthen the unyielding establishment of the OIC member governments.

Contrarily, the realization of Islamic globalization lies on the synergy of the grass-root to self-actualize itself. This grass-root comprises the intellectuals, educational institutions, the poor and deprived, the informed and the entire micro-level of society at large.

187

Political consciousness toward this end is essential. It must be clear to the agents of change, that the occident in its own way, grew out of the Spanish Inquisition into the light of its own rationalism. This rhythm is pervasive and perpetual in occidentalism. In the bi-polar world that has emerged during post-Cold War period between Islam and the West, the Islamic alternative has to realize itself within its own world view if the Muslims are to take their alternative seriously.

CONCLUSION

What is then the conclusion on globalization for the Muslim world? We have shown in this chapter that globalization is not an innocent word of occidental goodwill. Just like any other good delivered by the intrinsically conflicting and domineering model of Eurocentricity, globalization too is a product of that category embedded in neo-mercantilism. Thus the foundation of the occidental concept of globalization is grounded on its liberal neoclassical type political philosophy. International trade, privatization, market shares, foreign direct investments, are then treated as instruments to realize the Eurocentric capitalist gains. The industrialized nations treat these instruments to realize economic interests and strategic interests, either by choosing between the instruments or by submerging them in one dominance model. We have argued the cases where both of these instances of the Eurocentric model apply. To realize such interests, globalization and its instruments can be easily put into effect in desired ways by the occidental player by exercising the two key instruments: interest rate and exchange rate mechanisms.

The Muslim world is particularly vulnerable to these external sector policy variables, as her external sector condition is found to be in disequilibrium compared to the developing countries in general. Yet we found that this debility is compounded by the blind imitation of the Western models in science, technology, society, markets, economics and globalization by OIC member countries. This is proven by the obvious inaction of OIC instruments toward realizing authentic Islamic change; OIC's indifference to grass-roots democratic change in all fronts according to the *Shuratic* Process; and her subservience to occidental modalities in entirety. The authentically Islamic meaning and *modus operandi* of globalization was formalized in the framework of the pervasively embryonic *Shuratic* Process of development and change. The condition for this is reconstruction of thought in the direction of the *Tawhidi* episteme in the socio-scientific order. This discursively evolutionary knowledge process necessitates transformation of the Muslim countries and their institutions into grass-roots democratic and participatory institutions as cause and effect of the *Shuratic* Process.

Islamic thought, behaviour, methods, institutions, choices and socio-scientific dynamics in the framework of the *Shuratic* Process, now substantively ethicize the market order. In the midst of this, the twin concepts of privatization and globalization assume an authentically Islamic meaning. They make global Islamic solidarity possible. The same globalization model is also then opened up to the rest of the world.

CHAPTER 8

MALAYSIA AND THE MUSLIM WORLD: THE TWENTY-FIRST CENTURY AND BEYOND

Malaysia today is emulating the nations of the world and competing with the newly industrializing countries in the South-East Asian Region to fast grow into a fully industrialized economy by the year 2020. Yet many questions remain unanswered as to the *modus operandi* for attaining growth with development in the light of the internal and external assumptions of social, political and economic responsibilities that Malaysia will need to comprehend in her menu of change. This is a challenge that is not necessarily faced by the other newly industrializing countries. What vests this responsibility on Malaysia is her unique position as a nation and society in both the Muslim world and the total globalizing environment. There is thus an apparent push and pull between the interests of Malaysia towards optimally realizing an internal growth in the globalizing environment through interactions with the world seen as a homogeneous entity. Then there is the need for her diversion to the Muslim world with a conscious focus.

PREVALENT MALAYSIAN MODELS OF GROWTH AND DEVELOPMENT

Those familiar with the literature in economic growth with distribution will know that for sometime now the World Bank Group led by Chenery and Ahluwalia had promoted this idea (Chenery & Ahluwalia 1976). Their prescription in tandem with the outlook on structural adjustment and its complementarity with the IMF conditionalities, was based on outward orientation, market transformation and smaller government size. The Agenda for Accelerated Development of Sub-Saharan Africa under the Brady-Baker Plan subsequently went on to recommend a similar prescription (IDS Bulletin 1983). The result was impoverization of Africa, as small markets, plummeting world commodity prices, absence of infant industry protection for African commodities with the fiasco in the Common Fund and Integrated Commodities Arrangements, all defeated such a vile agenda on economic growth.

Ten years after the Agenda for Accelerated Development for Sub-Saharan Africa, the same prescriptions are embracing the wave of capitalist globalization throughout the world today. Its instruments now are market transformation, privatization, export-orientation with trade liberalization and institutional supervision under World Trade Organization along with the Bretton Woods Institutions in these areas. What proved to be a fiasco in Sub-Saharan Africa under the World Bank's Structural Adjustment and IMF's Conditionalities, are now being legitimated by the prosperous countries, who are wielding the stick and the carrot for bringing about global capitalist transformation but not necessarily democratic change.

The question then to address in a new socio-economic development paradigm is whether the old paradigm of growth with distribution is at all a workable one in the existing outlook of capitalist programs? If not, then what must be the alternative explanation of growth-distribution relationship in the midst of a new pattern of globalization?

The goal of growth with distribution is a central one in Malaysia's development perspectives and is built into her Vision 2020 (Government of Malaysia 1991). It is therefore so important to understand the conceptualization and the policy-analytic composition of this idea in development planning. To address the above problem on existing debility and then to provide a new perspective on the paradigm of growth and distribution for Malaysia, we proceed as follows.

192

We note first, that economic growth involves a particular structural arrangement of the economy. Such a program is supported by institutional and technological inputs that direct resources into industrialization and occupational skill development in order to man the secondary manufacturing-centred pattern of industrialization. One therefore finds that policies and programs of governments and multinational institutions generate incentives to fast industrialize through secondary manufacturing activities and then to evolve into a service economy. To bring these about, producers and investors both nationally and internationally, are interested in the efficiency performances of the economy.

Economic efficiency presents itself in the form of rapid economic growth, profitability, cost management among producers, controlling of social expenditure, price levels and external sector imbalance. All of these are needed to provide the climate of confidence for the potential investments on which the industrializing sectorial shifts depend. The World Bank's structural adjustment and IMF's conditionalities are aimed singularly at attaining economic growth, i.e. economic efficiency, profitability and market transformation. One can see the frantic enforcement of these goals during these post Cold-War times.

On the other hand, distributive equity is a social goal. Only when it is combined with the idea of sustainability of resources needed for future economic growth, does distributive equity become a socio-economic end in development planning. But distribution traditionally requires greater presence of government expenditure in social directions, such as, in poverty alleviation, public education, population maintenance, inculcation of universal ethics, values and morality, medical care and subsidy to the agricultural sector. Yet in received economic perspectives, these are found to go against the notion of minimal government. Hence there exists a perennial conflict in development planning between the two goals - economic efficiency focusing economic growth and distribution focusing social growth. Such a tradeoff has pervaded the entire outlook in the World Bank's prescription on growth with distribution.

Relating to these, technology enters the scene to promote a greater degree of flexibility between growth and distribution. But one notes that such a technology is the result of previously accumulated capital. The previous stage of development was indeed enabled by its focus on economic growth in the first place. Otherwise, the technology could not have been made possible. In this way, a technological change as the output of a growth regime, perpetuates the bias on economic growth, i.e. capital accumulation. Markets then become increasingly removed from government directives. What exists is the imposition of certain institutional policies aimed at creating and sustaining market transformation for realizing economic growth.

The present globalizing order along with its trade and developmental institutions, powerful nations, multinationals and national economies, are all fused together into this dominant paradigm of tradeoff between economic growth and distributive equity. What we are watching in the world scene is a theatre of institutional impacts on market transformation today as a grab for the self-interested end of capital accumulation and its attendant regime of economic growth.

Such a consequence is the result of neoclassical marginalist substitution - a mere assumption by itself, rather than a premise of human naturality. Marginalism is made to control both institutional minds and economic forces in the neoclassical capitalist system. According to it, scarce resources flow in the direction in which they are most productive, irrespective of the social goals of development. Any subsequent governmental and institutional intervention to alter such a direction of resource allocation is seen to distort the market process. Governmental expenditures are expensive; whereas, markets are cost-effective. Institutions are to promote markets by the same policies, programs and behaviour as if they were established by market process in the first place. Institutions are thereby seen as the result of previous regimes of capital accumulation. Technology as the product of this capital accumulation, becomes the joint

194

weapon of both markets and institutions to promote their common generic source of interest.

The project on economic growth with distribution that was taken up by the World Bank Group, does not therefore, answer the central issue of simultaneity between growth and distribution. This debility has harped itself through the structural adjustment and conditionality mediums. It is today entrenched in the capitalist globalization process, institutionally and by markets. This relationship is being well-coordinated by the interactions among markets, institutions and governments. All of these act in concert with each other under the dominant effect of politico-economic convergence. That dominance is introduced by the dictates of powerful nations, their transnationals and their sub-contractees for sharing of global resources (Bidwai 1993). Examples here are the U.S. hegemony over APEC, WTO's hegemony over South-East Asian regional trading pacts, the pitching of South-East Asian nations one against the other in trade and global market shares (Ollapally 1993).

In the neoclassical model of economic growth with development, followed by macroeconomic policing of disequilibria that emanate from the neoclassical economic arrangement, there will exist inevitable conflicts between the above two goals. This is the power centricity of all Western models of growth and development - with or without distribution. The global order will offer the prospect for rapid growth. But such a growth will be a risky one both economically and politically in the long run. Economically, uncertainties will arise from the continuing price-taking position that Malaysia would continue to hold indefinitely in the global economy.

Hence, the nature of technological change will remain concentrated in an overly reliance on foreign direct investments that are known to pursue sheer short-run profitability without any distinct built-in concern for social development and indigenous human capital growth or technological diversification. Sectorial linkages and the consequential productivity growth are not seen as built-in concerns of foreign direct invest-

195

ments. There is also the open-ended benefit for free repatriation of profits and reallocation of foreign direct investments, further intensified in a competing global environment that entraps these relations between FDI, technological change, sectorial linkages, productivity growth and pricing (Ali 1992).

The result is that distributions both across sectors and households will continue to remain skewed between the *rentier* class and recipients of transfer incomes (Mehmet 1986). Poverty alleviation and food security goals of the Malaysian Government will both remain entrenched in the kind of entrapped transfer and disabling relationships caused by the nature of technology, sectorial linkages, productivity change, pricing and distribution in the midst of globalizing relations. The position of Malaysia in these directions is made all the more precarious from the point of view of socio-economic development during these emerging years of the World Trade Organization post-Uruguay Rounds (Choudhury 1994, Salleh et al. 1988, Osman-Rani et al. 1990).

It is futile to believe that the primacy of growth will later trickle down to development, distribution and prosperity. The socio-economic world does not behave in this wishful manner. The conditions that defeat such wishful thinking are first, lost opportunities to the adversely affected people during the process of substitution. Skills, income, value of wealth and entitlement do not shift in accord with the sectorial shifts that take place for reasons of inability to adapt to technological change. Secondly, the fruits of growth are quickly syphoned off by investors to invest in other profitable sectors where the substituted factors do not matter spatially. Thirdly, the substitution in favour of capital are aimed at generating wealth and profits by owners of capital, while cost-minimizing wages are paid to labour. Thus, capital reaps its returns and power through the marginalist substitution process of neoclassical economic arrangements. Fourthly, policies in the industrialized nations make other national policies to follow suit. These cause external sector instabilities that tell adversely in domestic socio-economic conditions. The most vicious of such externally induced policies are interest rate and exchange rate mechanisms. Economic fundamentals are unable to predict precisely the relationship between interest rates and exchange rates.

THE ISSUE OF LABOUR MARKET AND TECHNOLOGICAL CHOICE IN MALAYSIA

There is a feverish pursuit among Malaysian policy-makers, academicians and employers today to adopt a capital-intensive and labour-saving technological change by the year 2020. The Malaysian Government is recommending that skill formation, productivity and economic growth being the economic goals of the Malaysian Government to the year 2020, therefore reduction in foreign labour requirements is to be targeted as the means to attain these ends in the face of her existing labour shortages. Let us examine critically the long-run consequences of such a policy recommendation.

Productivity and efficiency are interrelated concepts in the neo-classical substitution framework. They together marginalize consideration of distributive equity in development. On the one side, productivity measured by the unit output of production by a factor input, necessitates all other factors to be left unchanged. Thus technological change is fully absorbed by this particular factor. On the side of cost, the marginal cost of production caused by the variable factor increases, till it is above the average cost of production. In this way finally, price-output relationship in economic competition as the meaning of economic efficiency, becomes identical with optimal productivity.

In either of these measurements, the social and institutional effects of production are technically ignored. This is a methodological consequence of neoclassical productivity measurement. Planners cannot thereby, introduce technical and policy consequences in the measurement of the broader concept of socio-economic productivity. Many important factors that underlie a comprehensive concept and application of development

197

get ignored. Among them are self-reliant development, minimization of social and transactional costs and avoidance of external sector uncertainties. In a globalizing age, these other influences determine the direction of the most vulnerable indicators of growth and development, namely, external resource flow and internal economic stabilization.

External resource flow is controlled by the world interest rate and exchange rate mechanisms. These remain permanently with the industrialized nations today. Internal economic stabilization is generated by a proper adaptation between real sector activity and monetary and fiscal liberalization. Thus resources needed for real sector growth, which in turn fuels self-reliance and sustainable real economic growth, establish a one-to-one relationship with the quantity of money. Social expenditures are derived from fiscal measures.

In contrast to these important components that comprise the concept of socio-economic productivity, the sheer measure of economic productivity makes population growth a debilitating factor of development. Whereas, population increase remains an important political target for Malaysia. This in turn implies need for a growing labour force. Skill formation in the present scenario of economic growth presents a mere mechanical use of foreign technology by indigenous manpower. There is a difference between a mechanical use of imported technology and adaptive use of technology. The latter is indigenous to the extent that dependence on foreign technology is marginalized even as indigenous technology is progressively upgraded by means of imported ones.

Indigenous technology for Malaysia must mean economic growth and development in the perspective of the politico-economic importance of population increase. This long-term perspective must also be pursued by such a technology that can adapt to available labour and establish complementarity among activities that can promote the long-term politico-economic goals. Technology means investment in machines, people and society over the long haul. So is also human resource development. The two must adapt to each other over this long haul. Hence, there exists a one-to-one relationship among technology-population-labour-development and economic growth that must be recognized. In this menu of complementarity, neither short-run nor long-run capital-intensive and labour-saving technology is meaningful for Malaysia.

QUESTION OF PRODUCTIVITY IN A KNOWLEDGE-BASED SOCIETY

Even when we take up the knowledge-based economy as the premise for productivity measurement and still retain the shifting developmental patterns as experienced by the industrial change in the West, the problem of complementarity between efficiency and equity is not solved. Hence the broader concept of socio-economic productivity is not realized. Why is this?

Knowledge as treated in the neoclassical framework that is used to explain industrial shifts, is itself a form of capital. Just as capital ownership creates wealth in the segment that has it, so also knowledge ownership will create wealth in the ones who will have this to produce with. However, this by itself is not the source of the problem. But when such a pattern of ownership is taken to the level of industrial shifts, then the consequential presence of sectorial delinkages will create the shifts in the use and intensity of knowledge in the dominant directions. Thus the relationships caused by the industrial shifts will themselves cause knowledge as capital to accentuate the privileges and skewness of ownership.

Transfer incomes in these industrial growth situations do not help out, for then self-reliance as the source of empowerment and ownership is not enhanced. On the other hand, it is adaptability between available skills, its integration in appropriate technology and then to recreate technology as skills adapt and grow in the use of technology, that generates socio-economic sustainability. Now production by means of sectorial linkages can generate the much needed simultaneity between efficiency and equity and not simply the generation and diffusion of knowledge for realizing economic efficiency alone.

199

It is well known that in the sense of knowledge as stock of formal education, the neoclassical idea of human resource development has not helped out over the years in creating this simultaneity, although immense amounts of sophisticated knowledge and skills have been introduced. Such a pattern of knowledge acquisition has always proved to be increasingly efficiency-creating along the trajectory of growth that tilts always towards this direction. Here Drucker's knowledge society does not help either, for this futurism is construed as an engine of capitalist transformation driven by information supremacy. Drucker's idea does not help in treating the issue of knowledge as interactions across systems, integration and dissemination derived from and leading to the global grassroots perspective of socio-economic transformation (Drucker 1989). This is an idea of knowledge subsumed by disguised neoclassicism of the information age global order, where the same neoclassical assumption of homogeneity of technological flows and standards among all nations, is upheld.

ABSOLUTE VERSUS RELATIVE INEQUALITY WITH SKILL FORMATION

All the above is not to say that with the advance of knowledge, skills and efficiency, incomes and ownership will not increase among the once underprivileged. Absolute poverty, as in Malaysia, has been effectively reduced. Yet relative poverty remains, particularly between rural and urban sectors, between Bumiputeras and other groups, between states, specially for Sabah, Sarawak and Kelantan (Johari 1991).

Absolute poverty creates non-competing groups and is a condition of political dysfunctionalism. It is relative poverty that becomes the source of conflict and unrest in a growing economy. Relative poverty and inequality brings into confrontation contending groups in society in light of the expectations of changing developmental regimes, preferences, organizations and policies enacted at large. A very important one of such conditions to consider among is the unbridled privatization of the economy now sweeping Malaysia to emulate and compete with the countries around in a bid to step up economic growth. Thus goals and methods of realizing economic efficiency and distributive equity once again conflict.

The Malaysian Sixth Plan states (Government of Malaysia 1991): "During the Fifth Plan period, despite progress achieved in the implementation of the Bumiputera Commercial and Industrial Community (BCIC), the overall impact in terms of creating a viable participation of Bumiputera in the modern sectors of the economy remained limited. The major factors that contributed to the low performance were the small and narrow base of their business enterprises, inadequate experience and lack of management capabilities." In the face of this trend, sustained government expenditure for ameliorating the Bumiputeras, is causing mismatch between labour productivity and social expenditure per capita. This is a major cause for the recent burst of inflation, which the Government of Malaysia is now trying to control by means of demand management policies.

The continuing relative inequality in asset-holding by Bumiputeras is taking place in the face of a massive shift from agricultural to manufacturing, with secondary manufacturing instead of resource-based diversification, leading the value added in the manufacturing sector. It is in this kind of delinked development that it becomes so very difficult for such skills and knowledge to be realized, as are to be found in sectorial and occupational complementarities. A very important kind of complementarity in the political economy is participation of all levels. Indeed, it is the participatory sense of ownership and hence empowerment, that alone can tamper with the otherwise conflicting situation that relative inequality causes in society.

The final question remains to be addressed: Are the industrial shifts that have been used in economic history to legitimate the given nature of industrial transformation, natural and universal prescriptions of socio-economic change? To answer this we note that technologies and preferences among consumers, producers and institutions act interactively in response to say, incomes, opportunities, stability, ownership and empowerment. The study of these under extensive interactions needs alternative paradigms based on interrelationships between political and market forces. Here, rather than hegemony as dictated by powerful governments, what is required are grass-roots participation and discourse to bring about the desired pattern of change. Governments can act as catalysts towards this realization, but they should not accept the Western hegemony nor practise it themselves to impose a technology that is not adaptable to themselves and that does not emanate from and reinforce wide degrees of socio-economic complementarity. In this alternative pattern of change it is unnatural to accept forced induction. It is natural to ground change on adaptation caused by the widest range of complementarities.

Only complementarity and relevant reorganization among the above-mentioned socio-economic goals with appropriate planning and policies, can generate the broader measure of socio-economic productivity. On the other hand, the deliberate labour-saving and capital-intensive technological change that is presently being framed for Malaysia Incorporation 2020, is a move towards costly external sector dependency on capital. In this way, it causes inter-sectorial substitution of capital for labour. Such a substitution can make Malaysian economic growth and social well-being highly uncertain and unsustainable in the long run, unless sheer economic productivity is substituted by a complementary concept of socio-economic productivity in the more universal sense.

The long-run condition can be particularly hurtful for Malaysia in view of her responsibility to the target groups, the Bumiputeras. It will also increasingly individuate the greater relationship that Malaysia is expected to promote with a future self-reliant Muslim world and in opposition to the hegemonic controls of the global economy. Such an individuation can arise from various quarters: Malaysia's diversion of capital to finance expensive capital-intensive development at home; abandonment of appropriate and intermediate technology that should otherwise promote interlinkages in a future Islamic Common Market; Mal-

202

aysia's restriction on labour-use from the Muslim world that otherwise can generate income distribution through the division of labour across the future *Ummah* (world nation of Islam as a unified political economy).

THE NEED FOR A NEW OUTLOOK IN MALAYSIAN DEVELOPMENT

There is thus every reason for Malaysia to seriously diversify attention to the Muslim world. But here too, applying a neoclassical model of international trade and investments will mean sacrificing the benefits of Malaysia's look-East policies. Such a situation would be equally unwarranted. It can worsen the socio-economic position of Malaysia in the face of an inevitable trade diversion policy that must otherwise be adopted against the trade creation prospect of look-East policy.

An inherent resource 'tradeoff' scenario reflecting something called rational choice in economic textbooks, is thus posed for Malaysia in the neoclassical and Keynesian models of growth with development. The final outcome is that neither growth nor development engendered by sheer economic efficiency, can coexist in the long-run neoclassical and Keynesian models of economic growth and development.

Alternative Paradigm of Growth With Development for Malaysia

How do we then examine alternative socio-political and socio-economic development paradigm for Malaysia? There are three processes involved here and the paradigm is one of establishing global complementarities among these processes in this three-sector world.

The first sector is Malaysia's internal socio-political and socio-economic arrangements in the midst of a maturing, value-creating and interacting society. The second sector comprises the global order without the Muslim world with which Malaysia trades and on which she depends for her technological change. Trade creation is predominant in this relationship. The third sector is the Muslim world to which Malaysia must turn for her rational long-term socio-political and socio-economic bene-fits. Here trade diversion in the world scene would be the nature of the game.

In all of these, socio-political considerations involve the realization of a society-wide, community-based orientation in generating national decisions, policies and programs. This would necessitate widely inter-acting and tolerantly participatory democracy at all levels. The citizens must be allowed to and must involve themselves in all rungs of issues and problems at the helm of Malaysian development perspectives. Merely a capitalist driven transformation backed by Government-centred dominant role in all decisions, renders the participatory perspectives absent.

Now social costs cumulate. The costs are felt on the side of a naïve, almost unmoved desire by society to participate in its own outlook of the future. The consequential dominant role of the Malaysian Government in all socio-political affairs, results in a picture of self-righteousness without objective political credibility on the issue, wherein the nation and its objective machinery as a whole can participate.

MEANING OF SOCIO-POLITICAL AND SOCIO-ECONOMIC INTERACTIONS

Socio-political and socio-economic interactions within Malaysia must therefore mean the future order of participatory democracy by the people. The Government and civil servants in all departments must not be capitalizing in all things big and small. A participatory democracy must be broadly based at all levels, starting from the grass-roots to the higher echelons, objectively interconnected with each other. There would then exist interactions in circular flows among all these echelons and decision makers in every issue. The issues themselves must interrelate and no national issue is to be left out in this, starting from sensitive religious dialogues; the nationally desired nature of privatization, the appropriate nature of technology and goods; the nature of Malaysia's participation in

global organizations, and so on. Such strengths based on internal complementarities, would then determine the nature of technology, development,
growth and distributional futures that Malaysians would want and share
with intellectually, politically and in terms of adapting skills with
appropriate technology for growth, values, self-reliance and sustainability
in complementary ways.

Socio-political and socio-economic interactions taken up at the level
of the Muslim world, must bring forth Malaysia's emerging importance
in influencing collective choices in the same areas. These are, socio-
political change, grass-roots and communitarian focus in national
development plans, greater influence in these directions fundamentally
to change the existing development organizations in the Muslim world in
terms of their philosophy and focus, realizing objective regional economic integration with a fervour of Islamic Common Market. The issues
of human resource development, choices of technology, intra-communal
pricing of own assets and tradables, markets and vigorous interactions on
these fronts, will subsequently follow.

SOME COMPLEMENTARY POLITICO-ECONOMIC POLICIES
RELATING TO A FUTURE ISLAMIC COMMON MARKET

The resulting implications of trade diversion into an Islamic Common
Market are establishing of an Islamic Common Fund, Investment Guar-
antees, Customs Union aspects of free flow of professionals and skilled
labour, a well-funded Centre for Upgrading of Intermediate Technologies, and Joint Defence Pact. Above all, the focus on equal voting
principle by OIC member states must adopt weighting by national
population size of Muslim nations. Such weights must determine the per-
capita share contributions to the common fund of various members. The
OIC and her institutions have thus to be revamped and changed in
substantive ways in such an *Ummatic* overhaul.

The centralization of power in the hands of given autocratic Muslim governments would thereby be neutralized by the increasing per-capita contributions at the micro-enterprise level. This will enhance itself with increasing population size. Funds required for such contributions would be generated at the grass-roots levels and from sources favourable to such a transformation, internationally among Muslims at all levels of enterprise. Funds may also be borrowed between Muslim countries based on the contracts of *Musharakah/Mudarabah* (equity participation/profit-sharing). Private sector Islamic financial institutions would be activated for mobilizing resources through such outlets. In this way, common interests would be served and resources would be mobilized, while autocratic political-centricity by Muslim governments against the common expression and will, is neutralized. In recent years, such political-centricity has proved to be of the same oppressive nature as Eurocentricity is against the Muslim countries in general. Muslim national dominance has deeply strengthened Eurocentricity against their own peoples.

The socio-political and socio-economic perspectives in Malaysia's position on her look-East policy would mean international trade and resource allocation (FDI), technological futures and pricing in view of the social cost-benefit comparisons between trade diversion and trade creation, given the above-mentioned perspectives. Thus over a period of transition, there would be an inverse relationship between trade diversion and trade creation, as the above-mentioned transformations start to take effect. Now trade diversion may occur in the global scene; but there will be trade creation within the Muslim bloc, resulting in greater trade flows between Muslim countries. Thus as a developmental instrument, trade diversion of this type becomes a powerful tool of development cooperation and cannot replace trade creation within the Muslim world.

In the longer run, a homogeneous concept of objective globalization process may return, with Muslim nations determining their own direction of trade and developmental resources. Foreign direct investments (FDIs) would now flow not as exogenous technologies, but rather to finance such appropriate technologies that can match the emergent manpower-technology adaptation in Muslim nations. Such technologies would complement with intermediate technologies and upgrade themselves into advanced technologies. Consequently in such a case, a transformation toward price-setting capability by Muslim trading countries in the world scene is realized. The present state of price-taking commodity economies is overcome.

MALAYSIA'S GROWTH-DISTRIBUTION PERSPECTIVES

Malaysia's development outlook in Vision 2020 aims at attaining the goals of economic growth and distributive equity simultaneously, not by a tradeoff. Thus Malaysia must be wary of keeping her development paradigm outside of the neoclassical prescriptions. She must likewise, insulate herself from the domineering agenda of powerful nations and their institutions. How can these be accomplished?

The manufacturing shift towards industrialization must keep its focus on establishing interlinkages in resources, inputs and output with the agricultural and service sectors. In this way, manufacturing growth would be centred around the availability of the abundant indigenous capacity of Malaysia, namely, agricultural primary commodities, in order to develop the corresponding kinds of industrial linkages. This does not mean a sheer primary sector developmental focus. Rather, the focus here is on resource-based manufacturing while using all secondary manufacturing and service sector developments for establishing the widest inter-sectorial linkages.

Examples of Activities on Sectorial Interlinkages

Examples here are legion. Let us consider converting of agricultural waste into methanol/ethanol-type energy sources; fruits and their wastes into processed fodder. The technology to be adopted here must in turn comply with agricultural-manufacturing interlinkages, so that the two sectors are served by such a technological adaptation and not simply in isolation of each other. Another example here is the processing of raw materials within production sites, adopting environmentally appropriate methods. Yet another one is the treatment of all kinds of wastes into fertilizers and technological development to reduce waste at production source.

The service sector diversification of the above type of agricultural-manufacturing-secondary interlinkages can be taken up, for example, by establishing marketing sources and information systems at production sites. In this way, the primary producers can be informed of prices in global markets. Such an information flow can provide the necessary directions for selling or controlling inventories and for pursuing new/ alternative production lines. Agricultural by-products could be used for packaging of electronic and heavy material equipments, replacing thus the existing environmentally unfriendly foams. The foam products would accordingly be converted into housing insulation materials that can prove to be good exportables.

Above all, it is an encouraging sign to see high demand in financial markets for the various issues of shares for the target groups - *Amanah Saham Nasional* and *Amanah Saham Bumiputera*. Both of these are equity shares for increasing the assets of underprivileged target groups in Malaysia. These are aimed at increasing the share of assets by the poor. This is an area that can clearly develop into financing of projects to serve as interlinkages between the micro-enterprises of target Bumiputeras and the well-to-do businesses. The cooperative nature and participatory diversification of such financial resources and assets, can bring about a good deal of sectorial interlinkages in Malaysia.

There are substantial socio-economic returns to be earned from such interlinkages. First, wealth and resources are ploughed back to the agricultural sector. This generates purchasing power in the agricultural sector, enabling it to buy the joint outputs of the manufacturing-agricultural sectors. There are also returns from the manufacturing sector that flow into reinvestments, wages and dividends in the agricultural sector. The low cost micro-enterprises that can be generated on an extensively participatory basis using Amanah Saham shares, can mobilize human and capital resources for the benefit of the consumers and marginal businesses. This would increase the stock of wealth in the nation as a whole.

These processes are accompanied by occupational and skill development as permanent human resource developments. With such an increase in a diversified environment of production, structural change and service sector evolution, comes about greater self-reliance in development. This will help to insulate the Malaysian economy from the external sector shocks by the development of markets at home.

The argument presented here is not to belittle the great importance of trade in small population economies, as is the case of Malaysia. However, the specific nature of such products and their steady prices would make them particularly attractive tradables in the South-East Asian region. The same idea of interlinkages across appropriate goods and technologies needs to be popularized regionally by capitalizing on the diversities of indigenous structures at the rural-urban levels interlinked nationally and regionally.

In the globalizing age, wherein South-East Asia is enacting its own developmental paradigms, such an interlinked developmental perspective should be both a prescription and a possibility. To Malaysia it arises from within her Vision 2020 - a complementarity process in realizing moral-material well-being and as leader of the developing world.

Every one of such agricultural-manufacturing-service interlinkage will carry with it the necessary occupational and skill developments. Such human resources will come both from the rural and urban sectors. The on-site-productions would generate service-sector and housing complexes away from the congested cities. Socio-economic distribution would arise from the human capital formation, capital formation, entitlement and structural transformation of production, technology and growth within the market venue of change.

The principal differences between the ethicized market transformation based on interlinkages and the alienating markets pronounced by global dominance that have proved to be ecologically disparaging, are the former's capacity to enable society at large to engage in a participatory venue of change. Ethicized market and hence the consequential globalization process with extensive politico-economic interlinkages and socio-economic productivity gains, is a cause and effect of complementarities.

Thus there are many ways of developing indigenous sectorial interlinkages. These will carry along the diversification needed in skills and occupations. They will engage the Malaysian society, institutions, government and economy at large, to attend to the simultaneous realization of the goals of economic growth and distributive equity. This is also the target of Malaysian Vision 2020. Complementarities promote, substitutions marginalize social change.

Such a prescription is thoroughly different from the one on 'growth with distribution' prescribed by the World Bank and its neoclassical economic basis, which we have referred to earlier. In the new politico-economic and ethicized prescription, market, society, institution, government and the globalization process of sustainability, are found to be interlinked with each other. Realizing such interlinkages in a participatory civil and caring society, is also Malaysia's total Vision 2020. It comprises the moral-material well-being in a civil caring society and of Malaysia as a leader of the developing world.

OVERALL INTERACTIONS IN GLOBAL ECONOMY AND SOCIETY

The final interactions occur at all levels. For Malaysia, socio-political interactions lead to the conscious reinforcement of values, self-reliance, technological change and growth with development through the most important human force. This is self-actualization in all fronts, realized by individuals and groups through the medium of participatory democracy applied at all levels of decision-making. Overly Government involvement in all matters is to be replaced by grass-roots-markets-Government interface. Indeed, the grass-roots future provides the unique model of universal interactions. The monolithic model, of which is the Government as a dominant polity, is being increasingly rejected.

The growing human power sets in motion Malaysia's relevant position towards influencing future events. It realizes such targets of development and transformations that would complement with the Malaysian interests and transformation when brought to complement within the Muslim world and in herself.

Finally, the emerging price-setting and politically enhancing position of Malaysia in the future Islamic Common Market, would bestow a global order that generates equalizing benefits globally and special benefits to both Malaysia and the Muslim world. Unfortunately we fail to see such a cooperative relationship coming out of the recent International Conference on Smart Partnership among government, the private sector, society and the global order. The conference sponsored by the Government of Malaysia and commemorated by the Prime Minister Dr Mohammad Mahathir, was held in July 1995 at Langawi, Malaysia (T.V.3 1995).

THE META-THEORY OF DEVELOPMENT BY APPLICATION OF THE PRINCIPLE OF UNIVERSAL COMPLEMENTARITY

It is high time that the paradigm shifts of peoples turn to new epistemologies that otherwise industrial post-modernity will be unable to offer in its perceived continuation of the Western Eurocentric models. In the entire socio-political, socio-economic and also in the socio-scientific order, this occidental continuity is manifest in its meta-theory of methodological individualism. It presents itself as marginalist substitution

211

(tradeoff) in economics; as Eurocentricity in politics and development; as egocentric self-interest in social psychology; as value-neutral conjecturism in the sciences; as ethical neutrality in technology determined outside of human interface.

The unique and powerful alternative for developmental change in all fronts that both embrace and uplift the human presence, is premised only in interacting systems. This premise formulates the Principle of Universal Complementarity, for it replaces occidental meta-theory of methodological individualism by its own meta-theory of intra- and inter-systemic interactions, integration and evolution. In political economy, this meta-theory pronounces an endogenously ethical transformation of markets by the joint preferences and benefits of interacting groups comprising polity, society, markets and individuals. In the sciences, it presents itself as the epistemology of an extensively interacting universe beyond the confined domain of the Invariance of Physical Constants. In technology, it presents itself as the conversion of that scientific knowledge into processes that serve as the medium premised upon and activating the interactions and integration as explained here.

CONCLUSION

The shape of things to come for Malaysia should be such a world view of society, political economy, scientific and technological vision. Development regimes are to be thought out carefully, away from blindly adopting borrowed model prescriptions of the West. They are to be thought out instead, within a world view of moral-material simultaneity. In this prescription, ways and means of attaining ethicized markets and objective globalization are to be thought out carefully. Trade creation within the Muslim world and in ways that can be taken up within a developmental effect of such trade on the *Ummah*, are to be considered. This would secure the Muslim countries in general, and Malaysia in particular, from the Eurocentric consequences in the future. Such consequences have been overly proven to go against these countries in the entire history of Muslim-West politico-economic relationship.

Such processes of transformation will then prove to be both the newly acquired strength - revolutionary to the core, and enhancing globally over the long haul. In the absence of these tripartite globally interactive processes of transformation, the Malaysian economy, polity and society, run the uncertainty of being submerged in an intensively bi-polar post-modern world. Today, with the ignominious fall of Muslim states in the Middle East and beyond to Western and Zionist forces, the last frontier of Muslims, and thereby, of a truly just and prosperous future for the world, importantly rests on Malaysia. These human and ecological values can then be launched to greater heights therefrom. The *Qur'an* promises this limitless victory over space and time in the following words (Asad 1993):

O you who believe! God has promised you many war-gains (i.e. gains against all kinds of antagonism) which you shall yet achieve; and He has vouchsafed you these worldly gains well in advance, and has stayed from you the hands of hostile people, so that this your inner strength may become a symbol to the believers who come after you, and that He may guide you all on a straight path (Chapter: Victory (48), v. 20).

CHAPTER 9

INSTITUTIONAL REFORMATION: THE ORGANIZATION OF ISLAMIC CONFERENCES SYSTEM

The Organization of Islamic Conferences today stands as the prime institution for promoting Islamic transformation among Muslim countries in the areas of economic and political cooperation. The aims and goals of OIC are nobly stated (OIC 1995): The objectives of OIC are to strengthen, (1) Islamic solidarity among member states; (2) cooperation in political, economic, social, cultural and scientific fields; (3) the struggle of all Muslim people to safeguard their dignity, independence and national rights. The OIC also aims at coordinating ways and means toward safeguarding the Islamic Holy Places; support the struggle of the Palestinian people and assist them in recovering their rights and liberating their occupied territories. OIC also aims at eliminating racial discrimination and all forms of colonialism; and to create a favourable atmosphere for the promotion of cooperation and understanding between Member States and other countries.

The OIC is also a well-developed institution. Figure 9.1 shows how this politico-economic institution integrates its functions across heads of states, subsidiary support sister organizations involved in research (e.g. SESRTCIC, IRTI) policy-making and special areas of science (e.g. IFSTAD, COMSTECH) and economics (e.g.COMCEC, IDB). There are also several autonomous sister organizations that carry on similar objectives of economic and technological development of member states (IDB, IRTI, ICCICE) (Nienhaus 1986). Hence we find that the OIC as a comprehensive institution, embodies fairly decentralized levels of sister organizations that can devote to the full gamut of economic, social and political functions.

Figure 9.1: The OIC System.

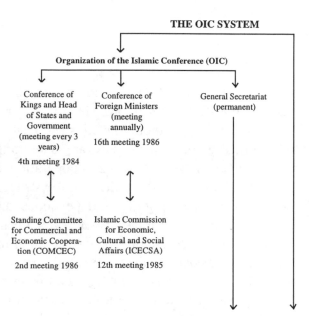

THE OIC SYSTEM

Organization of the Islamic Conference (OIC)

Conference of Kings and Head of States and Government (meeting every 3 years)

4th meeting 1984

Conference of Foreign Ministers (meeting annually)

16th meeting 1986

General Secretariat (permanent)

Standing Committee for Commercial and Economic Cooperation (COMCEC)

2nd meeting 1986

Islamic Commission for Economic, Cultural and Social Affairs (ICECSA)

12th meeting 1985

(Selected) **Subsidiary Organs of The OIC** Statistical, Economic and Social Research and Training Centre for Islamic Countries (SESRTCIC), Ankara Islamic Centre for Vocational and Technical Training and Research (ICVTTR), Dhaka Islamic Centre for Development of Trade (ICDT), Casablanca Islamic Foundation for Science, Technology and Development (IFSTAD), Jeddah Islamic Civil Aviation Council, Tunis

Independent Members of the OIC System (Selection) Islamic Development Bank (IDB), Jeddah Islamic Research and Training Institute (IRTI), Jeddah Islamic Chamber of Commerce, Industry and Commodity Exchange (ICCICE), Karachi International Association of Islamic Banks (IAIB), Jeddah Islamic Shipowners Association, Jeddah Islamic Telecommunications Union, Karachi Islamic Cement Union, Ankara

The members of the OIC now stand at 51 in number. These members extend from Europe to Central Asia, the Middle East, South East Asia and the Far East. Hence they bring with them an extensive texture of diversity that can be harnessed for their political coordination and economic development. The prospect for economic cooperation in a world that sees diversity as the medium of globalization and increasing possibilities for trade, skill and technological complementarity among the members, appears as the logical consequence for the vast Muslim world endowed as it is with rich and diverse resources.

In general therefore, the OIC presents a scope for an effective politico-economic superstructure for the resolution and collective determination of the many woes that disparage the Muslim world today. Such an involvement should make it possible for the OIC system to embrace a vast portfolio of goals. Among these are the promotion of collective social well-being, poverty alleviation, development of the common aspirations of people in a productive participation within a self-determined, motivated, driven toward a bright politico-economic future, and creating a science, technology and human resource complementarity in the membership through the exercise of instruments such as, trade, development and economic cooperation.

CRITICAL QUESTIONS RELATING TO THE OIC SYSTEM

Yet why is it that these very ideals although enunciated in the preamble, remain far from attainment by the OIC system? It was mentioned in Chapter 7 that a very small percentage, about 8-10 percent of world trade done by Islamic countries flows between themselves. For the year 1994, intra-OIC exports stood at only 7.38 percent of world imports by this bloc; exports to developed countries comprised 59.12 percent; exports to developing countries stood at 30.11 percent. Intra-OIC imports as a percentage of world imports by this bloc was 10.82 percent; from developed countries it was 63.59 percent; from developing countries it

217

was 25.59 percent (IMF 1995). In 1993, intra-trade among Gulf Cooperation Council stood at 7.36 percent of world trade; among Economic Cooperation Members (Pakistan, Iran, Turkey, Afghanistan and others) it was 2.93 percent; among IDB-Asean members it was 1.52 percent; among Arab Maghreb Union it was 3.21 percent; among the IDB-Economic Community of West African States it was 3.56 percent (Islamic Development Bank 1995a).

Yet statistics on cumulative approved financing of operations by the Islamic Development Bank for the period 1991-95 shows that 72.11 percent of this went into Foreign Trade Financing and only 24.00 percent into Project Financing (Islamic Development Bank 1995b). A contradictory message is evident between a low inter-communal trade level and a high Foreign Trade Financing percentage. An obvious inference is that Foreign Trade Financing has not been looked upon as a development financing instrument and its impact on inter-communal trade flow being relatively minimal, much of the Foreign Trade Financing would have been either in oil-related products or in items imported from outside the Muslim countries. A breakdown of such external import dependency is provided elsewhere (Choudhury 1989).

Besides, human resource development too is at its lowest compared to any standards (Haniff 1992). The mean literacy rate of Muslim countries in the eighties was at 38 percent compared to 59 percent for the Third World countries and 98 percent for the industrialized countries. Among these, 77 percent of those in ages 25+ had no education as compared to 64 percent for the Third World countries and 3 percent for the industrialized countries. Only 43 percent in age group 5-19 years were in schooling as compared to 51 percent for the Third World countries and 76 percent for the industrialized countries. There were only 3,593 scientists and engineers per million of people in the Muslim countries compared to 6,691 per million of population in the Third World countries and 23,824 per million of population in the industrialized countries.

These are despicable statistics for the Muslim countries in terms of their development in spite of the prevalence of OIC in this front.

The OIC has managed to call forth teems of resolutions for the economic development, human resource development, labour mobility and social security and for economic and political cooperation in its membership, which it refers to as the *Ummah* (SESRTCIC 1993). The technical report of IFSTAD points to many resolution and highlights important needs for the scientific and technological rehabilitation of the *Ummah*, especially by focusing on critical areas of food sufficiency and industrial development (Islamic Foundation for Science, Technology and Development 1993). Yet after twenty-three years of its existence, OIC could improve neither the economic nor the political conditions of the Muslim countries. The Muslim fiasco in the Gulf War 1991, the inaction of the OIC in the Iraq-Iran war, in Bosnia and in Somalia, are just a few examples of the intrepid role that OIC has played in resolving conflicts among Muslim countries (Choudhury 1991a).

This state of affairs and the questions respecting the inability of OIC in realizing its goals or its Islamic mission, deem an examination in this chapter. In light of the Islamic regenerative model and future prospect of transformation that the earlier chapters have pointed out, we will once again examine Figure 9.1. Two basic points are obviated.

We note first, that the organizational picture shown in Figure 9.1 is one of top-down and and heavily concentrated hegemony by the category termed, 'Kings and head of states'. This very perspective of political hegemony is seen as the stereotype in the organizational complex by means of the civil service cadre on which the decentralized sister organizations of the OIC system are based. The hegemonic preferences of the superstructure that are behind self-interest of principal agents and decision-makers, are repeated to reflect privileged institutional preferences and control. The deadlock between the unchanging nature of political order in the Muslim countries and the absence of participatory democracy by the citizens make the nature of decentralization in the OIC system a perpetuating factor of hegemonic control.

PUBLIC CHOICE-THEORETIC EXPLANATION OF
OIC DECISION-MAKING

According to public choice theory, decision makers in the OIC as an international organization would be viewed as maximizing their self-interested preferences. Hence, actual events in the political and socio-economic sphere are seen to be manipulable according to the direction of self-interest and the underlying power of the role players. This manipulation takes place in ways and by means that lead to the perpetuation of the unchanging preferences that maximize self-interest (Ansari 1986). At the end of the public choice-theoretic game thereby, one finds that development finances are used as carrots and sticks by the dominant players over the weaker ones.

Such hegemonic states have endlessly characterized the politics of the Muslim countries for a long while now. Recent incidents of such dominance were found during the Gulf War 1991 when countries that opposed the Western Alliance were ostracized by the hegemonic capital surplus Arab countries. Consequently, the OIC and the Arab League became inept to resolve the ensuing regional conflicts. This matter has not ended to date, as we find the human costs of the sanctions against the Iraqi people to continue unabated (Clarke 1995).

The public choice theory of international organizations emulated by the OIC system and its hegemonically decentralized structure, can be invoked to explain her economic distributions of communal resources. In this regard, now we come to the second cause of OIC's inability on the politico-economic front. A systemic view of interactions among agents and sectors, big and small, that should characterize any effective and socially enhancing decision-making, is found to take place in Figure 9.1 in one of the following ways: First, the top-to-down hegemonic structure allows for interactions among the sister organizations, entrenching this same structure within the OIC system. Secondly, a total independence of decision-making is found to exist among the sister organizations of the OIC.

We note that the rule of political convergence found to arise from the maximizing of power and self-interest in the model of public choice endowed to the OIC system in the present case, means that the concept of *Ummatic* social well-being ensuing from the system, is based simply on an assignment of predetermined rules of the game provided exogenously by the most powerful players. The social well-being function now becomes a monotonic transformation of the perception of well-being of the most dominant player (Choudhury 1993). In present times, the latter type of agents happen to be the capital surplus Muslim countries. The state of control so emanating from the hegemonic transference of power and control in and through the superstructure, consequently defies the most fundamental premise of socio-economic development, which is freedom and liberty of the citizens to determine their destinies by participation to make choices and by collectively defining the development mandates. In this latter case otherwise, the predetermined, unchanging and self-perpetuating preferences of decision makers would give way to interactive and dynamic preferences of role players across decentralized agencies and sectors of the total politico-economic order.

If on the other hand, the assumption of independence among the sister agencies of the OIC system is made to explain organizational decision-making, the concept of social welfare derived from Figure 9.1 reduces to a lateral addition of the utilities of each decision-making group (sub-system). Such a perception of well-being is identical to the utilitarian method of aggregating the utilities of self-interested agents, each motivated by its own goals of maximizing material happiness (social well-being) (Quinton 1989). The intrinsic linearity of the process by which commands and adaptation in the system now flow, causes each of the group-specific utilities to be ordinally scalar values of the other. The common factor in the preferences defining the agent-specific utilities is lineage to the most dominant exogenous preference assigned in the system. The social well-being concept now reverts to the concept of hegemonic convergence as discussed above.

Consequently, there exists no substantive difference between the two ways of viewing how decisions are made - either in an environment of compliance to the most dominant preference to which the system converges through mechanical convergence, or by way of independence of the decision-making but indirect dependence on the prescribed and dominant rule of the game. From neither of these aspects of decision-making within the OIC system can emerge the participatory concept of decentralization and democracy to guide the future transformation process of the *Ummah*. The loss of freedom and empowerment of the common people causes inertia in the human spirit to rise to higher levels of aspirations. The OIC as a developmental institution trapped in her hegemonic world-system, is then seen to be the cause and effect of the debilitating picture of the *Ummah's* future.

THE *SHURATIC* PROCESS ORIENTED TRANSFORMATION OF THE OIC SYSTEM

1. Empowerment by Participation

The negation of human development by the powers of hegemony and control, means the possibility of human prospects in the midst of an empowering and participatory future collectively established in and by the *Ummah*. This modality of reforming the future, takes us to the application of the *process* model of participatory decision-making, resource allocation, agent and sectorial and capital market and global interactions, all of which are conducted in the absence of any kind of hegemony and control.

What can that origin of politico-economic experience be? Any human system, be this democracy or other, leads to some form of hegemonic state. History is replete with the way that democracy has been used as a law of large numbers to support the most heinous acts. In this book we have shown that the unique way to liberate oneself and hence human institutions from the hegemonic authority, is the medium of anthropic discursions for deriving rules from sources that are truly Divine. These comprise the seat of the Universal Moral Law.

In Islam, this source is called the *Shari'ah* (Islamic Law), and the derivation and application by the consensus according to the epistemological sources of *Qur'an, Sunnah* and *Ijtehad*, comprise the *process* of the *Shura* in the widest range of its decentralization across domains of thought and organization. We have referred to this process in this book as the *Shuratic* Process. Its principal essence was to discover unification epistemology from the Precept of the Oneness of God and translate this episteme to understand and explain all systems big and small, according to the unification model of reality. The most distinctive mark of *Shari'ah* is its sole premise of the Precept of Unity (*Tawhid*) and the externalization of this precept in lived experience and thought through its comprehension and application based on human discursions to know (Field of Unity).

The OIC system can hope to attend to its goal of *Ummatic* transformation if it is ready to embrace the Unity premise of the *Shuratic* Process and apply this to all its functions. Matters of economic cooperation and customs union must then be reformulated according to the principle of regionally interlinked models that promote skill use, labour mobility, resource, technological, scientific and educational developments in accordance with the development regimes that are authenticated by the participants in the *Shuratic* Process. Examples of such regimes of choice are dynamic basic needs approaches to development; complementing technology existing in the Muslim world while upgrading these subsequently to higher levels of technological enhancement; and authentic socio-scientific development in accordance with the total picture of social well-being in whose domain, science, technology, society, economy and institutions must interconnect as systemic wholes.

2. Using *Zakah*, Islamic Wealth Tax as International Finance

Zakah is mandatory tax on the rich for the well-being of the poor at a flat rate of 2.5 percent of annual savings and material wealth that either exists in liquid form or is derivable from invested funds. There are also *Zakah* levies on jewellery, animal stocks, agricultural produce and the like. The *Qur'anic* injunction is to collect *Zakah* from the well-to-do whose savings in all forms exceed an allowable exemption (*Nisab*). *Zakah* funds so collected in organized form by the Islamic Central Treasury (*Bait al-Mal*) are spent for the well-being of the poor, needy, those in debt, wayfarers, orphans, ransom slaves, for kins and for the cause of Islam (*Qur'an,* Chapter 2 v. 177). These categories can be extended by analogy (Abu-Saud 1988).

In present times, *Zakah* can be seen as an important source for alleviating poverty and rehabilitating them by means of productive activities at the grass-roots. This use of *Zakah* for ameliorating the poor is today being actively pursued in Malaysia. In the international scene, the *Shuratic* nature of OIC must examine ways and means of integrating an international flow of *Zakah* for the uplift of the poor and in the direction of productively rehabilitating them. The use of *Zakah* now considered as a transfer of development resources, must be soundly integrated with the total Islamic financial transformation. Thus the endogenous treatment of money, interest-free banking, participatory institutions (*Mudarabah* and *Musharakah*) and financial instruments, are to be interactively integrated together toward channelling the *Zakah* funds through them for the well-being of the recipients. In this way, the recipients themselves become participants in determining the use of *Zakah* funds in microenterprises of their own making, thus increasing empowerment, entitlement and productive transformation at the grass-roots.

The comprehension and practice of human equality and its collective participation for establishing well-being, means the Islamic transformation from the state of methodological individualism to the state of systemic interconnectedness by means of invoking the only primordial Truth, that is, the Oneness of God. This is the surest way for liberating human conditions from the bondage of hegemony and coercive control. While this primordial premise forms the Precept of Unity, the emanating financial and development instruments discussed here, such as participatory institutions, *Zakah*, interest-free financial sector and endogenous money etc., form the instruments of realizing the moral attributes on which the Precept of Unity stands. Such instruments form the premise of the Field of Unity. Let then the Muslim citizens participate freely and fully in such a transformation process and let the future OIC system along with new perceptions, governance and value of membership, become a catalyst in this authentic human development process.

STRUCTURAL CHANGE OF THE OIC SYSTEM IN LIGHT OF THE *SHURATIC* PROCESS

The attributes of global interactions (*Ijtehad*), integration (consensus =*Ijma*) and creative evolution into higher levels of knowledge characterized by the knowledge-based circular causation and continuity model of unified reality, are to depict the change in the OIC structure. The various sister agencies of the OIC as shown in Figure 9.1, now become interactive on the basis of participation that springs from the consensus of the global participants in the *Ummah*. The hierarchies of decision-making are then circularly interacted. The various groups are further decentralized to carry decision-making to the microenterprise levels. They are then interacted with other echelons of decision-making to make the total process truly representative and creatively evolutionary in the areas of human development and social well-being.

Figure 9.2 now presents this alternative view of the OIC system as a politico-economic international organization guided by the *Shuratic* Process for the future well-being of the true *Ummah*. In Figure 9.2, the two-way arrows denote the hierarchically organized flows of interactions

225

among groups. In each of these hierarchical levels carried to the micro-level of the grass-roots, there are strings of *Shuras* that interconnect within the total system. The grass-roots and higher echelons of decision-making groups now integrate in loops of feedbacks (Choudhury 1994).

Figure 9.2: The Organization of Islamic Conferences in Light of the *Shuratic* Process.

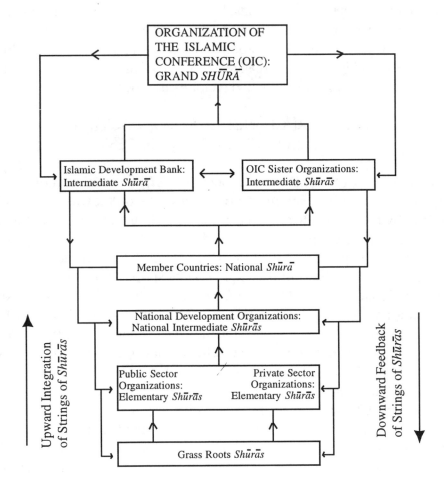

CHAPTER 10

POLICY CONCLUSION:
UMMATIC TRANSFORMATION

Three principal areas for reforming the Muslim world are to be pointed out in conclusion. These are as follows:

First, the Islamic institutions must change in favour of grass-roots orientation to development and participatory democracy. This needs transforming the OIC system and the present political milieu of the Muslim countries into *Shuratic* forms. The *Shuratic* Process must then be made to determine the political economy, institutions and scientific reconstruction of the Muslim people. The relationship of the Muslim world with the rest of the world must then be taken up in the same framework of the extension of the *Shuratic* Process respecting relationships with the global system.

The second principal area of reformation is to establish the infrastructure for the knowledge-based transformation in the educational curricula. Through this approach, a science-technology-society interface must be developed.

The third principal area of reformation is to establish a viable Islamic capital market system, well-coordinated and integrated in the Muslim world. On this basis, a comprehensive endogenous interrelationship among money and finance and goods would be made possible. The same capital market reorganization must be functional with the rest of the world.

- I-

HOW TO REALIZE SELF-RELIANCE?

The policy recommendation for reformation of the OIC system is now taken up and a redesign for OIC system is proferred. In Figure 10.1, the arrows indicate the flow of knowledge as cause and effect of interactions from one level to another of the total social system. Such interactions result in integration (consensus), which then is followed by evolution at reinforced levels. The process of interactions leading to integration and then followed by evolution in continuous cycles, is the essence of the *Shuratic* Process we have referred to in this book. Such a process emanates from the Divine Law of *Shari'ah*, from which the epistemology of the Islamic world-system is derived. The process that so emanates, defines the unification in the experiential universe, in which exist the interlinkages caused and reproduced by universal complementarity among possibilities. The circular flows of arrows in Figure 10.1 prove all these components of the *Shuratic* process.

The schema presented in Figure 10.1 points to the dire need for focus on economic, institutional and organizational aspects of development cooperation within the Muslim world in the first place. This alone in turn, will help develop self-reliance in the Muslim world and thus neutralize the military, political and economic deterrence of the West against the Muslim world. There remains little meaning in combating the technology and military might of the West by sheer armed conflict and confrontation. The politico-economic and socio-economic reorganizations of the Muslim world are centrally important because of their potential to help reallocate resources effectively within the Muslim countries and thus to empower themselves to sustain this state by means of appropriate policies on intercommunal cooperation, world trade, finance and pricing to their mutual benefit. From such a position onwards can arise the possibility to finance the defence and deterrence within the Muslim world.

228

On the other hand, the common claim by the Muslim world by popular demand of the people will legitimate the process of self-reliance, to which the West will have to submit on the basis of democratic legitimacy. In the post-Cold War period, wars are increasingly being replaced by trade, finance and diplomacy (Ihonvbbere 1992). That is where the Muslim world with its massive resources and with new organizational outlook must stand, if there is to be a future realization of the above kind of collective self-reliance leading to the rise of a future *Ummah*, the Islamic world-system, and its empowering forum of the Islamic Common Market (Islamic globalization). This indeed is the *Ummatic* transformation premised in the idea of *Khilafah,* the Divine vicegerency granted to the righteous by the *Shari'ah.*

The model given above also points to the gradual dissociation of the future *Ummah* from the political and development institutions of the West. This assertion should not be of any degree of alarm for the Muslims, after the sequence of defeating incidents that have been enacted upon them by Western institutions in Bosnia, Somalia, Iran, Iraq, and in the conflict between Islam and the West during the post-Cold War years. Such institutions are the United Nations, the Bretton Woods institutions and the regional economic integration and cooperation that are presently overshadowed by the growing presence of the Western presence. Among the latter ones are the Asia Pacific Economic Cooperation (APEC), the Association of South East Asian Economic Nations (ASEAN), the U.S. agenda for market-driven accelerated development of Sub-Saharan Africa (Institute of Development Studies Bulletin 1983), the brokering of an Israeli-PLO pact under the direction of the United States Government and the futile presence of Turkey in the North Atlantic Treaty Organization as an associate member. Each of these geo-political arrangements is a strategic power manifestation of the West upon Islamic change.

The question that needs to be investigated is how the dissociation can be phased in without abruptly causing political and economic disorder in

Figure 10. 1: The Blueprint of *Ummatic* Transformation.

Epistemology: *Qur'an, Sunnah*

↓

Deriving Content of Islamic World View: } *Shari'ah*
Ijtehad

↓

Developing Operational Rules: *Ahkam*
Impacting Upon the Total Social System

↓   ↓   ↓

Human Ecology:	Institutions:	Global Order:
Individual & Family	Government	*Ummatic*
Economy & Markets	Organizations	Other: This must
	Multinationals	be tacitly in
	Islamic movements	favour of
	microenterprises	Muslims.

↓   ↓   ↓

Unification Process: Interacting and Integrating Systemic
Preferences by Means of Appropriate *Ahkam*

↓   ↓   ↓

Internalization of	Internalization	Same as
Shari'ah in every	of *Shari'ah* in	the others
decision-making unit	every decision-	with emphasis
of human ecology.	making unit.	on the *Ummatic*
Education and Islamic	Education and	institutions.
value formation for	Islamic value	

developing capacity
to interact extensively:
Grass-roots dynamics

formation by
national development
cooperation:
establishing the
grass-roots
development process.

↓

Integrating the Grass-roots in the *Ummatic* Development Process: Economic Growth, Trade, Markets, Technology and Knowledge Formation to Enable Interactions Using *Shari'ah* at all levels: Ethicized Markets and *Ummatic* Development Cooperation, Policies and Programs, Activism and Change.

↓

The Islamic Global Order: *Shari'ah* Based Islamic Common Market with the Grass-roots Focus; Conscious Activism and Development of the Islamic Knowledge-Based World View.

← Evolution of the
   Shuratic Process

← ↓ →   Evolution of the →
              Shuratic Process

231

the Muslim world and between herself and the Western world? To examine this issue we have to understand that any move towards authentic Islamic change arising from the grass-roots in the Muslim world, will be vehemently opposed both by the hegemony of the West and the Muslim governments. This has been the nature of the opposition in recent times (Esposito 1994).

To phase in an authentic independence of the Muslim nations from the hegemonic political and economic grips of Western organizations, a national politico-economic change is mandatory. Here the grass-roots focus in the sense of its interactive and comprehensive hierarchy, becomes the engine of change. This is brought about, reinforced and driven by the knowledge basis of an authentically global Islamic transformation. Such a transformation is authentic by being epistemologically sound and definitely devoid of sheer emotions and polemics. That epistemological soundness means to centre the politico-economic transformation process in cooperation across indigenous technologies, resources development under the globally founded organization, that we termed in Figure 10.1 as the *Shuratic* Process. This presents the interactive, integrative and evolutionary process emanating from the systemic meaning of Islamic discursions (*Ijtehad*), herein called the process of *Shura* (universal consultation) premised on *Shari'ah*, the Islamic Law. Note here the supra-political nature of this process, which is at once a systemically politicizing process by virtue of the anthropic presence of God-Man-Universe interrelationship in science, organization and the world.

Since the power and prowess of the *Shuratic* Process depend upon the authentic Islamic change enabled by it, its relationship by cause and effect with the Western hegemonic arrangement will be inversely related. The growth of the *Shuratic* Process as a comprehensive world view in all parts of the *Ummah* must then be essential. This also means the knowledge-centred interactive-integrative process of Islam, which emanates directly from the *Qur'an* and is explicated by the *Sunnah* must remain fundamental in all issues of science and political economy.

The OIC with her sister organizations would thus be transformed along with the change in attitudes of existing Muslim nations toward collective self-reliance rather than hegemony and dependence. Such a change would carry with it both the organizational and technological re-thinking in the appropriate sense of the Islamic world view. It is indeed the resulting economic power by control and self-determination by the Muslim nations through their own order of regionally linked economic cooperations, that can enable the basis for the scientific, technological and politico-economic change. It is to be noted from the arguments presented in this chapter that any possibility toward neutralizing the military, economic and political dominance of the West over the Muslim world and affairs, is a matter of collective self-reliance of the grass-roots type invoked as an extensively interactive knowledge-centred process of comprehensive transformation.

In the meantime, before that final determination for self-reliance is effectively realized, the Muslim nations are to use such technologies from the West that are appropriate and adaptive for their transformation. Tech-nologies will be such that dependence on them must not be entrenched for the long haul. They must be easily replaceable by indigenous tech-nologies of the Islamic world advanced through integration in the medium run. The upgrading of intermediate technologies to more ad-vanced ones should lead to steady and self-reliant economic growth. Fur-thermore, in all such transformation process, the Principle of Universal Complementarity is to be applied.

In cases where the know-how does not presently exist in the Muslim world, as in the case with computerizing an algorithm for the interactive-integrative-evolutionary model for explaining science and technology in the *Shuratic* mould, a learning process is to be generated with scientists and technologists of the Muslim world and the Western world. Such levels of learning must always exist as the global dispensations of Islam to mankind. Hence there need not be segregation on this front. The focus and leadership of the Islamic inputs through cooperative efforts globally

233

in all authentic learning processes, must remain intrinsic to the meaningful Muslim-West relationship. This view is reflected in Figure 10.1 by means of the interconnections between the Muslin world and the other world. This kind of relationship must continue on knowledge-centred endeavours. The intellectual sharing is essential for the future realization of the *Ummah*.

It remains urgent for Muslim nations to transform into an *Ummah*. This new concept of the globalizing process necessitates shaping of the *Ummatic* transformation on grounds of the comprehensive knowledge-centred world view that is caused and driven by the Principle of Universal Complementarity, earlier referred to. This is also the practical expression of the unification process that derives its epistemology from Divine Unity (*Tawhid*).

- II -

TOWARDS ATTAINING SCIENCE-TECHNOLOGY-SOCIETY INTERFACE BY MEANS OF THE METHODOLOGY OF UNIFICATION EPISTEMOLOGY

Next we will summarize the recommendations in favour of realizing an educational transformation toward realizing the knowledge-based world view of the *Shuratic* Process in all areas of learning and science-technology-society interface. The model underlying the knowledge-based world view is the same as the circular causation and continuity model of unified reality that we have presented in this book.

1. The emergence of a study of circular causation and continuity model of unified reality in the framework of unification epistemology requires the introduction and conscious pursuit of an academic program and curricula reflecting substantive interdisciplinarity.

2. The goal of attaining substantive interdisciplinarity must aim at the development of courses or using existing ones in educational institutions

that can well integrate within the framework of delivering a whole program on unification epistemology and its application in various disciplines.

3. Such a program and curricula must be formulated at the introductory and advanced methodological levels, both being orientated toward understanding and applying unification epistemology in problems interfacing science-technology-society.

4. The orientation of the science-technology-society interdisciplinary program and curricula must be to integrate unification epistemology, methodology and its application in the natural and social sciences and humanities.

5. The conceptual and methodological levels of the program and curricula are to be at increasing depths in those methods that can be used and developed for computer algorithmic virtual reality of the simulations of relations in the interactive-integrative-evolutionary models.

6. Such a technique is to be made a marketable product in the knowledge-based markets of this information age.

7. Such computer applications of the methodology of circular causation and continuity model of unified reality are to be applied in laboratory experiments in the natural sciences both at the theoretical and applied levels to generate integrated scientific, technological and social realities.

8. Similar applications are to be carried out for policy-theoretic analysis of social, economic and institutional issues.

9. The academic programs and curricula on unification epistemology under the framework of the methodology of circular causation and continuity model of unified reality are to be interactively developed across institutions of higher learning. In the Muslim World today, there is an increasing number of Islamic research and training institutions. International Islamic universities have been established. These will provide the venue for learning the methodology suggested here.

- III -

DEVELOPMENT OF INDIGENOUS CAPITAL MARKET

The third area of Muslim reformation is development of an indigenous capital market in the Muslim world. A good choice would be to expand the Islamic capital market window at the Kuala Lumpur Stock Exchange with branches in all other stock markets in the Muslim countries. The latter could be coordinated by the Islamic banks and financial institutions.

On this front, it would be imperative for the Muslim world to combine an academic understanding of the endogenous concept of money, finance and markets to make the applications possible. There must be vigorous interface among academicians and practitioners to understand the idea of endogenous money and bring such a financial medium to application in an Islamic capital market. Towards attaining the above-mentioned goals of an Islamic capital market the following recommendations are offered here:

1. The academic pursuit of intellectuals, practitioners from banks, financial institutions and Governments of the Muslim world can start up from the existing dual system of endogenous and exogenous monetary and financial systems. But the focus must be towards fast transforming into the former, in which case all interest transactions and enterprises that depend upon interest transactions, will be replaced by profit-sharing instruments.

2. The conceptualization and construction of the monetary base, financial organization, balance of payments accounting and financial organizations, must be accordingly changed to reflect the new basis of valuation with endogenous money, in which the returns on money are reflected in the profitability of real goods transactions.

3. Serious efforts must be launched in such academic and practical directions of formulating the financial system in terms of endogenous

236

monetary base. This would take the form of conferences, workshops, advisory capacity among intellectuals, practitioners and other groups.

4. In the global economy, mutual consultation among all financial sectors is essential, but the leadership must come from the Muslim world taking bold steps toward realizing the future *Shuratic* transformation in general. The essence of the *Shuratic* Process is now specifically introduced into the monetary domain by cause and effect of the Islamic monetary, financial and market oriented economic integration and cooperation in the Muslim world.

CONCLUSION

In conclusion, reforming the Muslim world is a serious undertaking on a total transformation of thought, learning and institutions in the Muslim world in accordance with the substantive world view of the *Shuratic* Process. This is an epistemology, a methodology and a model of scientific theory and practical application on all fronts. Its theory and applications have been established in this book in terms of the primal reference to unification epistemology (*Tawhidi* epistemology) and its externalization to thought, experience and the world. At the end, the reformation as a transformation process must comprehend a global knowledge-based outlook. In this regard, the central and most urgent pursuits are as follows:

1. A well-integrated academic program and curricula development would have to establish increasing interactions with the mainstream courses and disciplines, so that more and more of such courses and programs are transformed into the curricula and programs dealing with the methodology of the interactive-integrative-evolutionary model of the *Qur'anic* world view.

2. At the progressive levels of program and curricula development the methodology of circular causation and continuity model of unified reality

237

and its applications are to be divulged to businesses and governments at large.

3. This popularization of the academic program and courses based on the circular causation methodology (equivalently interactive-integrative-evolutionary model) must take place by means of publications in periodicals, journals, books, demonstration of computer algorithms based on the circular causation and continuity model of unified reality, seminars, workshops and conferences.

4. At a well-developed stage, the introduction of the program and curricula on substantive interdisciplinarity must become a central focus of the national post-secondary educational policy.

5. This completeness of the academic program along with its interface among scientists, businesses and policy makers at all levels in the Muslim world, is to be simultaneously expanded by its externalization to the world scientific community.

NOTES AND REFERENCES

INTRODUCTION

al-Umari, A.D. 1991 (trans. Khattab, H.), **Madinan Society at the Time of the Prophet, Vols I and II** (Herndon, VA: International Institute of Islamic Thought) Note particularly the controversies that this author points out in Chapter 10. We for our arguments on the Essence and not simply the outer details of the Madinah Charter take it to be associated with the experience of the Prophet Muhammad during his celestial flight to the knowledge-realm of *Sidrathul Muntaha*, as quoted in the *Qur'an*. Much more on this topic is developed by the author. See Choudhury, M.A. 1995, **The Epistemological Foundations of Islamic Economic, Social and Scientific Order**, Vol. 6, Chapter 9: The Madinah Charter, *Sidrathan Muntaha* and the Precept of the 'Seven Heavens' (Ankara, Turkey: Statistical, Economic and Social Research and Training Centre for Islamic Countries).

Berggren, J.L. 1992, "Islamic Acquisition of the Foreign Sciences: A Cultural Perspective", **The American Journal of Islamic Social Sciences**, Vol. 9, No. 3, Fall, pp. 310-24.

Boisard, M.A. 1988, **Humanism in Islam** (Indianapolis, IN: American trust Publications).

Choudhury, M.A. 1995, **The Epistemological Foundations of Islamic Economic, Social and Scientific Order**, in six volumes plus Glossary (Ankara, Turkey: Statistical, Economic and Social Research and Training Centre for Islamic Countries).

----- 1993, **The Unicity Precept and the Socio-Scientific Order** (Lanham, MD: University Press of America) Chapter 6: "Toward a General Theory of Islamic Social Contract".

Crocker, L.G. (trans.) 1967 [1762], **Jean-Jacques Rousseau The Social Contract and Discourse on the Origin of Inequality** (New York, NY: Pocket Books).

Hammond, M. Howarth, J. & Keat, R. 1991, **Understanding Phenomenology** (Oxford, U.K.: Basil Blackwell).

Huntington, S.P. 1993, "The Clash of Civilizations?" **Foreign Affairs**, Summer.

Husserl, E. 1965, **Phenomenology and the Crisis of Philosophy** trans. Lauer, Q. (New York, NY: Harper & Row Publishers). Husserl wrote (trans. Lauer, Q) p. 155: Blinded by naturalism, the practitioners of humanistic science have completely neglected even to pose the problem of a universal and pure science of spirit and to speak of a theory of the essence of spirit as spirit, a theory that pursues what is unconditionally universal in the spiritual order with its own elements and its own laws. Yet this last should be done with a view to gaining thereby scientific explanations in an absolutely conclusive sense. (Author edited.)

----- 1970, **The Crisis of European Sciences and Transcendental Phenomenology** trans. Carr, D. (Evanston, Il: Northwestern University Press).

Kolb, D. 1986, **The Critique of Pure Modernity, Hegel, Heidegger and After** (Chicago, Il: The University of Chicago Press) Chapter 4: "Categories for Modernity". A typical ignorance of the Islamic world view of change and progress against individualism, is to be found in Kolb's comment: "One common understanding of progress and development urges the creation or liberation of something like a pure personal individuality and a pure human society... Throughout the world there are reassertions of tradition and reactions against modernization.... I am not thinking just of such strongly antimodern movements as those in the Islamic world." (p. 5).

Mahdi, M. 1964, **Ibn Khaldun's Philosophy of History, A Study in the Philosophic Foundations of the Science of Culture** (Chicago, Il: The University of Chicago Press).

Makkreel, R.A. 1990, **Imagination and Interpretation in Kant** (Chicago, Il: The University of Chicago Press) Chapter 2: The "Figurative Synthesis of Experience and the Meaning of Experience".

Mazrui, A.A. 1993, "Islam and the End of History", **The American Journal of Islamic Social Sciences**, Vol. 10, No.4, Winter, pp. 512-35.

Nasr, S.H. 1978, **An Introduction to Islamic Cosmological Doctrines** (Boulder, CO: Shambhala) Part I.

Parson, T. 1964, **The Structure of Social Action** (New York, NY: The Free Press of Glencoe) pp. 60-84.

Schleifer, A. 1985, "Ibn Khaldun's Theories of Perception, Logic and Knowledge: An Islamic Phenomenology", **American Journal of Islamic Social Sciences**, Vol. 2, No.2, pp. 225-31.

240

The Holy Qur'an, Text, Translation and Commentary (A. Yusuf Ali) (Brentwood, Maryland, U.S.A.: Amana Corporation, 1989, reprinted).

CHAPTER 1: THE EPISTEMOLOGICAL PREMISE OF REFORMATION

Bartley, W.W. 1988, "Theories of Rationality", in **Evolutionary Epistemology, Rationality, and the Sociology of Knowledge**, Radnitzky, G. & Bartley, W.W. eds. (La Salle, Il: Open Court) pp. 205-14.

Choudhury, M.A. 1995a, **The Epistemological Foundations of Islamic Economic, Social and Scientific Order, 6 Vols** (Ankara, Turkey: Statistical, Economic and Social Research and Training Centre for Islamic Countries).

----- 1995b, "The Process-Centred Worldview", **Proceedings of the Pakistan Academy of Sciences**, Vol. 32. pp. 123-26.

Daly, H.E. 1991, "From Empty-World to Full-World Economies: Recognizing a Historical Turning Point in Economic Development", in **Environmentally Sustainable Economic Development: Building on Brundtland**, Goodland, R. Daly, H. el-Serafy, S. & von Droste, B. eds. (Paris, France: UNESCO) pp. 29-38.

Hawking, S.W. 1988, **A Brief History of Time** (New York, NY: Bantam Books).

Maddox, I.J. 1970, **Elements of Functional Analysis** (Cambridge, Eng.: Cambridge at the University Press)

Neurath, O. 1970, "Foundations of the Social Sciences", in **Foundations of the Unity of Science, Vol. 2**, Neurath, O. Carnap, R. & Morris, C. eds. (Chicago, Il: University of Chicago Press) pp. 1-51.
This Vienna School laid the way for logical positivism as the groundwork for unification in the sciences. Consequently, this limited view of material unification did not yield abiding results. The same limitation is found in Einstein's field theory in theoretical physics. It is found today in the problems of unifying the forces of nature in Grand Unified Theory (GUT).

CHAPTER 2: THE SCIENTIFIC PREMISE OF REFORMATION

Bakar, O. 1991, **Tawhid and Science** (Penang, Malaysia: Secretariat for Islamic Philosophy and Science).

Choudhury, M.A. (forthcoming), **Studies in Islamic Social Sciences** (London, Eng.: Macmillan & New York, NY: St. Martin's Press).

----- 1995a, **The Epistemological Foundations of Islamic Economic, Social and Scientific Order, 6 Vols** (Ankara, Turkey: Statistical, Economic and Social Research and Training Centre for Islamic Countries).

----- 1995b, **Islamic Socio-Scientific Order and World System** (Penang, Malaysia: Secretariat for Islamic Philosophy and Science).

----- 1995c, "A Systems Model of the Malaysian Macroeconomy", **Kybernetes: The International Journal of Systems and Cybernetics**, Vol. 24, No. 7, pp. 75-90.

----- 1994, "The Epistemic-Ontic Circular Causation and Continuity Model of Unified Reality: The Knowledge Premise", **International Journal of Social Economics**, Vol. 21, No.1, pp. 3-18.

----- 1993a, **The Unicity Precept and the Socio-Scientific Order** (Lanham, MD: University Press of America) pp. 49-88.

----- 1993b, **Comparative Development Studies: In Search of the World View** (London, Eng.: Macmillan & New York, NY: St. Martin's Press).

Choudhury, M.A., Malik, U.A. & Adnan, M.A. (eds.) 1996, **Alternative Perspectives of Third-World Development: The Case of Malaysia** (London, Eng.: Macmillan & New York, NY: St. Martin's Press).

Descartes R. 1952, "Discourse on the Method of Rightly Conducting the Reason", in **Great Books of the Western World** (London, Eng.; Encyclopedia Britannica).

Einstein, A. 1949, quoted in **Albert Einstein: Philosopher-Scientist** P.A. Schilpp ed. (LaSalle, Il: Open Court).

----- (trans. Lawson, R.W.) 1954a, **Relativity, The Special and the General Theory** (London, Eng.: Methuen).

----- 1954b, "The Problem of Space, Ether, and the Field in Physics", in Commins, S. & Linscott eds. **Man and the Universe: The Philosophers of Science** (New York, NY. Pocket Books) pp. 173-84.

Faris, N.A. 1991, **The Book of Knowledge** (Being a Translation with Notes of *The Kitab al-'Ilm* of Al-Ghazzali's **Ihya' `Ulum Al-Din** (Lahore, Pakistan: Sh. Muhammad Ashraf).

Faruqi, B.A. 1977, **The Mujadid's Conception of *Tawhid*** (Delhi, India: Idarah-i-Adabiyat-i-Delhi) pp. 45-84.

Friedrich C.J. 1949, **The Philosophy of Kant - Immanuel Kant's Moral and Political Writings** (New York, NY: The Modern Library).

Hammond, M. Howarth, J. Keat, R. 1991, **Understanding Phenomenology** (Oxford, UK.: Basil Blackwell).

Hassan, M.A. 1992, **The *Tawhidic* Approach in Management and Public Administration** (Kuala Lumpur, Malaysia: National Institute of Public Administration) pp. 59-82.

Hawking, S.W. 1988, **A Brief History of Time, From the Big Bang to Black Holes** (New York, NY: Bantam Books).

Hegel, G.W.F. (trans. Sibree, J.) 1956, **The Philosophy of History** (New York, NY: Dover Publications, Inc.).

Holton, G. 1979, "Einstein's Model for Constructing a Scientific Theory", in Aichelburg, P.C. & Sexl, R.U. eds. **Albert Einstein: His Influence on Physics, Philosophy and Politics** (Weisbaden: Friedr. Vieweg & Sohn).

----- 1975, **Thematic Origins of Scientific Thought** (Cambridge, MA: Harvard University Press).

243

Hume, D. 1992, **Treatise on Human Nature**, Book I (Buffalo, NY: Prometheus Books).

Infield, L. 1963, **Immanuel Kant - Lectures on Ethics** (Indianapolis, IN: Hackett Publishing Co.).

Intrilligator, M.D. 1971, **Mathematical Optimization and Economic Theory** (Englewood Cliffs, N.J.: Prentice-Hall, Inc.).

Karim, F. undated, **Imam Ghazzali's Ihya Ulum-Id-Din Vol.1: The Book of Worship** (Lahore, Pakistan: Sh. Muhammad Ashraf Press).

Kuhn, T.S. 1970, **The Structure of Scientific Revolutions**, in Vol. 2 of **International Encyclopedia of Unified Science** (Chicago, Il: University of Chicago Press).

Leibniz, (trans. Ariew, R. & Garber, D.) 1989, **Philosophical Essays** (Indianapolis, IN: Hackett).

Marcuse, H. 1964, **One Dimensional Man** (London, Eng.: Routledge & Kegan Paul).

Paton, H.J. (trans.) 1964, **Immanuel Kant - Groundwork of the Metaphysic of Morals** (New York, NY: Harper & Row Publishers).

Popper, K.R. 1963, **Conjectures and Refutations** (London, Eng.: Routledge & Kegan Paul).

Smith, T.S. 1992, **Strong Interactions** (Chicago, Il: University of Chicago Press).

Stigler, G.L. 1967, "The Nature and Role of Originality in Scientific Progress", in **Essays in the History of Economics** (Chicago, Il: The University of Chicago Press) p. 12.

Welldon, J.E.C. trans. 1987, **Aristotle's The Nicomachean Ethics**, Book I (Buffalo, NY: Prometheus Books).

Whitehead, A.N. (edited) Griffin, D.R. & Sherburne, D.W. 1979, **Process and Reality** (New York, NY: The Free Press).

CHAPTER 3: THE SOCIO-SCIENTIFIC PREMISE OF REFORMATION: FROM MODERNITY TO POST-MODERNITY

[Imam] Al-Ghazzali, (trans. Karim, M.F.) 1982, **Ihya Ulum-id-Din, Vol.1: The Book of Worship** (New Delhi, India: Kitab Bhavan).

[Imam] Al-Shatibi, undated, **Al-Muwafaqat Fi Usul Al-Shari'ah** (Cairo, Egypt: Abdallah Draz Al-Maktabah Al-Tijariyyah Al-Kubra).

Asad, M. 1984, **The Message of the** *Qur'an* (Gibraltar: Dar al- Andalus). Asad comments on the Prophetic experience of *Sidrathul Muntaha* as given in the *Qur'an* (Chapter 53, v. 9-11); see footnote 10: On the occasion of his mystic experience of the 'Ascension' (*mi'raj*). Explaining the vision conveyed in the expression *sidrat al-muntaha*, Raghib suggests that owing to the abundance of its leafy shade, the *sidr* or *sidrah* (the Arabian Lote tree) appears in the *Qur'an* as well as in the Traditions relating to the Ascension as a symbol of the 'shade' - i.e. the spiritual peace and fulfilment - of paradise.

Barrow, J.D. 1991, **Theories of Everything, the Quest for Ultimate Explanation** (Oxford, Eng.: Oxford University Press).

Bayrakli, B. 1992, "The Concept of Justice (A'dl) in the Philosophy of Al-Farabi", **Hamdard Islamicus**, Vol. V, No. 3, Autumn).

Bennington, G. & Young, R. 1990, "Introduction: Posing the Question", in Attridge, D. Bennington, G. & Young, R. (eds.) **Post-Structuralism and the Question of History** (Cambridge, Eng.: Cambridge University Press).

Bohr, N. 1985, "Discussions with Einstein on Epistemological Issues", in Folse, H. **The Philosophy of Niels Bohr: The Framework of Complementarity** (Amsterdam: North Holland Physics Publishing).

Breuer, R. 1991, **The Anthropic Principle, Man as the Focal Point of Nature** (Boston, MA; Birkhauser).

Buchanan, J. & Tullock, G. 1962, **The Calculus of Consent** (Ann Arbor, Michigan: Michigan University Press).

Callaghy, T.R. 1993, "Visions and Politics in the Transformation of Global Political Economy: Lessons from the Second and Third World", in R.O. Slater, B.M. Schutz & S.R. Dorr (eds.) **Emerging Global Economic Interdependence** (Boulder, CO: Lynne Rienner).

Childers, E. & Urquhart, B. 1994, "Renewing the United Nations System", **Development Dialogue**, Vol.1, pp. 77-86.

Chittick, W.C. 1989, **Sufi Path of Knowledge** (Albany, NY: State University of New York).

Choudhury, M.A. 1996, "Why Cannot Neo-Classicism Explain Resource Allocation and Growth in Islamic Political Economy?", in E. Ahmed ed. **Islamic Perspectives on Economic Growth and Privatization** (Herndon, VA: The International Institute of Islamic Thought) pp. 17-44.

----- 1995, "Ethics and Economics: A View from Ecological Economics", **International Journal of Social Economics**, Vol. 22, No.2, pp. 40-60.

----- 1994a, "Islamization of Knowledge", **Journal of the Faculty of Islamic Studies and Arabic** (University of Peshawar), Vol. No.2, pp. 168-215.

----- 1994b, "The Concept of Sustainable Development: From Rio to Ethics", **Malaysian Economic Journal**, Vol. 28, Dec. pp. 69-92.

----- 1994c, "The Concept of Substantive Interdisciplinarity in Curriculum Development", **Intisari**, University Kebangsaan Malaysia, Sept.

----, 1993a, **Comparative Development Studies: In Search of the World View** (London, Eng.: Macmillan and New York, NY: St. Martin's Press).

----- 1993b, **The Unicity Precept and the Socio-Scientific Order** (Lanham, MD: The University Press of America) discusses some aspects of the utilitarian groundings in the topic of *Maslaha*, Chapter 6, pp. 105-48.

----- 1990, "Islamic Economics as a Social Science", **International Journal of Social Economics**, Vol. 17, No. 6, pp. 35-59.

246

Dampier, W.C. 1961, "Scientific Philosophy and Its Outlook", in **A History of Science and Its Relations with Philosophy and Religions** (Cambridge, Eng.: Cambridge at the University Press).

Davies, P. & Gribbin, J. 1992, **The Matter Myth** (New York, NY: Simon & Schuster) p. 26.

Dodd, D.H. & White Jr. R.M. 1980, **Cognition, Mental Structures and Processes**, Boston, MA: Allyn & Bacon, Inc.). A definition of cognition in cognitive forms is as follows: "The objective of Skinner's approach is the prediction and control of behavior. The theory explains human cognition in terms of functional connections between environmental conditions stimulating the organism and some resulting behavior."

The Economist, "Living With Islam", April 4-10, 1992.

Ekins, P. 1992, **A New World Order, Grassroots Movements for Global Change** (London, Eng.: Routledge).

Esposito, J.L. 1992, **The Islamic Threat: Myth or Reality?** (New York, NY: Oxford University Press).

Fukuyama, F. 1992, **The End of History and the Last Man** (New York, NY: The Free Press).

Giddens, A. 1983, **A Contemporary Critique of Historical Materialism** (Berkeley, CA: University of California Press).

Hawking, S.W. 1988, **A Brief History of Time** (New York, NY: Bantam Books, 1988) says, "The eventual goal of science is to provide a single theory that describes the whole universe." (p. 10).

Holton, G. 1975, **Thematic Origins of Scientific Thought** (Cambridge, MA: Harvard University Press).

Hubner, K. 1983, "Foundations of a Universal Historistic Theory of the Empirical Sciences", in **A Critique of Scientific Reason** (Chicago, Il: University of Chicago Press).

247

Hume, D. 1992. "Part I: Of the Understanding", in **Treatise of Human Nature** (Buffalo, New York: Prometheus Books, reprinted).

Huntington, S.P. 1993, "The Clash of Civilizations?" **Foreign Affairs**, Summer.

Kant, I. (trans. C.J. Friedrich) 1977, "Metaphysical Foundations of Morals", in **The Philosophy of Kant** (New York, NY: The Modern Library, reprinted).

Maddox, I.J. 1970, **Elements of Functional Analysis** (Cambridge, Eng.: Cambridge University Press).

Mahdi, M. 1964, **Ibn Khaldun's Philosophy of History** (Chicago, Il: University of Chicago Press).

Masud, M.K. 1984, **Islamic Legal Philosophy** (Islamabad, Pakistan: Islamic Research Institute).

Minford, P. & Peel, D. 1983, "The Political Economy of Democracy", in **Rational Expectations and the New Macroeconomics** (Oxford, Eng.: Martin Robertson & Co.).

S. Moussalli, 1990, "Syed Qutb's View of Knowledge", **American Journal of Islamic Social Sciences**, Vol. 7, No. 3, pp. 315-33.

Nagel, E. 1961, "The Reduction of Theories", in **The Structure of Science, Problems in the Logic of Scientific Explanation** (New York, NY: Harcourt, Brace & World, Inc.).

Rozenthal, F. 1958, trans. in 3 volumes, Ibn Khaldun's **The Muqaddimah: An Introduction to History** (London, Eng.: Routledge & Kegan Paul).

Schumpeter, J.A. 1968, "The Scholastic Doctors and the Philosophers of Natural Law", in **A History of Economic Analysis** (New York, NY: Oxford University Press).

Sherover, C.M. 1972, **Heidegger, Kant and Time** (Bloomington, IN: Indiana University Press).

Skinner, B.F. 1957, **Verbal Behavior** (New York, NY: Appleton-Century-Crofts).

Smith, H. 1989, **Beyond the Post-Modern Mind** (New York, NY: Crossroads).

Welldon, J.E.C. trans. 1987, **Aristotle, The Nicomachean Ethics, Book I** (Buffalo, New York: Prometheus Books).

White, H. 1989, "New Historicism", in Veeser, H.A. (ed.) **The New Historicism** (New York, NY: Routledge).

Wisman, J.D. 1990, "Beyond Foundationalism and Relativism: What Hope for Sciences of Society?", **Humanomics**, Vol. 6, No. 2.

Wordsworth, A. 1990, "Derrida and Foucault: Writing the History of Historicity", in **Post-Structuralism and the Question of History**, op cit.

CHAPTER 4: THE POLITICAL ECONOMY OF REFORMATION

Abu-Rabi, I.M. 1990, "Beyond the Post-Modern Mind", **The American Journal of Islamic Social Sciences**, Vol. 7, No. 2.

Bank Islam Malaysia 1994, **1994 Annual Report** (Kuala Lumpur, Malaysia).

Becker, G. 1989, "Family", in J. Eatwell, M. Milgate & P. Newman (eds.) **Social Economics, The New Palgrave** (New York, NY: W.W. Norton) p. 72.

Berman, H.J. 1989, "Beyond Marx, Beyond Weber", in H.B. McCullough (ed.) **Political Ideologies and Political Philosophies** (Toronto, Ont.: Wall & Thompson) pp. 144-47.

Bowles, S. 1991, "What Markets Can - and Cannot - Do", **Challenge**, Vol. 34, No. 4, July/Aug; pp. 11-16.

Chittick, W.J. 1989, **Sufi Path of Knowledge** (Albany, NY: State University of New York Press).

Choudhury, M.A. 1995, "Epistemological Questions of Science and Political Economy: Between Islam and the Occident", **Islamic Thought and Scientific Creativity**, Vol. 6, No. 1, pp. 29-48.

----- 1994, "A Critique of Modernist Synthesis in Islamic Thought with Special Reference to Political Economy", **The American Journal of Islamic Social Sciences**, Vol. 11, No. 4, Winter, pp. 475-503.

Drucker, P.F. 1993, **Post-Capitalist Society** (New York, NY: Harper Collins Publishers, Inc.) pp. 181-210.

----- 1989, **The New Realities** (New York, NY: Harper & Row Publishers, Inc.) pp. 232-52.

Ferry, L. & Renault, A. (trans. F. Phillip) 1992, **From the Rights of Man to the Republican Idea** (Chicago, Il: University of Chicago Press) Ch. 4: "The Division of Society and the State as a Value: Liberalism and Human Rights." Also see Chapter 2.

Foucault, M. trans. A.M. Sheridan, 1972, **The Archaeology of Knowledge and the Discourse on Language** (New York, NY: Harper Torchbooks).

Fukuyama, F. 1992, **The End of History and the Last Man** (New York, NY: The Free Press) pp.181-91.

Government of Malaysia, 1991, **The Second Outline Perspective Plan 1991-2000** (Kuala Lumpur, Malaysia 1991).

Hammond, P.J. 1987, "On Reconciling Arrow's Theory of Social Choice with Harsanyi's Fundamental Utilitarianism", in G.R. Feiwel (ed.) **Arrow and the Foundations of the Theory of Economic Policy** (London, Eng.: Macmillan Press Ltd.).

Hayek, F.A. 1976, **Law, Legislation and Liberty, the Mirage of Social Justice, 2** (Chicago, Il: The University of Chicago Press).

----, 1967, **Studies in Philosophy, Politics and Economics** (Chicago, Il: Chicago University Press).

Hegel, G.W.F. trans. J. Sibree, 1956, **The Philosophy of History** (New York, NY: Dover Publications).

Notes and References

Holton, R.J. 1992, **Economy and Society** (London, Eng.: Routledge) pp. 259-62.

Howard, D. 1985, **From Marx to Kant** (Albany, NY: State University of New York) pp. 1-47.

Hubner, C. Trans. Dixon, P.R. Jr. & Dixon, H.M. 1983, **A Critique of Scientific Reason** (Chicago, Il: University of Chicago Press) pp. 105-24.

Iqbal, M. 1934, **Reconstruction of Religious Thought in Islam** (Oxford University Press).

Karim, F. trans. undated, **Imam Ghazzali's Ihya Ulum-Id-Din, 4 Vols.** (Lahore, Pakistan: Shah Muhammad Ashraf Press).

Lombardini, S. 1989, "Market and Institution", in T. Shiraishi & S. Tsuru (eds.) **Economic Institutions in a Dynamic Society** (London, Eng.: Macmillan Press, Ltd.).

Maddox, I.J. 1970, **Elements of Functional Analysis** (Cambridge, Eng.: Cambridge University Press).

Ma'sumi, A.H.M. 1974, **Al Razi's Mufassira** (Baghdad, Iraq: Dar al Harriyah).

Minford, P. & Peel, D. 1983, "The Political Economy of Democracy, Nordhaus Model", in **Rational Expectations and the New Macroeconomics** (Oxford, Eng.: Martin Robertson & Co.).

Myrdal, G. (trans. P. Streeten) 1953, **The Political Element in the Development of Economic Theory** (London, Eng.: Routledge & Kegan Paul).

Nasr, S.H. 1978, **An Introduction to Islamic Cosmological Doctrines** (Boulder, CO: Shambala).

Nozick, R. 1974, **Anarchy, State and Utopia** (Oxford, Eng.: Blackwell).

Polanyi, K. 1944, **The Great Transformation** (New York, NY: Rinehart).

Popkin, S.L. 1979, **The Rational Peasant: The Political Economy of Rural Vietnam** (Berkeley, CA: University of California Press).

Rawls, J. 1971, **A Theory of Justice** (Cambridge, MA: Harvard University Press).

Reichenbach, H. trans. M. Reichenbach & J. Freund, 1958, **The Philosophy of Space & Time** (New York, NY: Dover).

Resnick, S.A. & Wolff, R.D. 1987, **Knowledge and Class, A Marxian Critique of Political Economy** (Chicago, Il: University of Chicago Press) pp. 1-37.

Rousseau, J-J. (trans. M. Cranston) 1968, **The Social Contract** (London, Eng.: Penguin Books) p. 71.

Schumpeter, J.A. 1934, **Theory of Economic Development** (Cambridge, MA: Harvard University Press) Ch. II: "The Fundamental Phenomenon of Economic Development".

[Imam] Shatibi undated, **Al-Muwafaqat fi Usul al-Shari'ah** (Cairo, Egypt: Abdallah Draz al-Maktabah al-Tijariyah al-Qubra).

Staniland, M. 1985, **What is Political Economy? A Study of Social Theory and Underdevelopment** (New Haven, CO: Yale University Press).

Steiner, H. 1989, "Entitlements", in **Social Economics**, pp. 40-4.

Sullivan, W.M. 1989, "The Contemporary Crisis of Liberal Society", in **Political Ideologies and Political Philosophies**, pp. 57-9.

Taylor, O.H. 1967, "The Future of Economic Liberalism", in **Economics and Liberalism** (Cambridge, MA: Cambridge University Press) pp. 294-311.

Viederman, S. 1993, "Sustainable Development: What Is It and How Do We Get There?", **Current History**, April. pp. 180-85.

Wallerstein, I. 1989, **The Modern World-System III** (New York, NY: Academic Press, Inc.) p. 256 & Ch. 1.
In this work Wallerstein traces the early development of capitalism in Western organization within the Western World and in her relationship with trading nations. This seemingly capitalist relationship in the Western World instituted her world-system.

-----, **The Modern World-System I**, Ch. 7.

CHAPTER 5: THE INSTITUTIONAL BASIS OF REFORMATION: ORGANIZATIONAL THEORY OF THE FIRM

Arrow, K.J. 1971, **Essays in the Theory of Risk-Bearing** (Chicago, Il: Markham).

Chapra, M.U. 1985, **Towards a Just Monetary System** (Leicester, Eng.: The Islamic Foundation).

Choudhury, M.A. 1995a, **The Epistemological Foundations of Islamic Economic, Social and Scientific Order, 6 Vols** (Ankara, Turkey: Statistical, Economic and Social Research and Training Centre for Islamic Countries, Organization of Islamic Conferences). The work derives the circular causation and continuity model of unified reality from the *Qur'an*, treats *Akhira* as a scientifically functional reality and derives the theories of topological time and supercardinality, among others.

----- 1995b, "A Theory of Renewal and Continuity in Islamic Science", **International Journal of New Ideas**, Vol. IV, No. 1, pp. 69-84.

----- 1994a, "The Muslim Republics of the CIS: Their Political Economy under Communism, Capitalism and Islam", in John C. O'Brien ed. **The Evils of Soviet Communism and Other Critical Essays: Part II** (Bradford, Eng.: MCB University Press) being the Special Volume 21, No. 5/6 of **International Journal of Social Economics**.

----- 1994b, **Economic Theory and Social Institutions** (Lanham, MD: University Press of America).

----- 1993a, "A Generalised Theory of Islamic Development Finance", **Managerial Finance: Topics in Development Finance**, Vol. 19, No. 7, pp. 47-69.

----- 1993b, "A Critical Examination of the Concept of Islamization of Knowledge in Contemporary Times", **Muslim Education Quarterly**, Vol. 10, No.4, pp. 3-34.

----- 1992, **The Principles of Islamic Political Economy: A Methodological Enquiry** (London, Eng.: Macmillan & New York, NY: St. Martin's Press) Chapter 6.

----- 1991, "The *Tawhidi* Precept in the Sciences", **MAAS Journal of Islamic Science**, Vol. 7, No.1, Jan-Jun. pp. 19-44.

Choudhury, M.A. & Che Hamat, A. Fatah (forthcoming), "Markets, Globalization and Structural Change", in Gupta, D. & Chaudhry, N. eds. **Political Economy Perspectives of Globalization Vol. Three** (Norwell, MA: Kluwer Academic Publishers).

Choudhury, M.A. & Malik, U.A. 1992, **The Foundations of Islamic Political Economy** (London, Eng.: Macmillan Press Ltd. & New York, NY: St. Martin's Press) pp. 184-92.

Debreu, G. 1970, "Economies with a Finite Set of Equilibria", **Econometrica**, Vol. 38, No. 3, May. pp. 387-92.

Dhrymes, P.J. 1970, **Econometrics** (New York, NY: Harper & Row) Chapters 9 & 10.

Friedrich, C.J. ed. 1977, **The Philosophy of Kant** (New York, NY: The Modern Library).

Georgescu-Roegen, N. 1981, **The Entropy Law and the Economic Process** (Cambridge, MA: Harvard University Press).

Grandmont, J-M. 1989, "Temporary Equilibrium", in Eatwell, J. Milgate, M. & Newman, P. eds. **The New Palgrave, General Equilibrium** (New York, NY: W.W. Norton) pp. 297-304.

Hahn, W. 1963, **Theory and Application of Liapunov' Direct Method** (Englewood Cliffs, NJ: Prentice-Hall, Inc.).

Henderson, J.M. & Quandt, R.E. 1971, **Microeconomic Theory, A Mathematical Approach** (New York, NY: McGraw-Hill, Inc.).

Hildenbrand, W. 1989, "Core of an Economy", in Arrow, K.J. & Intrilligator, M.D. eds. **Handbook of Mathematical Economics 3 Vols** (Amsterdam: North Holland) Chapter 18.

Hirshleifer, J. 1970, **Investment, Interest and Capital** (Englewood Cliffs, NJ: Prentice-Hall, Inc.) Chapter 9.

Notes and References

----- 1991, "Social Choice in an Islamic Economic Framework", **American Journal of Islamic Social Sciences**, Vol. 8, No. 2, pp. 259-74.

----- 1989, **Islamic Economic Co-operation** (London, Eng.: Macmillan & New York, NY: St. Martin's Press).

General Agreements of Tariffs and Trade 1993, **Final Act Embodying the Results of the Uruguay Round of Multilateral Trade Negotiations** (Geneva, Switzerland, Dec. 15).

International Monetary Fund 1993, **World Economic Outlook** (Washington, D.C. U.S.A.)

Islamic Development Bank various years, **Annual Reports** (Jeddah, Saudi Arabia).

Lessard, D.R. & Williamson, J. 1987, **Capital Flight and Third World Debt** (Washington D.C.: Institute of International Economics).

Mehmet, O. 1990, "Alternative Concepts of Development: A Critique of Eurocentric Theorizing", **Humanomics**, Vol. 6, No. 3, pp. 55-67.

Phelps, E.S. 1989, "Distributive Justice", in J. Eatwell, M. Milgate & P. Newman eds. **New Palgrave: Social Economics** (New York, NY: W.W. Norton) pp. 31-4.

Statistical, Economic and Social Research and Training Centre for Islamic Countries (SESRTCIC) 1993, **Documents Presented by SESRTCIC at the Twenty-First Islamic Conference of Foreign Ministers**, Karachi, Pakistan, April 24-9.

Tisdell, C. 1989, "Imperialism, Economic Dependence and Development: A Brief Review of Aspects of Economic Thought and Theory", **Humanomics**, Vol. 5, No. 2, pp. 3-20.

United Nations 1991, **Global Outlook 2000** (New York, NY).

United Nations Conference on Trade and Development Secretariat 1989, **The Least Developed Countries 1989 Report**.

Wallerstein, I. 1974, **The Modern World System** (New York, NY: Academic Press, Inc.).

CHAPTER 8: MALAYSIA AND THE MUSLIM WORLD: THE TWENTY-FIRST CENTURY AND BEYOND

Ali, A. 1992, "Technology Transfer in Manufacturing Industries Via Direct Foreign Investment", **Journal of Economic Cooperation Among Islamic Countries**, Vol. 13, Nos. 3-4, pp. 137-59.

Asad, M. trans. 1993, **The Message of the *Qur'an*** (Gibraltar: Dar al-Andalus).

Bidwai, P. 1993, "Unfree Trade", **New Statesman and Society**, Nov. 19.

Chenery, H. Ahluwalia et al. eds. 1976, **Redistribution with Growth** (Oxford, Eng.: Oxford University Press).

Choudhury, M.A. 1994, "Uncertainty After Marrakesh Declaration", **New Straits Times: Saturday Forum** (Kuala Lumpur, Malaysia), May 1.

Drucker, P.F. 1989, **The New Realities** (New York, NY: Harper & Row).

Government of Malaysia (Kuala Lumpur, Malaysia, 1991) **The Second Outline Perspective Plan 1991-2000**.

Institute of Development Studies Bulletin 1983 (University of Sussex, Eng.)

Johari, M.Y. 1991, "Poverty Profiles in Sabah and Rural Development Strategies After 1990", in **Issues and Strategies in Rural Development**, ed. Johari, M.Y. (Kota Kinabalu, Sabah, Malaysia: Institute for Development Studies Sabah & Konrad Adenauer Foundation) pp. 3-48.

Mehmet, O. 1986, **Development in Malaysia: Poverty, Wealth and Trusteeship** (London, Eng.: Croom Helm).

Ollapally, D. 1993, "The South Looks North: The Third World in the New World Order", **Current History**, April.

Osman-Rani, H. & Piei, H.M. 1990, "Malaysia's Industrialisation and Trade: Issues, Options and Strategies", **Jurnal Ekonomi Malaysia**, Vol. 21 & 22, pp. 13-44.

Notes and References

Salleh, K. Piei, H.M. & Sahathavan, M. 1988, "Trade Policy Options for Malaysia", in Ariff, M. & Loong-Hoe, T. eds. **The Uruguay Round: ASEAN-Trade Policy Options** (Singapore: Institute of Southeast Asian Studies) pp. 65-103.

Television Channel 3 Program 1995, **Money Matters**, "Smart Partnership", Malaysia, Sunday, July 30.

CHAPTER 9: INSTITUTIONAL REFORMATION: THE ORGANIZATION OF ISLAMIC CONFERENCES SYSTEM

Abu-Saud, M. 1988, **Contemporary Zakat** (Cincinnati, Ohio: Zakat and Research Foundation).

Ansari, J. 1986, **The Political Economy of International Economic Organization** (Boulder, CO: Lynne Rienner) pp. 19-24.

Choudhury, M.A. 1994, "Muslims, Islam and the West Today", **Hamdard Islamicus**, Vol. XVII, No. 1, Spring, pp. 19-34.

----- 1993, "A Mathematical Formulation of the Knowledge-Based Worldview of Development", in Ahmad, E. ed. **Economic Growth and Human Resource Development in an Islamic Perspective** (Herndon, VA: International Institute of Islamic Thought and Association of Islamic Social Scientists) pp. 17-29.

----- 1991a, "Islamic Futures After the Desert Storm", **Hamdard Islamicus**, Vol. IV, No. 4, Winter. pp. 5-21.

----- 1989, **Islamic Economic Co-operation** (London, Eng.: Macmillan Press Ltd & New York, NY: St. Martin's Press).

Clarke, R. 1995, "A Crime of Colossal Magnitude, 82 k tons of bombs in 42 days: 7.5 Hiroshima", **Impact International** (London, September).

Haniff, G. 1992, "Muslim Development at Risk: The Crisis of Human Resources", **American Journal of Islamic Social Sciences**, Vol. 9, No. 4, Winter, pp. 515-32.

International Monetary Fund 1995, **Direction of Trade** (Washington D.C.: International Monetary Fund).

Islamic Development Bank 1995a, **Annual Report 1415 (1994-1995)** (Jeddah, Saudi Arabia: The Islamic Development Bank).

----- 1995b, **Report on Operations and Activities of Islamic Development Bank 1415H (1994-1995)** (Jeddah, Saudi Arabia: IDB, Dec.).

Islamic Foundation for Science, Technology and Development 1993, **Update of the OIC Plan of Action, Amendments by IFSTAD, Second Consultation Among the OIC Institutions** (Jeddah, Saudi Arabia: IFSTAD, Nov).

Nienhaus, V. 1986, **Economic Cooperation and Integration Among Islamic Countries** (Jeddah, Saudi Arabia: Islamic Development Bank) pp. 55-69.

Organization of Islamic Conferences 1995, **Guide to the Organization of the Islamic Conferences** (Ankara, Turkey: Statistical, Economic and Social Research and Training Centre for Islamic Countries).

Quinton, A. 1989. **Utilitarian Ethics** (La Salle, Il: Open Court) pp. 1-10.

SESRTCIC 1993, **Report, Ninth Session of the COMCEC** (Istanbul, Turkey).

CHAPTER 10: CONCLUSION: *UMMATIC* TRANSFORMATION

Esposito, J.L. 1994, "Political Islam: Beyond the Green Menace", **Current History**, January.

Ihonvbbere, J.O. 1992, "The Third World and the New World Order in the 1990s". **Futures**, December.

Institute of Development Studies (IDS) 1983, Accelerated Development of Sub-Saharan Africa, **Bulletin**, Vol. 14, No.1.

INDEX

A

a posteriori 9, 34-5, 46-8, 50, 53, 81, 83, 102, 125, 151

a priori 9, 34-5, 38, 44-8, 50, 53, 76-7, 81, 83, 94, 102, 124-5

aggregation 32, 61, 75, 84

Ahkam 32-3, 40, 57, 64-6, 68-70, 126-7, 129, 131, 182-5, 230

   Ahkam-formation 40, 57, 64-5

atomism 52, 82, 89-90, 92, 94

   atomistic 52, 75, 107, 116

attributes 29-30, 36, 38, 40, 118, 124-5, 128-30, 132-3, 136-8, 140-1, 184, 225

   Divine attributes 30, 138

B

balance 36, 38, 40, 58-9, 61, 63, 101, 127, 133, 137-8, 141, 160, 236

biodiversity 55

Bretton Woods 166, 168, 170-1, 192, 229

C

capitalism 48, 51, 56, 78-9, 81-2, 87-8, 166, 172

categorical imperative 34-5, 40

circular causation 26, 32, 41-2, 53, 56-7, 64, 68-9, 73-4, 95-6, 99, 103, 114, 117-8, 121, 124, 128, 130, 132, 136, 138, 142, 153, 225, 234-5, 237-8

complementarity 9, 32, 41, 46, 52, 55, 59-60, 64, 68-70, 72-3, 120-1, 128-31, 134, 136-8, 140-2, 149, 153, 169, 172, 175, 178, 182, 184-6, 191, 199, 201-3, 205, 209, 211-2, 217, 228, 233-4

cooperation 96, 107, 136-40, 166, 186-7, 215, 217-9, 228-9, 231-3, 237

economic cooperation 96, 138, 140, 166, 186-7, 217-8, 229, 233

curriculum 42, 71, 70, 73, 227, 234-5, 237-8

D

Darwinian 9, 16, 18-9, 55, 82, 118, 138

debt 162, 173-6, 224

deconstruction 52, 92

   (also deconstructionism) 43, 49, 75, 78, 82-6, 89, 91-3, 95

development 12, 41, 46-9, 55-7, 62, 66, 71-3, 76, 79-80, 84, 89-90, 92, 95, 100-1, 121, 162-3, 166-7, 169-70, 173, 175, 178, 181-7, 189, 191-212, 217-9, 221-5, 227-9, 231-2, 235-7

   economic development 217, 219

   sustainable development 71, 89

   socio-economic development 192, 196, 203, 221

distributive equity 86, 135-6, 169, 185, 193-4, 197, 201, 207, 210

diversification 136-7, 139, 142, 195, 208, 210

duality 13, 120

   (also dualism) 9, 12-3, 16, 18-9, 23, 35, 41, 45, 47, 49-52, 54, 56, 62, 74, 77, 82-3, 85, 87-90, 92, 102-3, 170-1, 180-1, 211-2, 224

E

ecological 54, 60, 64, 66, 90-1, 93-4, 96-101, 121, 210, 213

   ecology 182, 230

economic efficiency 135-6, 138, 169, 193, 197, 199, 201, 203

   growth 72, 88, 100, 173-4, 191-5, 197-99, 201-3, 207, 210, 231, 233

economism 16, 19, 76, 78, 87, 113
   economistic 15, 76
educational system 70-1
   institutions 187, 235
empowerment 199, 201, 222, 224
endogeneity 9, 15-6, 19, 21-2, 32, 41,
   95, 98-9, 121, 124, 127, 137, 154,
   157
   ethical endogeneity 21-2, 41, 95,
   98-9
endogenous 14-5, 19, 23, 48, 76, 80,
   98, 104, 109, 129-30, 154-7, 159-
   63, 178, 224-5, 227, 236
   money 155, 160-3, 225, 236
   monetary (base)154, 156, 237
entitlement 85, 87, 139, 169, 196,
   210, 224
episteme(s) 9, 15, 44, 50, 80, 95, 182-
   3, 189, 223
   epistemic(s) 112-3
epistemic-ontic 26, 69
epistemology 70-1, 73, 76, 80-1, 91,
   93-8, 102-4, 113, 123-5, 127, 132,
   138, 140, 142, 148, 234-5, 237
   epistemological 1, 3, 11, 14, 16,
   20, 23, 35, 40-1, 43-4, 46, 50, 53,
   60, 62, 74, 81, 83, 89, 102, 110,
   117, 142, 232
equilibrium 23, 66, 77, 85, 91, 96, 98,
   105-13, 117, 119-20, 123, 126,
   128, 141, 144, 151, 154-5, 158-9,
   168, 175, 188
   equilibria 28, 58, 106-8, 126, 128,
   138, 141, 154-5, 158-9, 195
Eurocentric 18, 43, 49, 103, 170-1,
   178, 181, 188, 211-2
   Eurocentricity 17, 43, 51, 74,
   167, 173, 178, 185, 188, 206, 212

evolutionary 6-7, 10, 23, 25-8, 32-3,
   36, 38, 40, 53, 48, 60, 62-4, 71-3,
   82, 89, 97-99, 102-3, 117-8, 123-
   5, 132-3, 137, 141, 144, 148, 150,
   159, 163
   evolution 3, 5, 6-9, 16, 18, 19, 25,
   27, 35, 41, 45, 52, 53-4, 58-9, 62-
   6, 76-7, 81-2, 98-9, 102, 117-8,
   122, 125, 127, 129-30, 132-3, 135,
   137-8, 141-3, 149, 158-9, 175,
   209, 212, 225, 228, 231
   evolutionary epistemology 38, 98,
   182

F
falsification 18
   falsificationism 18
field 1-3, 9-10, 12-3, 15-6, 20-1, 32,
   54, 68-9, 71, 91, 96, 108-10, 116,
   118, 124-6, 163, 166, 215, 223,
   225
flows 4, 6-10, 25-8, 31-4, 38-40, 57-
   60, 63, 65-6, 68, 97, 106, 108-9,
   117, 125-31, 140, 173, 177, 184,
   186, 200, 204, 206, 217, 225, 228
   knowledge flows, 4, 6-10, 25, 28,
   38, 40, 57-60, 63, 65-6, 97, 125-6,
   128-9, 130-1, 140
foreign investments 175, 179
   foreign direct investments 170,
   188, 195-6
   foreign trade financing 184, 218
foundationalism 47, 49-50, 64, 102

G
general relativity 14-5
Ghazzali (also Al-Ghazzali) 24, 29,
   31-2, 36, 38-9, 61

grass-roots 72, 100-1, 184-7, 189, 200, 202, 204-6, 211, 224, 226-7, 231-3
Gulf War 180, 218-20

H
heteronomy 34-6
Hisbah 131, 138-9
historicism 16-7, 43-4, 51-3, 56, 62-4, 77-8, 83, 86, 93, 103
Husserl, E. 12, 16-7

I
Ibn Khaldun 61, 93
Ijma 29, 31, 33, 57, 66, 142, 183, 225
Ijtehad 57, 63, 66, 142, 223, 225, 230, 232
individualism 18-9, 23, 35, 49-52, 54, 56, 74, 77, 82-3, 85, 87-90, 92, 102-3, 170-71, 181, 211-2, 224
individuation 7, 44-5, 47, 49, 50, 52, 63, 74, 85, 88, 92, 97, 103-4, 185, 202
industrialization 175, 193, 207
institutionalism 49, 76, 84-5, 87, 89, 172, 183, 187
Islamic 1, 10-2, 23-4, 29-30, 32-3, 30, 44, 49, 56-8, 60, 62, 64, 66, 69, 73-5, 94, 100-3, 105, 114, 121-3, 129-33, 135-45, 147-50, 152-4, 156, 158, 160, 162-3, 174, 176, 178, 180-2, 184-9, 202, 205-6, 211, 215, 217-9, 223-4, 226-37
Islamic Common Market 186, 202, 205, 211, 229, 231

Islamic political economy 102, 105, 137, 145, 148-50, 152-4, 156, 160-2
Islamic World Trade Organization 184-5, 196
interactions 6-9, 13, 16-23, 25-7, 32-3, 38-9, 41, 44, 48, 50, 52, 53, 56-9, 63-6, 69-72, 80, 83, 87, 91, 96, 98-9, 105, 108, 110-6, 121-3, 125-6, 129-30, 132-3, 137, 140-3, 148-50, 157-8, 163, 181, 183-4, 191, 200, 202, 204-5, 210-2, 220, 222, 225, 228, 231, 237
interactive-integrative-evolutionary 27-8, 53, 57, 60, 71-3, 89, 123-4, 148, 150, 163, 233, 235, 237-8
interdisciplinarity 70-3, 234-5, 238

J
Justice 58, 61, 63, 74, 78, 85-7 125-7, 130, 135, 141, 183

K
Kant 11-2, 20, 24, 34-6, 38, 46,76, 77, 78
Keynesian 76, 150, 154-6, 168, 203
  Keynesianism 168, 170
knowledge-based 1, 7, 26-7, 29, 41, 113, 118, 122, 126, 128-9, 142-5, 149, 163, 199, 225, 227, 231, 234-5, 237
  knowledge-induced, 25, 58-9, 63, 91, 94, 98-9, 112, 123-4, 126-7, 129, 132, 137, 141-2, 148, 158-9
  knowledge-centred 26-8, 62-3, 69, 81, 110, 118, 233-4

L
Lauh Mahfuz 33, 38-9, 57, 60, 125
liberalism 51-2, 61, 86, 88, 93

M
Madinah Charter 34, 62
markets 65-6, 72, 76-80, 82, 84-8, 93, 101-2, 107-9, 131, 142, 148, 151, 156, 162, 166, 169, 172-3, 175, 177, 186, 188, 192, 194-5, 205, 208-12, 230-1, 235-6
meta-theory 53, 74, 92, 103, 211-2
moral law 34-5, 84, 223
Mudarabah 123, 136-7, 206, 224
Musharakah 123, 136-7, 206, 224

N
neoclassical 54, 59, 69, 76-7, 80, 85-7, 90, 92-4, 96-8, 102-3, 109, 121, 131, 133, 140, 147, 149, 200, 203, 207, 210
neoclassicism 81, 86, 91, 93, 95, 103, 169, 170, 172, 200
newly industrializing countries (NICs) 170, 178, 191

O
occidental 11-2, 19, 23-4, 32, 35, 41, 43-4, 47-54, 56, 58, 62, 64, 68, 73-4, 77, 80, 83, 102-4, 181, 184-5, 188-9, 211-2
occidentalism 11, 43, 45, 51-2, 56, 74, 102, 188
ontic 39-40, 46, 50, 76-8, 99
ontology 125
optimal control theory 22, 106, 128
optimality 22, 32, 98, 106, 109, 112
optimization 22, 32, 106, 114, 120, 122, 126

optimality-equilibrium 109, 113, 117, 126
Organization of Islamic Conferences (OIC) 173-80, 185-9, 205, 215-7, 219-26, 227-8, 233

P
paradigm 192, 194, 203, 211
perception 7-9, 47, 53, 56, 89, 102, 147, 221
perceptual 17, 35, 47-8, 92, 97, 102
phenomenology 16-7, 39
plurality 17-8, 47, 58, 62-3, 74, 92, 103
pluralism 17, 23, 35, 41, 49, 74, 77, 80, 82, 89, 90, 92, 103
policy variables 22, 129, 131-3, 138, 141, 188
poverty 90, 101, 169, 193, 196, 200, 217, 224
preferences 50-2, 60-2, 65-6, 68, 70, 74-6, 82-3, 86, 90, 92, 94, 96, 98, 105, 108-9, 114, 121, 130-3, 136, 163, 183-4, 200, 212, 219-21, 230
privatization 165, 170, 173, 176, 185, 189, 192, 200, 204
process 1-2, 4, 6-7, 16-7, 19-21, 23, 25, 38-40, 43, 45-9, 51-3, 56-64, 66-74, 76-81, 84, 86-7, 89, 92-6, 98, 102-3, 105-6, 114-33, 136-8, 140, 142, 144, 148, 154, 157-8, 163, 165-6, 170-1, 173, 175, 178-9, 181-7, 189, 194-6, 203, 206, 208-10, 212-13, 221-23, 225-8, 230-4, 237
Shuratic Process 56, 58, 60, 63-4, 73, 102, 105, 125-30, 137-8, 142, 157, 163, 183-7, 189, 222-3, 225-8, 231-2, 234, 237

profit-sharing 100, 136, 140, 160, 161, 206, 236
production 59, 65-6, 70, 79, 90, 92, 96, 105-6, 110, 119-21, 123, 130-1, 134-40, 151, 156
    function 105-6, 120, 140
    menu 105, 131, 136-7, 140, 156

Q

Qur'an 10-1, 24-5, 29, 38-40, 56-8, 60-2, 66, 74, 94, 103, 124-5, 128-30, 135, 138, 182-3, 213, 223-4, 230, 232
    Qur'anic 2, 24, 32-3, 41-4, 57-8, 61-4, 69, 73-4, 93-4, 103-4, 125-8, 142, 183, 224, 237

R

rate(s) 152, 167-8, 174-7, 188, 197-8, 218, 224
    exchange 167-8, 174-7, 188, 197-8
    inflation 176
    interest (also *Riba*) 123, 152, 154, 167-8, 174-7, 188, 197-8
rationalism 7-9, 12-3, 15-6, 19, 24, 32, 34-5, 44-5, 47, 50-1, 53, 74, 76, 78, 81, 94, 102, 104, 123, 188
rationality 86, 98, 114-5, 117, 120
revelation 8, 25, 29-30, 34, 57, 60

S

satisfycing 114-5
self-actualization 30-1, 211
self-reliance 163, 198-9, 205, 209-10, 228-9, 233
Shari'ah 29, 40, 61-2, 64, 69-70, 126-7, 131, 135, 162, 183, 223, 230-1
Shatibi (also Al-Shatibi) 61, 94

Shura 56, 58, 64, 66, 69, 73, 125-6, 182-5, 223, 226, 232
    Shuratic 56, 58, 60, 63-4, 73, 102, 105, 125-30, 137-8, 142, 157, 163, 182-9, 222-7, 231-4, 237
simulation 96-7, 99, 126, 128, 131-3, 136, 141, 150, 152-3, 158, 235
simultaneity 8, 14, 117, 119, 135, 137, 149, 195, 199-200, 212
social 13, 15-6, 22-4, 29-30, 32, 36, 41-2, 47-8, 51-2, 54-7, 61-2, 65-6, 69, 73-6, 78, 81, 83-93, 101, 111, 115-6, 121, 123, 130-1, 133-40, 142, 146, 149, 169-70, 172, 178, 183-4, 191, 193-5, 197-8, 201-2, 204, 206, 210, 212, 215-7, 219, 221, 223, 235, 228, 230, 235
    causation 84-5
    contract 86
    economy 30
    goods 65-6, 85, 121, 123, 130-1, 133, 137
    system 123
space-time 13-7, 20, 149
speculation 112, 147-9, 157, 162-3, 168
state variables 22, 106, 109, 111, 113-8, 120-2, 127, 132, 134, 136, 138
Stock of Knowledge 2-3, 5-6, 8, 10, 25, 27, 32, 39, 57, 125, 127
    Complete Knowledge 2, 4, 57, 60, 115
structural 48, 54, 62, 64, 90, 108, 166, 169-70, 176, 187, 191-3, 209-10
    adjustment 166, 169-70, 176, 191-3, 195
    change (also structural transformation)108, 187, 209-10
structuralism 48-52

structuralist 43, 48-9, 53, 75, 78,
  83, 89
  post-structuralism 49-52, 63, 75
subspaces 3-5
  sub-universes 14
substitution 41, 54-6, 59, 69, 90, 98,
  119-21, 138, 140, 149, 169, 196-7,
  202, 210
  substitutional 56
Sunnah 29, 32-3, 62, 66, 69, 74, 223,
  230, 233
sustainability 24, 40, 72, 92, 103, 193,
  199, 205, 210

T
Tawhid 27, 29-33, 38, 124, 128
  Tawhidi 25-8, 32-3, 36, 39-40,
  124, 127-8, 130, 138, 140, 182-3,
  189, 237
technology 41, 55, 62, 68-74, 82, 96,
  105, 109, 120, 130-1, 139, 167,
  175, 187-8, 194, 196, 198-9, 201-
  2, 204-5, 207-10, 212, 217, 219,
  223, 228, 231-3
  technological 71, 79-80, 108,
  120, 138, 140-2, 175, 184, 193-7,
  200, 203, 206, 208, 210, 212, 215,
  217, 219, 223, 233, 235
time 14-5, 20-1, 23-4, 29, 31, 38, 40,
  44, 48, 61-2, 66, 89, 101, 103,
  106, 108-9, 111-20, 128, 132, 136,
  146, 148-9, 151-4, 158-9, 211,
  213
  timal 16, 110

topological 3, 7, 9-10, 64, 97-8, 118,
  122, 126, 128, 149
  topology 3-4, 97, 128
trade 146, 165-70, 172-3, 176-8, 183-
  6, 188, 192, 194, 196, 203-6, 209,
  212, 217-8, 228-9, 231
  creation 206, 212
  diversion 203-6

U
Ummah 102, 178, 184-6, 203, 212,
  219, 222, 225, 229, 232, 234
Ummatic transformation 163, 227,
  229-30, 234
unification 1, 5-7, 9-10, 12, 17, 23-6,
  28-9, 33, 34, 38, 40, 48, 50, 53-4,
  56, 58-60, 63-5, 68-71, 73, 78, 81,
  89, 93-7, 103-4, 123-5, 132-3,
  138, 142, 144, 148, 181, 184-5,
  223, 228, 230, 234-5, 237
  unification epistemology 1, 5, 10,
  28, 40, 56, 58-60, 64-5, 68, 70-1,
  73, 93-7, 103-4, 123-5, 132, 142,
  181, 184-5, 223, 234-5, 237
Unity 1-3, 7-10, 23-5, 27, 41, 56, 60-3,
  95, 114, 124-6, 142, 148, 181,
  185, 223, 225, 234
  Precept of Unity, 1-2, 5, 8, 10, 23,
  95, 124, 126, 223, 225
  Field of Unity 10, 126, 223, 225
Uruguay Rounds 166
utilitarian 32, 46, 61-2, 75, 85, 87,
  221
  utilitarianism 9, 84, 93
utility 61, 83, 93, 152

W

well-being 58-9, 62-3, 65, 70, 72, 123, 125, 130-1, 133-9, 141, 202, 209-10, 217, 221, 223-5

World Trade Organization 184-5, 196

world view 8-12, 18, 23-5, 32, 41, 44, 50, 53, 55-6, 61, 63-4, 70, 74-5, 89, 93, 97, 103-4, 117-8, 121, 125-6, 138, 142, 181, 184-8, 212, 230-4, 237

Z

Zakah 123, 224-5